EDWARD DE LA BILLIÈRE specializes in natural history, conservation, travel and adventure travel stories, writing regularly for *The Daily Telegraph* and *The Independent* as well as various magazines, and freelancing for the BBC's Natural History Unit on Radio 4 and BBC1.

His training for the Pennine Way, 'the big one', included climbing Alaska's Mt McKinley with a blind and half-paralysed man (filmed for the BBC's *QED* series) and running the 1200-mile Iditarod sled dog race across Alaska (filmed for the BBC's *Extreme Lives* series).

He lives in the Peak District National Park with his wife Pips and their two boys, Barnaby and Toby, and he

moonlights as a white-collar crime lawyer in Manchester.

KEITH CARTER'S interest in the great outdoors was kindled on a school trip to Snowdonia which hooked him for life. Work became what he did between walks and he has since explored almost every corner of the British Isles with occasional forays into France, Austria and the USA.

Writing articles for magazines led him into guide-book writing and he now spends most of his time rediscovering Scotland, cultivating organic vegetables and growing willow. He is the author of *Offa's Dyke Path*, also from Trailblazer.

Pennine Way
First edition: July 2004

Publisher
Trailblazer Publications
The Old Manse, Tower Rd, Hindhead, Surrey, GU26 6SU, UK
Fax (+44) 01428-607571
www.trailblazer-guides.com

British Library Cataloguing in Publication Data
A catalogue record for this book is available from the British Library

ISBN 1-873756-57-7

Editor: Charlie Loram
Additional research and writing:
John King, Anna Jacomb-Hood,
Bryn Thomas and Patricia Major
Series editor: Charlie Loram
Layout and proof-reading: Anna Jacomb-Hood
Illustrations: © Nick Hill (p59)
Photographs (flora): © Bryn Thomas except: C2 middle right,© Edith Schofield;
C2 bottom left and centre, C3 middle right, C4 top left and middle © Charlie Loram
Photograph (top) opposite p240: © Bryn Thomas (thanks to Jacqui and Sue)
Cover photograph: © John Cleare/Mountain Camera 2004
All other photographs: © Keith Carter unless otherwise indicated
Cartography: Nick Hill
Index: Jane Thomas

The maps in this guide were prepared from out-of-Crown-
copyright Ordnance Survey maps amended and updated by Trailblazer.

Warning: hill walking can be dangerous
Please read the notes on when to go (p18) and on health and outdoor safety (pp248-50).
Every effort has been made by the author and publisher to ensure that the information
contained herein is as accurate and up to date as possible. However, they are unable
to accept responsibility for any inconvenience, loss or injury sustained by anyone
as a result of the advice and information given in this guide.

Printed on chlorine-free paper by
D²Print (☎ +65-6295 5598), Singapore

PENNINE WAY

EDALE TO KIRK YETHOLM

planning, places to stay, places to eat
includes 135 large-scale walking maps

EDWARD DE LA BILLIÈRE
KEITH CARTER

TRAILBLAZER PUBLICATIONS

Dedications

From Edward: To Pips, who carried the real load
while I was out walking and having fun in the name of work.

From Keith: For Annie

Acknowledgements

From Edward: It was when I started putting this book together that I fully realized how much work goes into keeping the Pennine Way open. It is not just the stewardship put in by the countless number of farmers through whose land you will walk over: there is an army of people who maintain the stiles, the path, the signposts, and even decide on whether a section of the route needs varying. I cannot thank all of them enough for keeping this route going.

Additionally the work of the Edale Tourism Association deserves high praise for ensuring your walk can get off to a good start. The information centre in Edale is also run by highly informed and extremely friendly people. Their charm will go a long way towards your transition from the hectic life you may be trying to escape and the deep peace that will imbue you once you have started walking.

All of the national parks have been extremely helpful – the Peak District, the Yorkshire Dales and Northumberland – as have the huge number of tourist offices on the route. The Association of National Parks was a great help in aiding my understanding of how these vital national treasures, the parks themselves, came about and fit into the wider community.

Along the route the people I met, asked questions of, and those whose hospitality at B&Bs and pubs I enjoyed, coloured the Pennine Way in rosy glow for me; even though it is as green as Britain gets.

Finally, and most sincerely, I must thank Keith Carter for stepping in to help me out with a project that became impossible for me to finish because of the upset caused by the Foot and Mouth epidemic. His skill, dedication and artistic flair gave the book you have bought (most wisely!) most of its appeal. And above both of us stands Charlie Loram, whose editorial skill, lawyer-like attention to detail, and passion for all things kind to Mother Earth, led me, and then Keith, along the path to print. Thanks to you all.

From Keith: Thanks to those who helped me complete this book particularly the series editor, Charlie Loram, for his insistence on attention to detail. Also at Trailblazer, thanks to John King, Patricia Major, Anna Jacomb-Hood, Nick Hill for all his work on the maps, and Jane Thomas for the index.

Thanks also to my companions on the trail, to all those who patiently answered my questions along the way, in particular the Bayes family at the Pen-y-Ghent Café in Horton-in-Ribblesdale and to Annie, my wife.

A request

The author and publisher have tried to ensure that this guide is as accurate and up to date as possible. Nevertheless things change. If you notice any changes or omissions that should be included in the next edition of this book, please write to Trailblazer (address on p2) or email us at info@trailblazer-guides.com. A free copy of the next edition will be sent to persons making a significant contribution.

Updated information will be available on the Internet at
www.trailblazer-guides.com

Front cover: On the Cheviots; view eastwards from the final leg of the Pennine Way
© John Cleare/Mountain Camera 2004

CONTENTS

Of all the long-distance trails in the British Isles the Pennine Way, 256 miles (412km) along the backbone of northern England, is pre-eminent. The first to be opened as a National Trail, to some it's the best; it's certainly the best known and it's arguably the hardest.

Anyone who completes the Pennine Way will refute the suggestion that it was easy. It isn't. It requires fitness, determination, good humour and adaptability because your walk won't go smoothly all the time. There will be days when nothing seems to go right and you wish you'd never got out of bed; then again, there will be others when you feel invincible, when you can walk all day and arrive at your next stop, still with a spring in your step – when to be alive is 'very heaven'.

The Way takes you through most of the different habitats of flora and fauna in this country and you'll see a wonderfully varied and wide range of plant and animal life. You'll start with a testing trudge over the peat moors of the Peak District and continue through the South Pennines past such milestones as Stoodley Pike and Calder Vale where a short detour to Hebden Bridge is recommended. You are into Brontë country and will pass Top Withens, said to be the Wuthering Heights of Emily's great novel. The parsonage where the family lived in nearby Haworth is well worth visiting.

Your path continues past reservoirs and windswept moorland until the millstone grit turns to limestone and a delightful riverside walk leads to Malham. Next you climb Fountains Fell and Pen-y-Ghent and then down into Horton-in-Ribblesdale. Now you are in Three Peaks country, a land of wide skies and magnificent views that go on forever. Through Swaledale the Way continues, where Hawes and Keld lead to lonely and deserted Baldersdale: the halfway point.

You continue via the fantastic glaciated chasm of High Cup and move on to the lush meadows of Teesdale and the attractive village of Dufton, respite before the inevitably stormy traverse of Cross Fell. Leaving the excitement of the landscape of the North Pennines you reach Hadrian's Wall, one of the most evocative places, archaeologically and historically, in Britain. For many, the walk from Greenhead to Once Brewed is one of the many outstanding days of the entire trail.

From the Wall you enter the vast forests of Wark and Redesdale eventually reaching the village of Bellingham. One more day to the lonely forest outpost of Byrness followed by the biggest day of all – the 27-mile (43km) crossing of the Cheviots to the end of the Way at Kirk Yetholm.

Some who have walked the Pennine Way say it has changed their lives. It certainly gives everyone a chance to prove to themselves what they are capable of: 'I never thought I could do it', they say yet the Way has shown them there's nothing you can't do once you set your mind to it. Spiritual experience or great fun, hard work or the walk of a lifetime, maybe a combination of all four, the Pennine Way stands supreme.

About this book

This guidebook contains all the information you need; the hard work has been done for you so you can plan your trip from home without the usual pile of books, maps, guides and tourist brochures. It includes:

- All standards of accommodation from campsites to luxurious guesthouses
- Walking companies if you want an organized tour
- A number of suggested itineraries for all types of walkers
- Answers to all your questions: when to go, degree of difficulty, what to pack and the approximate cost of the whole walking holiday

When you're all packed and ready to go, there's detailed information to get you to and from the Pennine Way and 135 detailed maps (1:20,000) and 10 town plans to help you find your way along it. The route guide section includes:

- Walking times in both directions
- Reviews of accommodation including camping, hostels, B&Bs and guesthouses
- Cafés, pubs, tea-shops, restaurants, and shops for buying supplies
- Rail, bus and taxi information for all the towns and villages on or near the Way
- Street maps of the main towns
- Historical, cultural and geographical background information

Minimum impact for maximum insight

Nature's peace will flow into you as the sunshine flows into trees. The winds will blow their freshness into you and storms their energy, while cares will drop off like autumn leaves. **John Muir** (one of the world's earliest and most influential environmentalists, born in 1838)

Why is walking in wild and solitary places so satisfying? Partly it is the sheer physical pleasure: sometimes pitting one's strength against the elements and the lie of the land. The beauty and wonder of the natural world and the fresh air restore our sense of proportion and the stresses and strains of everyday life slip away. Whatever the character of the countryside, walking in it benefits us mentally and physically inducing a sense of well-being, an enrichment of life and an enhanced awareness of what lies around us.

All this the countryside gives us and the least we can do is to safeguard it by supporting rural economies, local businesses, low-impact methods of farming and land-management and by using environmentally-sensitive forms of transport – walking, of course, being the best.

In this book there is a detailed and illustrated chapter on the wildlife and conservation of the region and a chapter on minimum impact walking with ideas on how to tread lightly in this fragile environment; by following its principles we can help to preserve our natural heritage for future generations.

The springs of enchantment lie within ourselves; they arise from our sense of wonder, that most precious of gifts. **Eric Shipton**

PART 1: PLANNING YOUR WALK

About the Pennine Way

HISTORY

Tom Stephenson used the title 'Wanted: A long green trail' for an article he wrote in 1935. He was the first to suggest a public trail along the backbone of England, the Pennines, ending just over the Scottish border. His quest was taken up by many and over the years new rights of way were created until one long chain of 256 miles (412km) had been established from Edale in Derbyshire to Kirk Yetholm in Scotland. It officially opened as the Pennine Way in 1965, making it the first official long-distance footpath in Britain.

In its early days the Pennine Way was very hard going and not just because of the endless ups and downs. A substantial part of the route is over water-logged peat and bog which make doing it impossible without getting your feet wet somewhere. But they won't get wet nearly as often as 20 or even 10 years ago because of the Herculean efforts that have been made to lay stone slabs for people to walk on. Some people love these, others hate them. They are but an example of how the face of the British countryside has changed, and will continue to change, over the relatively short time that the route has been open.

HOW DIFFICULT IS THE PENNINE WAY?

The Pennine Way is a walk to do if you are looking for a challenge. If you want easy ambling along well established and level paths choose another one. The Pennine Way is difficult; there is no denying it. Some of the countryside is incredibly inhospitable (and all the more natural and, to many people, rewarding as a result). The weather can whip in unchallenged from the western coast and leave you drenched and sometimes frozen. The views can be barren, the navigation aids minimal and people few and far between. Half the Pennine Way is on open moorland, one quarter on rough grazing and only a tenth through forest, woodland or along riverbanks.

This level of difficulty is exactly what gives it its special identity. You will end each day feeling as if you have battled and come through. Your evening meal will taste all the better for it and can justifiably be bigger. With Britain's huge number of cultural differences packed into such a small area you will see the greatest variety of cultures of any long-distance walk in the country. And for years to come you will be able to bask in the reflected glory of your achievement.

Do not be put off. Around 10,000 people a year make the trek and despite the impressions of the first couple of days the Way is not too steep. There are 178 miles (286km) on gentle slopes of less than five degrees, 20 miles (32km) on slopes of ten to fifteen degrees, and only 3½ miles (6km) on steep slopes of more than fifteen degrees. If you can read a map and can walk 12 miles (19km) in a day without too many problems you should be able to make it. It's just not going to be a walk in the park.

Route finding

Navigation can be tricky although in peak season the path will be well trodden, if only by day trippers, and there are wooden signposts along the route marked  with an acorn symbol. They are not infallible though and great care must be taken at all times to ensure you are on the right route and not taking the one that looks easier because you are tired or it looks better trodden. The signposts are considerably less frequent in the wilder areas because of a policy to try and be sensitive to the area. In these parts take a map and compass and know how to use them.

HOW LONG DO YOU NEED?

The record for completing the 256 miles (412km) of the Pennine Way stands at around 3½ days. If 75 miles (121km) a day sounds a little too quick for you, you could aim for the average of 17 days. This will make for some very long days of well over 20 miles (32km), but should also afford some shorter ones and at least one rest day. Of course you could decide to do it in 40 days, or even longer. There is much to see and admire along the route and the slower you go the more you will take in. The variety of the scenery is one of the great attractions of this walk and you should not hurry by.

Practical information for the walker

ACCOMMODATION

Places to stay are relatively numerous and well spaced along most of the Pennine Way, allowing for some flexibility in itineraries. All bunkhouses, hostels and B&Bs should, however, be booked ahead if possible, especially from May to August when visitors have places booked up months in advance. You can avoid a lot of this accommodation mayhem at the busy times of the year by walking mid-week to put you out of synch with the hordes that start their walk on a weekend. If you're walking in winter be warned that many places to stay will be closed.

Camping

Even in the crowded British Isles camping can nurture a sense of freedom and simplicity which beautifully complements the act of walking. Your rucksack will of course be heavier, but carrying all the necessary equipment for sleeping out and cooking your own meals lightens the load in other ways; there's no need to book accommodation, you can make and change your plans as you go and it's by far the cheapest option (generally less than £5 per person).

Pitching your tent wherever you like is not allowed along the Pennine Way unless you gain the permission of the landowner. Official sites along the Way range from those with a basic toilet and little else to luxurious establishments with shop, laundrette and restaurant.

Camping barns, bunkhouses and hostels

The Pennine Way is liberally dotted with an assortment of cheap places to stay from simple stone barns to top-of-the-range hostels. If you need to keep your expenses to a minimum but don't relish carrying a tent and struggling with a sheet of flapping canvas in the pouring rain these are the answer. With prior planning (see Suggested itineraries p21) it is possible to stay in this type of accommodation on almost every night of your walk.

The simplest and cheapest of all are **camping barns** (£3-4 per person) which, at a minimum, provide a roof over your head, a sleeping platform on which to lay your sleeping bag and mat, a cooking area for your stove and a toilet. They're often referred to as 'stone tents' because you need to bring everything you would normally have for a camping trip apart from the tent. Some barns also provide hot water, showers, cooking facilities and a wood-burning stove for heating.

Bunkhouses (£5-11.50) are a couple of rungs up the comfort ladder, equipped with bunkbeds, full cooking facilities (cooker, pans, crockery and cutlery), showers and a drying room. Most assume you will have your own sleeping bag with you, although it is often possible to hire bedding for the night. A few even provide breakfast and an evening meal.

There are a total of 18 **youth hostels** along the Pennine Way most of which are ideally positioned a day's walk from the next. Their size and facilities vary enormously from simple wood cabins to purpose-built concrete institutions with prices to match: £8.50 to £11.80 including breakfast. Accommodation is usually in bunk-bedded same-sex rooms and there's always a fully-equipped self-catering kitchen for your use. In addition, a good-value three-course evening meal costing £5.20 (£3 for a child) and a packed lunch (£3.20-4.10) are available at all the youth hostels along the route except (currently) Mankinholes, Earby, Bellingham, Byrness and Kirk Yetholm.

To stay at a youth hostel you need to be a member of the **Youth Hostels Association of England and Wales** (☎ 0870-870 8808, 🖳 www.yha.org.uk, Trevelyan House, 8 St Stephen's Hill, St Albans, Hertfordshire, AL1 2DY) which costs £14 per year (£7 for under 18s, £28 for a family) and you can join at any of the hostels. You can either book accommodation online through the

YHA website or by phone: the YHA's Pennine Way Bureau (see p15) will book all your accommodation for you or you can use the relevant booking number given in Part 4. If booking less than a week in advance phone the youth hostel direct (the number is given beside each hostel name in Part 4).

Bed and breakfast

B&Bs are a great British institution. For anyone unfamiliar with the concept, you get a bedroom in someone's home along with an enormous cooked breakfast the following morning. It is a brilliant way to walk the Pennine Way as you can travel with a light pack. You also gain an insight into how people live in other parts of the very varied British Isles by spending the night in someone's home. One night you may be staying in a suburban 'semi', the next on a remote hill farm. They do, however, vary greatly in standard: in one you may find yourself shut away in a tiny cell-like bedroom for the night; in the next you may be welcomed as a true guest of the family and made to feel really at home.

What to expect This guide tries to pick out B&Bs that are 'walker friendly'; arriving in muddy boots doesn't matter, they have drying facilities and understand that you may well want to do nothing more than collapse.

An **en suite** room attracts a premium and often this is just for a cramped cubicle squeezed in next to the loo. So don't automatically turn your nose up at a bathroom across the corridor. It may be a room with a deep, white, clean, inviting bath just waiting for you to turn the taps on and settle in for a long hot soak.

Single rooms are usually poky 'box' rooms. **Twin** rooms have two single beds while a **double** is supposed to have one double bed, although just to confuse things, twins are sometimes called doubles. **Family** rooms sleep three or more.

Some B&Bs provide an **evening meal**, particularly if there is no pub or restaurant nearby. Check what the procedure is when you book. Many will do a packed lunch, too, but always ask the night before.

Prices B&B prices are usually quoted on a per person per night basis and range from £17 to £20 in a simple room with a shared bathroom to over £40 per person for a very comfortable room with private bathroom and all mod cons. Most places listed in this guide are less than £25. Be warned that if you are staying on your own some places may charge you a single person's supplement of between £5 and £10, particularly if you take a twin or double room. Owners change their prices at a moment's notice in response to the number of visitors, so only use the prices in this book as a rough guide. In the off season (September to March) prices may come down to some extent.

Guesthouses, hotels, pubs and inns

These businesses are much less personal and generally slightly more expensive (£30-35 per person) but do offer more space, an evening meal and a comfortable lounge for guests.

Pubs and inns often turn their hand to mid-range B&B accommodation in country areas. They can be good fun if you plan to drink in the bar until closing time (and beyond if you want to: bars can stay open as long as there is a demand from a resident). Equally, if you want an early night you may be kept awake by the hum of convivial conversation below, or drunken voices out in the street.

Hotels in the true sense of the word have comparatively high prices, around £60-85 for the room, usually inclusive of breakfast. Some are fantastic places with great character, others the ubiquitous chain-hotel style. If you feel in need of some TLC (tender loving care) a decent hotel is possibly your best bet.

Booking

Always book your accommodation. Not only does this ensure you have a bed for the night but gives you an opportunity to find out more about the place, check the price and see what's included. If you have to cancel please telephone your hosts; it will save a lot of worry and possibly allow them to provide a bed for someone else.

You may also want to consider using the services of one of the walking companies listed on p15 who will happily book accommodation for you, for a small fee, saving you a considerable amount of work.

Holiday cottages

Self-catering cottages make sense for groups walking part of the Way and returning to the same base each night. They are normally let on a weekly basis with prices starting from about £100 for those sleeping 4-6 people, but some will accept a booking for a long weekend. Cottages haven't been listed in this book; contact the tourist information centre in the area you want to stay for further details (see p35).

FOOD AND DRINK

Drinking water

It is now widely accepted among the walking fraternity that an adequate intake of water is essential on a day's walk. What is adequate will depend on the weight and size of the individual but a person of average height and build needs between two and four litres a day. Many walkers now carry their water in a crafty plastic pouch (eg a Platypus) kept in your pack, with a tube that runs over your shoulder to enable you to take a sip on demand. This is the best way to keep your water level topped up without having to stop to get a bottle out of the rucksack.

Filling up the water container can be done before setting out and refilled during the day at public conveniences, garages or cafés and pubs along the trail. On the longer days over wild country remember to take extra supplies of water and look out for opportunities for refills. Farmsteads will often oblige if asked politely. There are days, however, when there is very little in the way of places where water can be replenished unless you resort to using streams which regrettably cannot be assumed to be unpolluted. Livestock use the streams and rivers and hence will have been in contact with the water that you would like to drink. The answer is to use water-purifying tablets or iodine, both of which give an unpleasant taste, or a portable water filter/pump.

Beer, incidentally, is not a substitute for water and tea and coffee are diuretics and hence don't stay in the body for very long.

Buying camping supplies

There are enough shops to allow campers doing all their own cooking to buy supplies along the way. Obviously those wanting to merely prepare a packed lunch are also catered for. All the shops are listed in Part 4. The longest you should need to carry food for is two days. Village shops are open year-round but those on campsites are typically only open in the main holiday season. Fuel for camp stoves requires a little more planning. Gas canisters and methylated spirits are available in many general stores and campsite shops; Coleman Fuel is not so widely distributed.

Pubs

Pubs vary, as much as B&Bs, and along the length of the Pennine Way there is something for all tastes. Not only a good place to revive flagging spirits in the middle of the day or early afternoon, the local pub is often your only choice for an evening meal. Food at some is merely whipped from the freezer, bunged into the microwave and served to you in the bar, while at others you can find yourself enjoying the comfort of their à la carte restaurant. Most menus include at least two vegetarian options.

Beer is equally varied. Lager is always available, but in northern England people tend to drink bitter; be warned that it can get very personal.

Other places to eat out

In the larger villages and towns you'll have a wider choice with both take-aways and restaurants offering culinary selections from around the world.

MONEY

You will need to carry a fair amount of **cash** with you on the walk, although you should come to a bank every two days or so, but don't always expect it to have a cash machine. Small independent shops will prefer you to pay in cash as will most B&Bs, bunkhouses and campsites but will generally accept cheques from a British bank as an alternative. Shops that do take cards, such as supermarkets, will sometimes advance cash against a card as long as you buy something at the same time. **Travellers' cheques** can only be cashed at banks, foreign exchange bureaux and some large hotels.

Using the Post Office for banking

Several banks in Britain now have agreements with the Post Office allowing customers to make cash withdrawals using either a chequebook and debit card or just a debit card (with PIN number) at post offices throughout the country. However, the era of the country post office seems to be coming to an end and many are closing down so check in advance if you are planning to rely on one.

OTHER SERVICES

Many of the settlements that the Pennine Way passes through have little more than a public **telephone**, **village shop** and a **post office**, and some not even that. If you find you are carrying unnecessary equipment do consider posting it home; the expense is probably worth it if it means you will enjoy your walk all the more.

Where they exist, special mention has also been made in Part 4 of other services which are of use to walkers such as **banks**, **cash machines**, **outdoor equipment shops**, **laundrettes**, **pharmacies**, **medical centres** and **tourist information centres**.

WALKING COMPANIES

For walkers wanting to make their holiday as easy and trouble free as possible there are several specialist companies offering a range of services from accommodation booking to fully-guided group tours.

Accommodation booking

Arranging all the accommodation for your walk can take a considerable amount of time. For a small fee you can get someone else to do the phoning for you.

● **Brigantes Walking Holidays** (☎ 01729-830463, 🖳 www.pikedaw.freeserve .co.uk/walks), Rookery Cottage, Kirkby Malham, Skipton BD23 4BX
● **Pack and Go** (☎ 01254-680793, 🖳 www.pack-and-go.co.uk), 1 Woodsend Close, Blackburn, Lancashire, BB2 3WR
● **Sherpa Van Project** (☎ 020-8569 4101, 🖳 www.sherpavan.com), 131a Heston Rd, Hounslow, Middlesex, TW5 0RF
● **Spotlight Guides** (☎ 08453-454245, 🖳 enquiries@thepennineway.co.uk), Roseberry Ct, Ellerbeck Way, Stokesly Business Park, Stokesly, TS9 5QT
● **Tourist information centres** (TICs; see p35); local TICs will book accommodation for you for a small fee
● **Tyne Valley Holidays** (☎ 0191-284 7534), 21 Celandine Close, Gosforth, NE3 5JW
● **YHA** (☎ 0870-770 6113; 🖳 www.yha.org.uk), PO Box 67, Matlock, Derbyshire, DE4 3YX; their Pennine Way Bureau will book accommodation at youth hostels along the Way for you.

Baggage carriers

The thought of carrying a large pack puts a lot of people off walking long-distance trails. The following companies offer a baggage-carrying service either direct to your campsite/accommodation each night or to a drop-off point in each village; all you need to carry is a small daypack with essentials in it. If you are finding the walk harder than expected you can always join one of these services en route. Please, however, bear in mind the extra environmental impact of using one of these services.

Some of the **taxi** firms listed in this guide (see Part 4) can provide a similar service within a local area if you are having problems carrying your bags for a day or so. Using a taxi is only likely to be cost-effective if you are in a small group and can share the expense.

- **Brigantes Walking Holidays** (see p15)
- **Pack and Go** (see p15)
- **Spotlight Guides** (see p15)
- **Sherpa Van Project** (see p15)
- **Tyne Valley Holidays** (see p15)

Self-guided holidays

The following companies provide all-in customized packages for walkers which usually include detailed advice and notes on itineraries and routes, maps, accommodation booking, daily baggage transfer, and transport arrangements at the start and end of your walk. If you don't want the whole all-in package some of the companies can simply arrange **accommodation booking** or **baggage carrying** services on their own.

- **Brigantes Walking Holidays** (see p15)
- **Pack and Go** (see p15)
- **Sherpa Expeditions** (☎ 020-8577 2717, 🖳 www.sherpa-walking-holidays.co.uk), 131a Heston Rd, Hounslow, Middlesex, TW5 0RF
- **Tyne Valley Holidays** (see p15)

Group/guided walking tours

Fully-guided tours are ideal for individuals wanting to travel in the company of others and for groups of friends wanting to be guided. The packages usually include meals, accommodation, transport arrangements, mini-bus backup, baggage transfer, as well as a qualified guide. Companies' specialities differ widely with varying size of groups, standards of accommodation, age range of clients, distances walked and professionalism of guides; it's worth checking out several before making a booking.

- **Avalon Trekking** (☎ 01889-575646 and 0777-596 7644, 🖳 www.avalon-trekking.co.uk), 40 Waverley Gardens, Etching Hill, Rugeley, Staffordshire, WS15 2YE
- **Brigantes Walking Holidays** (see p15)
- **HF Holidays** (☎ 020-8905 9558, 🖳 www.hfholidays.co.uk), Imperial House, Edgware Rd, London, NW9 5AL
- **Sherpa Expeditions** (see above)
- **YHA** (see above) Guided walks from Hawes to Alston only

Budgeting

Your trip budget depends on the level of comfort you desire. If you are happy sleeping under canvas and cooking for yourself you can walk the Pennine Way very cheaply. It is, however, not difficult to spend much more than you might intend. See p18 for some estimates of possible expenditure.

❏ **Information for foreign visitors**

● **Currency** The British pound (£) comes in notes of £100, £50, £20, £10, £5 and coins of £2 and £1. The pound is divided into 100 pence (usually referred to as 'p', pronounced pee) which comes in silver coins of 50p, 20p 10p and 5p and copper coins of 2p and 1p.

● **Rates of exchange** Up-to-date rates of exchange can be found at ⌨ www.xe .com/ucc.

● **Business hours** Most **shops** and main **post offices** are open at least from Monday to Friday 9am-5pm and Saturday 9am-12.30pm. Many choose longer hours and some open on Sundays as well. **Banks** have a variety of opening hours from as early as 9am to as late as 5.30pm. As a rule of thumb most are open from at least 10am to 4pm Monday to Friday, but in small places they may only be open for, say, three half days per week.

There is always talk in the press of licensing laws being relaxed in England. But at the moment **pubs** are allowed to open from 11am to 11pm Monday to Saturday and 12 noon-3pm, 7-10.30pm on Sunday. The rules are different for hotels if you are a resident. Once you arrive in Kirk Yetholm in Scotland you can expect a much longer evening at the bar if that is what you like.

● **National holidays** Most businesses in England are shut on New Year's Day (January 1st), Good Friday and Easter Monday (March/April), first and last Monday in May, last Monday in August, Christmas Day and Boxing Day (December 25th and 26th).

● **Weights and measures** Britain is attempting to move towards the metric system but there is much resistance. Food is now sold in metric weights (g and kg) due to a European law but most people still think in the imperial weights of pounds (lb) and ounces (oz). A couple of market stall holders have earned themselves the name 'metric martyrs' because they've taken their claim to be allowed to sell in whatever unit the customer wants to the highest court in the land. So far they've lost all their court hearings. There is as yet no threat from European bureaucrats to the traditional units of milk and beer, the pint. Road signs and distances are always given in miles rather than kilometres.

● **Telephone** The international access code for Britain is +44, followed by the area code minus the first 0, and then the number you require. To call a number with the same area code as the phone you are calling from you can omit the code. It is cheaper to ring at weekends and after 6pm and before 8am on weekdays.

● **Emergency services** For police, ambulance, fire brigade and mountain rescue dial ☎ 999. If you need emergency help at any stage of the Pennine Way ask for 'Police and Mountain Rescue'.

ACCOMMODATION

Camping

You can get by on as little as £8 per person per day if you camp on the cheapest sites. This assumes you would be cooking all your own food from staple ingredients rather than enjoying lots of convenience food. Most walkers would find it hard to live that frugally and know that part of the fun is the odd pint or two and a greasy burger and chips every now and then, in which case £10-12 per day would be more realistic.

Bunkhouses and hostels

You can't always cook your own food in hostels/bunkhouses so costs inevitably rise: £15-20 per day will allow you to have the occasional meal out and enjoy sampling a few of the local brews. If you don't want to carry a stove or are planning on eating out most nights you may need to add another £5.

B&Bs

Obviously you won't be cooking for yourself if you choose this style of accommodation. Bearing in mind that B&B prices vary enormously, £50 per day should see you snoozing with your head on a clean pillowcase and your stomach full.

EXTRAS

Incidental sundries can add up. Postcards, film, cream teas, beer, getting back home, foot massages …Cheap individually, expensive together.

When to go

SEASONS

The **main walking season** in England is from the Easter holiday (March/April) through to October. With global warming it is hard to predict the weather – or, rather, it is easier to predict that it will be unpredictable but it still holds that the best months to walk the Pennine Way are May, June and September.

Spring

The month of **April** is one of the most unpredictable for walkers. The weather can be warm and sunny, although blustery days with showers are more typical; there is often snow still lying on the hills. On the plus side, the land is just waking up to spring, there won't be many other walkers about but there will be plenty of wild flowers and the bird song will be at its best.

May and early **June** are traditionally a great time for walking and the Pennine Way can be busy then, but you are at least outside the school holidays. The temperature could be warm, the weather is as dry and clear as can be expected, and wild flowers are out in their full glory. The days will be at their longest in June.

Summer

July and **August** often herald the arrival of hordes of tourists. On some weekends it can feel as if the whole world has arrived; traffic makes the roads noisy and many hostels and B&Bs are fully booked days in advance. As always in England, there is a good chance of at least some rain during these months.

Autumn

A slower pace of life returns when the school holidays come to an end. Late **September** and early **October** see stunning autumn colours in the woods and on the hills. You are less likely to meet other walkers, but more likely to encounter rain and strong winds. The air temperature is still mild.

Winter

Late **October** and **early November** can occasionally be glorious with crisp clear days, but this is also the start of winter; the days are shortening, the temperature has dropped noticeably and many seasonal B&Bs, hostels, campsites and shops have closed.

You need to be pretty hardy to walk between late **November** and mid-**March**. True, some days can be fantastically bright and sunny and your appreciation will be heightened by snow on the hills and the general absence of people. You are far more likely however to be walking through driving rain (and sometimes snow), and finding the onset of darkness more sudden than you had planned for.

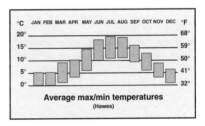

Average max/min temperatures
(Hawes)

TEMPERATURE AND RAINFALL

The Pennines are famous for being wet. However, if you pick your time of year you can minimize your chances of spending every day of your walk with soggy feet. They're equally well known for being cold, but as with rainfall you can plan around this. But, don't expect your plan to be fail proof. If there's one thing you can plan on with the English weather it is unpredictability. These tables provide a guide, which is all anyone can do.

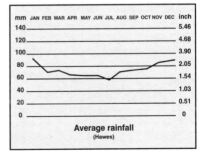

Average rainfall
(Hawes)

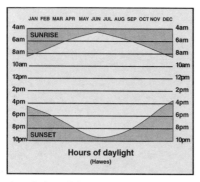

Hours of daylight
(Hawes)

DAYLIGHT HOURS

If walking in autumn, winter and early spring, you must take account of how far you can walk in the available light. It may not be possible to cover as many miles as you would in summer.

This table gives the sunrise and sunset times for the middle of each month at Hawes, a town about halfway along the Pennine Way. This gives a reasonably accurate picture for daylight for the whole trail. Depending on the weather you should get a further 30-45 minutes of usable light before sunrise and after sunset.

ANNUAL EVENTS

Many of the villages and towns on the Pennine Way have an agricultural show, gala and/or carnival in the summer months. These, and the events listed below, could add to your enjoyment of the walk but at the same time can mean accommodation in the relevant area gets booked up. For further details of any events in the region contact the tourist information centres (see p35).

Hebden Bridge
● **Green Week** The aim of this is to encourage people to shop locally (including at the farmers' market), use environmentally-friendly transport (bike taxis are available from the railway station), and events such as solar-powered Morris dancing. Held in the first week of June.
● **Arts Festival** A variety of music and arts events in the last week of June and the first week of July.

Horton-in-Ribblesdale
● Both the **Three Peaks Challenge** (🖳 www.threepeaksrace.org.uk, see box p127; held on the last Sunday in April) and the **Cyclocross** (last Sunday in September) involve getting up and down the Three Peaks (Ingleborough, Whernside and Pen y Ghent) either by running or cycling in as short a time as possible.

Hawes
● The **Hardraw Brass-band Contest** (every September) held by the waterfall in the grounds of the Green Dragon Inn.
● **Swaledale Arts Festival** (🖳 www.swaledale-festival.org.uk) held over two weeks at the end of May/early June every year. Brass bands, jazz and various art events.

Itineraries

All walkers are individuals. Some like to cover large distances as quickly as possible, others are happy to stroll along stopping whenever the whim takes them. You may want to walk the Pennine Way all in one go, tackle it over a series of weekends or use the trail for linear day walks; the choice is yours. To accommodate these differences this guidebook has not been divided up into rigid daily stages. Instead, it's been designed to make it easy for you to plan your own perfect itinerary.

The **planning map** and **table of village/town facilities** summarize the essential information and make it straightforward to make a plan of your own. Alternatively, to make it even easier, have a look at the **suggested itineraries** and simply choose your preferred type of accommodation and speed of walking. There are also suggestions (see below) for those who want to experience the best of the trail over a day or a weekend. The **public transport maps** on pp36-9 may also be useful at this stage.

Having made a rough plan, turn to **Part 4**, **Trail guide and maps**, where you will find summaries of the route; full descriptions of accommodation, places to eat and other services in each village and town; and detailed trail maps.

WHICH DIRECTION?

Most people head south to north. There are practical reasons for walking in this direction; the prevailing wind and rain (south-westerly) is behind you, as is the sun. But apart from that do whichever feels right to you.

The maps in Part 4 give timings for both directions and, as route finding instructions are on the maps rather than in blocks of text, it is straightforward using this guide back to front.

SUGGESTED ITINERARIES

The itineraries on p24, p25 and p26 are suggestions only; please feel free to adapt them to your needs. **Don't forget to add your travelling time** before and after the walk.

❏ **Walking with dogs**
Dogs are a pleasure to walk with providing they are well behaved. They must be under control at all times and kept on the lead when near livestock. You may know that your dog doesn't chase sheep but the farmer does not. You will be walking through many conservation areas so you must also carefully control your dog when there are nesting birds or fledglings around; they make tasty meals for a dog, and even if chased and not caught they can sometimes die later.

Place name Places in (brackets) are a short walk off the path	Distance from previous place approx miles/km	Cash Machine/ Bank	Post Office	Tourist Information Centre
Edale	Start		✔	✔
Crowden	16 (26)			
Standedge	11 (18)			
Mankinholes	10 (16)			
Calder Valley	4 (6)	✔	✔	✔
(for Hebden Bridge)				
Blackshaw Head	1 (2)			
Colden	1 (2)			
(Haworth)		✔	✔	✔
Ponden & Stanbury	10 (16)			
Ickornshaw & Cowling	4 (6)		✔	
Lothersdale	2 (3)			
(Earby)			✔	
Thornton-in-Craven	4 (6)			
East Marton	1.5 (2)			
Gargrave	2.5 (4)	✔	✔	
Airton	3.5 (6)			
Kirkby Malham	1.5 (2)			
Malham	1 (2)			✔
(Stainforth)				
Horton-in-Ribblesdale	15 (24)		✔	✔
Hawes	14 (23)	✔	✔	✔
Hardraw	1.5 (2)			
Thwaite	8 (13)			
(Muker)				
Keld	3 (5)			
Tan Hill	4 (6)			
(Bowes)			✔	
Baldersdale	10 (16)			
Lunedale	3 (5)			
Middleton-in-Teesdale	3.5 (6)	B	✔	✔
Holwick	2.5 (4)			
High Force	2.5 (4)			
Forest-in-Teesdale	3.5 (6)			
& Langdon Beck				
Dufton	12 (19)		✔	
Garrigill	16 (26)		✔	
Alston	4 (6)	CM	✔	✔
Slaggyford & Knarsdale	6 (10)			
Greenhead	11 (18)			
Once Brewed	7 (11)			✔
(Stonehaugh)				
Hetherington	9.5 (15)			
Bellingham	3 (5)	CM	✔	✔
Byrness	15 (24)			
(Uswayford)				
Kirk Yetholm & Town Yetholm	27 (43)		✔	

| TOTAL DISTANCE | 256 miles (412km) | | | |

TOWN FACILITIES

Eating Place	Food Store	Camp-site	Hostels* Bunkhouse Camping barn	B&Bs§ (B&B) = two or fewer	Place name Places in (brackets) are a short walk off the path
✓	✓	✓	YHA, CB, B	B&B	**Edale**
	✓	✓	YHA		**Crowden**
				(B&B)	**Standedge**
			YHA	(B&B)	**Mankinholes**
✓	✓			B&B	**Calder Valley**
					(for Hebden Bridge)
		✓		(B&B)	**Blackshaw Head**
✓	✓	✓			**Colden**
✓	✓		YHA	B&B	**(Haworth)**
✓	✓			B&B	**Ponden & Stanbury**
✓	✓	✓		(B&B)	**Ickornshaw & Cowling**
✓		✓		(B&B)	**Lothersdale**
✓	✓		YHA		**(Earby)**
				(B&B)	**Thornton-in-Craven**
✓		✓		(B&B)	**East Marton**
✓	✓	✓		(B&B)	**Gargrave**
			H	(B&B)	**Airton**
✓				(B&B)	**Kirkby Malham**
✓	✓	✓	YHA, B	B&B	**Malham**
			YHA		**(Stainforth)**
✓	✓	✓	YHA, B	B&B	**Horton-in-Ribblesdale**
✓	✓	✓	YHA	B&B	**Hawes**
✓		✓		(B&B)	**Hardraw**
✓				(B&B)	**Thwaite**
✓	✓	✓		B&B	**(Muker)**
	✓	✓	YHA	(B&B)	**Keld**
✓		✓		(B&B)	**Tan Hill**
✓	✓	✓		(B&B)	**(Bowes)**
		✓	YHA, CB	(B&B)	**Baldersdale**
				(B&B)	**Lunedale**
✓	✓	✓	B	B&B	**Middleton-in-Teesdale**
	✓	✓	B	(B&B)	**Holwick**
✓				(B&B)	**High Force**
		✓	YHA	(B&B)	**Forest-in-Teesdale**
					& Langdon Beck
✓	✓	✓	YHA	B&B	**Dufton**
✓		✓	YHA, B	(B&B)	**Garrigill**
✓	✓	✓	YHA	B&B	**Alston**
		✓		(B&B)	**Slaggyford & Knarsdale**
✓		✓	YHA, B	B&B	**Greenhead**
✓		✓	YHA	B&B	**Once Brewed**
		✓			**(Stonehaugh)**
				(B&B)	**Hetherington**
✓	✓	✓	YHA	B&B	**Bellingham**
✓	✓	✓	YHA, B	(B&B)	**Byrness**
				(B&B)	**(Uswayford)**
✓	✓		YHA	B&B	**Kirk Yetholm & Town Yetholm**

Hostels* YHA = Youth Hostel, H = Independent Hostel, B = Bunkhouse, CB = Camping barn
B&Bs§ This includes B&B-style accommodation in pubs, hotels etc

CAMPING

	Relaxed pace		Medium pace		Fast pace	
Night	**Place**	**Approx Distance** miles (km)	**Place**	**Approx Distance** miles (km)	**Place**	**Approx Distance** miles (km)
0	Edale		Edale		Edale	
1	Crowden	16 (26)	Crowden	16 (26)	Crowden	16 (26)
2	Standedge	11 (18)	Standedge	11 (18)	Mankinholes	21 (34)
3	Mankinholes	10 (16)	Blackshaw Head	15 (24)	Lothersdale	22 (35)
4	Ponden	16 (26)	Lothersdale	17 (27)	Malham	14 (23)
5	East Marton	11.5 (19)	Malham	14 (23)	Horton-in-Ribblesdale	15 (24)
6	Malham	8.5 (14)	Horton-in-Ribblesdale	15 (24)	Keld	26.5 (43)
7	Horton-in-Ribblesdale	15 (24)	Hawes	14 (23)	Middleton-in-Teesdale	20.5 (33)
8	Hawes	14 (23)	(Rest day)		Dufton	20.5 (33)
9	(Rest day)		Keld	12.5 (20)	Alston	20 (32)
10	Keld	12.5 (20)	Baldersdale	14 (23)	Greenhead	17 (27)
11	Baldersdale	14 (23)	Langdon Beck	15 (24)	Bellingham	21.5 (35)
12	Langdon Beck	15 (24)	Dufton	12 (19)	Byrness	15 (24)
13	Dufton	12 (19)	Alston	20 (32)	Kirk Yetholm	27 (43)
14	Garrigill	16 (26)	Greenhead	17 (27)		
15	Knarsdale	10 (16)	Once Brewed	7 (11)		
16	Greenhead	11 (18)	Bellingham	14.5 (23)		
17	Once Brewed	7 (11)	Byrness	15 (24)		
18	Bellingham	14.5 (23)	Kirk Yetholm	27 (43)		
19	Byrness	15 (24)				
20	wild camp in Cheviots	approx 13 (21)				
21	Kirk Yetholm	14 (23)				

STAYING IN HOSTELS, BUNKHOUSES AND CAMPING BARNS

	Relaxed pace		Medium pace		Fast pace	
Night	Place	Approx Distance miles (km)	Place	Approx Distance miles (km)	Place	Approx Distance miles (km)
0	Edale		Edale		Edale	
1	Crowden	16 (26)	Crowden	16 (26)	Crowden	16 (26)
2	Standedge*	11 (18)	Standedge*	11 (18)	Mankinholes	21 (34)
3	Mankinholes	10 (16)	Mankinholes	10 (16)	Ickornshaw & Cowling*	20 (32)
4	Haworth§	15 (24)	Ickornshaw & Cowling*	20 (32)	Malham	16 (26)
5	Earby•	9 (14)	Malham	16 (26)	Horton-in-Ribblesdale	15 (24)
6	Malham	12 (19)	Horton-in-Ribblesdale	15 (24)	Keld	26.5 (43)
7	Horton-in-Ribblesdale	15 (24)	Hawes	14 (23)	Middleton-in-Teesdale	20.5 (33)
8	Hawes	14 (23)	(Rest day)		Dufton	20.5 (33)
9	(Rest day)		Keld	12.5 (20)	Alston	20 (32)
10	Keld	12.5 (20)	Baldersdale	14 (23)	Greenhead	17 (27)
11	Baldersdale	14 (23)	Langdon Beck	15 (24)	Bellingham	21.5 (35)
12	Langdon Beck	15 (24)	Dufton	12 (19)	Byrness	15 (24)
13	Dufton	12 (19)	Alston	20 (32)	Kirk Yetholm	27 (43)
14	Garrigill	16 (26)	Greenhead	17 (27)		
15	Knarsdale*	10 (16)	Once Brewed	7 (11)		
16	Greenhead	11 (18)	Bellingham	14.5 (23)		
17	Once Brewed	7 (11)	Byrness	15 (24)		
18	Bellingham	14.5 (23)	Kirk Yetholm	27 (43)		
19	Byrness	15 (24)				
20	Uswayford*•	12 (19)				
21	Kirk Yetholm	15 (24)				

*No hostel; stay in B&B   § 3.5 miles (6km) off-route therefore +3.5 miles each way
• 1.5 miles (2km) off-route therefore +1.5 miles each way

STAYING IN B&Bs

	Relaxed pace		Medium pace		Fast pace	
Night	**Place**	**Approx Distance** miles (km)	**Place**	**Approx Distance** miles (km)	**Place**	**Approx Distance** miles (km)
0	Edale		Edale		Edale	
1	Crowden*	16 (26)	Crowden*	16 (26)	Crowden*	16 (26)
2	Standedge	11 (18)	Standedge	11 (18)	Mankinholes	21 (34)
3	Hebden Bridge	14 (23)	Hebden Bridge	14 (23)	Lothersdale	22 (35)
4	Ponden	12 (19)	Lothersdale	18 (29)	Malham	14 (23)
5	Thornton-in-Craven	10 (16)	Malham	14 (23)	Horton-in-Ribblesdale	15 (24)
6	Malham	10 (16)	Horton-in-Ribblesdale	15 (24)	Keld	26.5 (43)
7	Horton-in-Ribblesdale	15 (24)	Hawes	14 (23)	Middleton-in-Teesdale	20.5 (33)
8	Hawes	14 (23)	(Rest day)		Dufton	20.5 (33)
9	(Rest day)		Keld	12.5 (20)	Alston	20 (32)
10	Keld	12.5 (20)	Lunedale	17 (27)	Greenhead	17 (27)
11	Lunedale	17 (27)	Langdon Beck	12 (19)	Bellingham	21.5 (35)
12	Langdon Beck	12 (19)	Dufton	12 (19)	Byrness	15 (24)
13	Dufton	12 (19)	Alston	20 (32)	Kirk Yetholm	27 (43)
14	Garrigill	16 (26)	Greenhead	17 (27)		
15	Knarsdale	10 (16)	Once Brewed	7 (11)		
16	Greenhead	11 (18)	Bellingham	14.5 (23)		
17	Once Brewed	7 (11)	Byrness	15 (24)		
18	Bellingham	14.5 (23)	Kirk Yetholm	27 (43)		
19	Byrness	15 (24)				
20	Uswayford•	12 (19)				
21	Kirk Yetholm	15 (24)				

*No B&B; stay at hostel   • 1.5 miles (2km) off-route therefore +1.5 miles each way

❏ HIGHLIGHTS

The best day and weekend walks

One great way of experiencing the essence of the Pennine Way is to do it in a series of days or weekends that take in a section at a time, not necessarily consecutively. Over a period of time it would be quite possible to complete the entire route this way. The other advantage is to walk only the five-star sections, leaving the more boring bits out of the equation.

The following are some suggestions for linear walks intended to get the most out of the time available and stay on the trail for as long as possible. Getting back to the start is not always straightforward but by using bus and train timetables, taxi firms and some ingenuity it will be possible to do so.   *(continued opposite)*

❏ HIGHLIGHTS (CONTINUED)

Day walks

● **Edale to Kinder Downfall via Upper Booth, Jacob's Ladder and Kinder Low** – There and back is a walk of 10 miles (16km) which gives a true taste of the Dark Peak and the groughs and edges of the Kinder Plateau. The area gives a fine feeling of wilderness yet is not very far at any time from civilization. See pp66-73.

● **Standedge to the White House pub via Blackstone Edge** – 12 miles (19km). This walk covers some true peat moorland, mostly on slabbed paths laid to counter erosion but useful in keeping the boots out of the mire. It passes the celebrated snack caravan at Windy Hill, crosses the M62 on a fine, elevated footbridge and follows an ancient packhorse route in the closing stage that could have been used, if not built by, the Romans. See pp86-93.

● **Thornton-in-Craven to Malham via East Marton and the Leeds–Liverpool Canal** – 10 miles (16km) of super walking initially through meadows and fields, then on the canal towpath before visiting Gargrave, home of one of the best cafés on the whole Pennine Way. Beyond Gargrave we follow a lovely riverside path along the River Aire via Airton and Kirkby Malham to arrive at the delightful Malham where if time allows a visit to the Cove is a must. See pp115-25.

● **Middleton-in-Teesdale to Langdon Beck** – This walk of 9 miles (14km) follows the banks of the River Tees, an area rich in wild flowers and birds offering constant variety and many diversions to make this a truly exciting day out. The falls of High Force and Low Force can be seen, in spate an awesome sight. The path has been superbly maintained so the going is easy. By crossing the footbridge at Holwick Head, a visit to High Force Hotel can be made for lunch or a pint. See pp173-9.

● **Dufton to Garrigill over Cross Fell** – This one needs an early start so perhaps stay in Dufton the night before. It is 16 miles (26km) to Garrigill and the weather over Cross Fell is likely to be unpredictable so go well prepared. There's a mountain refuge hut just below the summit (Greg's Hut) where shelter can be sought if necessary. Then there's a long leg-stretching walk down the miners' track to the friendly village of Garrigill. See pp186-94.

● **Greenhead to Once Brewed** – This walk is a great introduction to Hadrian's Wall following the ramparts themselves as they swoop and soar along the Whin Sill. It's 7 miles (11km) and will only take a morning but if you take time to savour the Wall you will not regret it. Thirlwall Castle can also be visited, a later fortification than the Romans yet built using stone from the Wall itself. See pp208-14.

● **Kirk Yetholm to The Schil and return** – This 10-mile (16km) walk uses Kirk Yetholm as the starting point and follows the high-level alternative route south returning by the low-level route via Old Halterburnhead (ruin) and the road along the Halter Burn. It samples the Cheviots, visiting White Law and Steer Rig before finally topping out on the summit of The Schil. In good weather you should have fine views. See pp243-7.

Weekend walks

● **Edale to Standedge** – This 27-mile (43km) walk takes in the Kinder Scout, Bleaklow and Black Hill massifs and offers a chance to experience the true meaning of the name 'Dark Peak'. A night at the youth hostel in Crowden, one of the best, comes as a welcome break in the route, much of it slabbed to ensure you keep your boots relatively dry. See pp66-85. *(cont'd p28)*

❑ **HIGHLIGHTS**

Weekend walks *(continued from p27)*

● **Thornton-in-Craven to Horton-in-Ribblesdale** – This 25-mile (40km) route follows an outstanding section of the Way taking in the best of the limestone country with many hidden gems. After the lovely riverside walk along the gentle River Aire we arrive in Malham, a perfect spot for an overnight stop and the chance to visit the gift shops and sample the draught German beer in the Lister Arms. On day two you have some stiff climbing to do over Fountains Fell, then up to the windy heights of Pen y Ghent to end an exhilarating weekend at Horton. See pp115-34.

● **Hawes to Tan Hill** – This 16¹/₂-mile (27km) walk could be done in a day but is better split into two with an overnight stop in the tiny hamlet of Thwaite, perhaps taking advantage of a quality mini-break at the charming Kearton Country Hotel. Tan Hill could be reached for a late lunch on the second day, allowing the rest of the day to call a taxi to take you down into Kirkby Stephen where there is a train station. The walking is superb and includes a lovely stretch along the escarpment high above the Swale. See pp145-56.

● **Middleton-in-Teesdale to Dufton** – An outstanding weekend walk of 20 miles (32km). You'll take in the flower-filled meadows of the River Tees along with the spectacular High Force waterfall which, after heavy rain, thunders over the lip in a boiling peat-brown turmoil. Cauldron Snout is lower but equally impressive and the vast glaciated amphitheatre of High Cup adds further wonders to this magical walk. The walking is strenuous but rich in terms of views and the sense of lonely isolation among wind-swept moors. See pp169-85.

● **Byrness to Kirk Yetholm** – This weekender gives a flavour of the Cheviot Hills in all their splendour and can be made to include an overnight stop at the lonely Uswayford Farm. The full 27-mile (43km) crossing follows the Border fence, switching from England into Scotland and back again at will. There are two emergency refuges where shelter can be sought from the wind and rain. The walk is sometimes tackled in a single day but perhaps only by the very strong. Better to make it a two-day walk and get the most out of it, preferably in good weather as these hills become sponge-like in the wet. See pp231-47.

What to take

How much you take with you is a very personal decision which takes experience to get right. For those new to long-distance walking the suggestions below will help you strike a sensible balance between comfort, safety and minimal weight.

KEEP IT LIGHT

From small acorns do great oak trees grow, and so from lots of small unnecessary things do great big heavy rucksacks grow. When packing, if in doubt leave it out. A heavy rucksack will impinge on your enjoyment, and sometimes leave you walking in the 'head down, bottom up' posture, which is hardly the best way to see the countryside.

HOW TO CARRY IT

Today's rucksacks seem to have as much design and engineering put into them as a Formula 1 racing car. Most of them are fully adjustable so take the time to adjust it properly to suit you.

If you are carrying your world on your back you will need at least a 65-75 litre rucksack. If you're not taking a tent and staying in bunkhouses 40-60 litres should be ample. For people eating out every meal and staying in B&Bs a 30-40 litre pack should suffice.

Although many rucksacks claim to be waterproof there is always somewhere where the rain can get in; pack everything in a **waterproof rucksack liner** or strong plastic bin liners. It can also be handy to organize the contents of your rucksack into different coloured **stuff sacks** so you know what is where. This can prevent tipping the whole pack upside down just to find the can opener. Take some plastic bags for laundry, wet things, rubbish etc; they're always useful.

Of course, if you decide to use a **baggage-carrying service** (see p15) you can pack most of your things in a suitcase and simply carry a small day-pack with the essentials you need for the day's walking.

FOOTWEAR

Boots

Your feet will work extremely hard on the Pennine Way and in some nasty conditions. Give them as much comfort and support as you can. A quality three-season walking boot is ideal. They must fit well and be properly broken in. A week's walk is not the time to try out a new pair of boots. It does not matter how fit you are; if you get bad blisters you won't be going anywhere. Refer to p249 for more blister-avoidance strategies.

Socks

The traditional wearing of a thin liner sock under a thicker wool sock is no longer necessary if you choose a high-quality sock specially designed for walking. A high proportion of natural fibres makes them much more comfortable. Wool wicks well and keeps you warm when wet. Three pairs are ample.

Extra footwear

Some walkers like to have a second pair of shoes to wear when they are not on the trail. Trainers, sport sandals or flip-flops are all suitable as long as they are light.

CLOTHES

Tops

Always be prepared for wintry weather. It used to be the case that good synthetic clothing couldn't be beaten for keeping you warm and dry, but recently there's been a welcome resurgence of merino wool goods onto the market that are just as good and have the added benefit of being natural and recyclable. In terms of biodegradability there is no difference between a synthetic shirt and a plastic bag and they're both derived from petroleum.

The age-old layering system is still one of the best clothing principles to follow. The base layer transports sweat away from your skin; the mid-layer(s) keep you warm; and the outer layer or 'shell' protects you from the wind, rain and snow.

Avoid cotton at all costs; it chills you when wet and you'll be wet from sweat if not the skies. Take a change or two of **base layers** (including underwear), a good **fleece** or woollen jumper, plus an extra one if you're walking from September to May, and a decent **waterproof**. Keeping the wind chill to a minimum is a key factor in adding to your enjoyment. You can buy very **lightweight wind-proofs** that are invaluable if you prefer not to walk in your waterproof when it's windy but not raining. You may also want a **duvet jacket** if you're camping.

It is always useful to have a **complete set of dry clothing**, just in case the rain gods decide to attack you and so you're able to put on something different once you arrive at your destination. Always make sure you have a **dry base layer** in case you or someone you are with goes down with hypothermia. You have to keep them warm and wet clothes won't help.

Leg wear

Your trousers want to be light, quick-drying, non-restrictive and non-chaffing. Being windproof is an advantage. Many British walkers find polyester tracksuit bottoms comfortable. Poly-cotton or microfibre trousers are excellent. Denim jeans should never be worn; if they get wet they become heavy, cold and bind to your legs. A pair of **shorts** is nice to have on sunny days. Thermal **long johns** or thick tights are cosy if you're camping and necessary for winter walking. **Waterproof trousers** can be handy most of the year but in summer could be left behind if your main pair of trousers is reasonably windproof and quick-drying. **Gaiters** are not needed unless you come across a lot of snow in winter.

Other clothes

A **warm hat** and **gloves** should be carried at all times of the year. Take two pairs of gloves in winter. In summer you should carry a **sun hat** and possibly a **swimsuit** if you enjoy swimming in cold rivers. A small **towel** will be needed if you are not staying in B&Bs.

TOILETRIES

Only take the minimum: a small bar of **soap** in a plastic container (unless staying in B&Bs) which can also be used instead of shaving cream and for washing clothes; a tiny tube of **toothpaste** and a **toothbrush**; one roll of **loo paper** in a plastic bag. If you are planning to defecate outdoors you should also take a lightweight **trowel** for burying the evidence (see p43 for further tips). A **razor**; **deodorant**; **tampons/sanitary towels**; a high-factor **sun screen**; a good **insect**

❏ **Mountain Rescue**
If you need to call assistance dial ☎ 999 and ask for 'Police and Mountain Rescue'.
That way the operator will be able immediately to direct your call to those that can
help. Although Mountain Rescue teams are called out by the police and are answer-
able to the Home Secretary, all team members are volunteers. Most have full-time
jobs as well as families so would prefer not to hear their bleeper go off at 1am because
someone has come unstuck on the hills.

On average the Edale team attends three call-outs a fortnight which can be anything from a lost child or sprained ankle to searching for murder victims. They do all
their fundraising themselves so if you see a collection box for the local team please
give generously. You don't know when you may need them.

---

repellent for the summertime midges; and some system for **water purification**
(see p249) should cover all your needs.

FIRST-AID KIT

Medical facilities in Britain are excellent so you only need a small kit to cover
common problems and emergencies; pack it in a waterproof container. A basic
kit will contain **aspirin** or **paracetamol** for treating mild to moderate pain and
fever; **plasters** for minor cuts; '**moleskin**', '**Compeed**', or '**Second Skin**' for
blisters; a **bandage** for holding dressings, splints, or limbs in place and for supporting a sprained ankle, **elastic knee support** for a weak knee, a small selection of different-sized **sterile dressings** for wounds; **porous adhesive tape**;
antiseptic wipes; **antiseptic cream**; **safety pins**; **tweezers**; **scissors**.

GENERAL ITEMS

Essential
Anyone walking in the mountains should carry a 'Silva' type **compass** and
know how to use it; an emergency **whistle** for summoning assistance; a litre
water bottle; a **torch** (flashlight) with spare bulb and batteries in case you end
up walking after it's got dark; **emergency food** which your body can quickly
convert into energy; a **penknife**; a **watch**; and several **plastic bags** for packing
out any rubbish you accumulate (see p42 for further information). If you're not
carrying a sleeping bag or tent you should also take an emergency plastic **bivi-
bag**.

Useful
Many would list a **camera** as essential but it can be liberating to travel without
one once in a while; a **notebook** is more reliable than your memory for record-
ing sites, sounds and smells; a reading **book** to pass the time on train and bus
journeys; a pair of **sunglasses** in summer or when there's snow on the ground;
binoculars for watching wildlife; a **walking stick** or pole to take the shock off
your knees; and a **vacuum flask** for carrying hot drinks. Nothing aids admiring
the view from the top of a steep, high hill like a cup of hot tea.

SLEEPING BAG

If you're camping or planning to stay in camping barns and bunkhouses you'll need a sleeping bag. Some bunkhouses have bedding available but you'll keep your costs down if you don't have to hire it. All youth hostels provide bedding and insist you use it.

A three-season bag will cope with most eventualities although many walkers will be able to make do with one rated for one or two seasons; it's a personal choice. If in doubt, go warm.

CAMPING GEAR

If you're camping you will need a decent **tent** (or bivi bag if you enjoy travelling light) able to withstand wet and windy weather with netting on the entrance to keep the midges at bay; a **sleeping mat**; a **stove** and **fuel**; a **pan** with frying pan that can double as a lid/plate; a **pan handle**; a **mug**; a **spoon**; and a wire/plastic **scrubber** for washing up (there's no need for washing up liquid and it should never be used in streams, lakes or rivers).

TRAVEL INSURANCE

Visitors from other countries within the EU should complete form E111 which entitles you to medical treatment under the National Health Service. This is no substitute for proper medical cover on your travel insurance for unforeseen bills and getting you home should that be necessary.

All walkers should consider insurance cover for loss or theft of personal belongings, especially if you are camping or staying in hostels, as there will be times when you'll have to leave your belongings unattended.

MAPS

The hand-drawn maps in this book cover the trail at a scale of 1:20,000. In some parts, particularly on high moors where navigation points are scant, a map and compass will be essential, too, in case the mist comes down or you wander far from the trail by accident. Maps are available from Ordnance Survey (☎ 0845-200 2712, 🖥 www.ordsvy.gov.uk) or Harveys (☎ 01786-841202, 🖥 www.harveymaps.co.uk).

From south to north Ordnance Survey's yellow Outdoor Leisure range (currently being replaced by orange Explorer maps) covers the Pennine Way on the following sheets at 1:25,000: **1** The Peak District, **21** South Pennines, **10** Yorkshire Dales Southern Area, **2** Yorkshire Dales, **30** Yorkshire Dales Northern & Central Areas, **31** North Pennines, **43** Hadrian's Wall, **42** Keilder Water, **16** The Cheviot Hills.

Map buyers can reduce the often considerable cost of purchasing them: members of the **Ramblers' Association** (see p35) can borrow maps for up to six weeks at 50p per map from their library; members of the **Backpackers Club** (see p35) can purchase maps at a significant discount through their map service.

USEFUL BOOKS

Flora and fauna field guides

Any good field guide will do; the Collins Pocket Guide series is unfailingly practical:

● *Wild Guide British Wildlife – The essential beginner's guide*, Collins 2002. A useful compendium including birds, wild flowers, trees, insects, wild animals, butterflies and moths.

● *Birdwatcher's Pocket Field Guide*, Mark Golley, New Holland, 2003

● *The New Birdwatcher's Pocket Guide of Britain and Europe*, Peter Hayman and Rob Hume, Mitchell Beazley 2003

● *Wild flowers of Britain and Ireland*, Richard Fitter, Alastair Fitter and Marjorie Blamey, A & C Black, Domino Guide 2003

● *Birds*, Peter Holden, Collins Wild Guide 2004

● *Wild Flowers*, John Akeroyd, Collins Wild Guide 2004

● *Insects*, Bob Gibbons, Collins Wild Guide 1999

● *Trees*, Allen J Coombes, Dorling Kindersley, 2000

❏ **Getting to Britain**

● **By air** There are plenty of cheap flights from around the world to London's airports: Heathrow, Gatwick, Luton, London City and Stansted. However, Manchester and Edinburgh airports are the closest to the start and finish points of the Pennine Way. There are also airports at Newcastle and Leeds.

● **From Europe by train** Eurostar (☎ 020-7928 5163, 🖳 www.eurostar.com) operates a high-speed passenger service via the Channel Tunnel between Paris and London (3 hours) and Brussels and London (2 hours 40 minutes). Trains arrive and depart London from the international terminal at Waterloo station. Waterloo has connections to the London Underground and to all other main railway stations in London. There are also various rail/ferry services to and from Britain and the continent; for more information contact Rail Europe (☎ 08705-848848, 🖳 www.raileurope.co.uk).

● **From Europe by bus** Eurolines (☎ 08705 143219, 🖳 www.eurolines.co.uk) have a huge network of long-distance bus services connecting over 500 cities in 25 European countries to London. Check carefully, however: often, once such expenses as food for the journey are taken into consideration, it often does not work out that much cheaper than taking a flight, particularly when compared to the prices of some of the budget airlines.

● **From Europe by car** P&O Ferries (☎ 08705 202020, 🖳 www.POferries.com) and Hoverspeed (☎ 08702 408070, 🖳 www.hoverspeed.co.uk) run frequent ferries between Calais and Dover. The journey takes about 75 minutes.

Eurotunnel (☎ 08 705 353535, 🖳 www.eurotunnel.com) operates the shuttle train service for vehicles via the Channel Tunnel between Calais and Folkestone taking one hour between the motorway in France and the motorway in Britain. There are also countless other ferries plying routes between all the major North Sea and Channel ports of mainland Europe and the ports on Britain's eastern and southern coasts.

Getting to and from the Pennine Way

Travelling to the start of the Pennine Way by public transport makes sense. There's no need to worry about the safety of your abandoned vehicle while walking, there are no logistical headaches about how to return to your car when you've finished the walk and it's obviously one of the biggest steps you can take towards minimizing your ecological footprint. Quite apart from that, you'll simply feel your holiday has begun the moment you step out of your front door, rather than having to wait until you've slammed the car door behind you.

NATIONAL TRANSPORT

Manchester and Sheffield can both be used as gateways to the start of the Pennine Way being only 30-45 minutes from Edale by train, the most convenient way to get there. Berwick-upon-Tweed is the main transport hub at the northern end of the walk and is reached from Kirk Yetholm (the end of the Way) by bus changing at Kelso.

By rail

Manchester and Sheffield are served by frequent trains from the rest of Britain making it easy to get to the start of the Pennine Way, and Berwick-upon-Tweed is on the mainline between London, Newcastle and Edinburgh for the journey home. There are stations on the Pennine Way at Edale, Hebden Bridge, Gargrave and Horton-in-Ribblesdale. Other useful stations with good bus services linking them to various parts of the Way include Huddersfield, Skipton, Darlington, Haltwhistle and Hexham.

   National rail enquiries (☎ 08457-484950, 24hrs, 🖳 www.nationalrail .co.uk) will be able to give you the timetable and fare information for rail travel in the whole of Britain. It's worth planning ahead as you can save a considerable amount of money by buying a ticket in advance. These special rates are of limited availability so book as early as possible; at least two weeks if possible although you can often get some discount a week in advance. It helps to be as flexible as possible and don't forget that most of these tickets carry some restrictions; check what they are before you buy your ticket. Travel on a Friday may be more expensive than on other days of the week.

By coach

National Express (☎ 08705-808080, lines open 8am-10pm daily; 🖳 www .nationalexpress.com) is the principal coach (long-distance bus) operator in Britain. There are services from most towns in England and Wales to Manchester, Sheffield and Berwick-upon-Tweed. Travel by coach is usually cheaper than by train but does take longer. Advance bookings carry discounts so be sure to book at least a week ahead. If you don't mind an uncomfortable night there are overnight services on some routes.

By car

Both Edale and Kirk Yetholm are fairly easily reached using the motorway and A-road network from the rest of Britain. Unless you're just out for a day-walk however, you'd be better leaving the car at home as there is nowhere safe to leave a vehicle unattended for a long period.

❏ **FURTHER INFORMATION**

Trail information

Pennine Way website The latest information on the trail can be found on 🖥 www .pennine way.demon.co.uk.

National parks

The Pennine Way goes through the Peak District, Yorkshire Dales and Northumberland national parks; their administrative centres are useful sources of information. See p49 for contact details.

Tourist information

Tourist information centres (TICs) Most towns throughout Britain have a TIC which provides all manner of locally-specific information for visitors and an accommodation booking service (for which there is usually a charge). There are TICs on or near the Pennine Way in **Edale** (☎ 01433-670207), **Hebden Bridge** (☎ 01422-843831), **Malham** (☎ 01729-830363), **Horton-in-Ribblesdale** (☎ 01729-860333), **Hawes** (☎ 01969-667450), **Middleton-in-Teesdale** (☎ 01833-641001), **Alston** (☎ 01434-382244), **Once Brewed** (☎ 01434-344396) and **Bellingham** (☎ 01434-220616).

Organizations for walkers

● **Backpackers Club** (🖥 www.backpackersclub.co.uk, 29 Lynton Drive, High Lane, Stockport, Cheshire, SK6 8JE) A club aimed at people who are involved or interested in lightweight camping whether through walking, cycling, cross-country skiing or canoeing. They produce a quarterly magazine, provide members with a comprehensive information service (including a library) on all aspects of backpacking, organize weekend trips and also publish a farm pitch directory. Membership is £12 per year, family £15, under 18s and over 65s £7.

● **British Mountaineering Council** (☎ 0161-445 4747, 🖥 www.thebmc.co.uk) 177-179 Burton Rd, Manchester, M20 2BB. Promotes the interests of British hillwalkers, climbers and mountaineers. Among the many benefits of membership are an excellent information service, a quarterly magazine and travel insurance designed for mountain sports. Annual membership is £25, family £42.50 and under 18s £14.

● **The Long Distance Walkers' Association** (🖥 www.ldwa.org.uk) An association of people with the common interest of long-distance walking. Membership includes a journal (three a year) giving details of challenge events and local group walks as well as articles on the subject. Information on over 500 Long Distance Paths is presented in the LDWA's Long Distance Walkers' Handbook. Membership is currently £10 per year, family membership is £15.

● **The Ramblers' Association**, (☎ 020-7339 8500, 🖥 www.ramblers.org.uk), 2nd Floor, Camelford House, 87-89 Albert Embankment, London, SE1 7BR. Looks after the interests of walkers throughout Britain. They publish a large amount of useful information including their *Yearbook* (£5.99 to non-members); a full directory of services for walkers. Annual membership is £20, joint/family membership is £26 and under 16s can join for free.

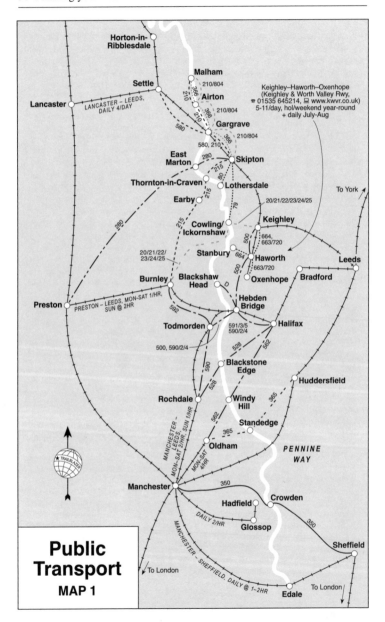

Horton-in-Ribblesdale

Malham
210/804
210
Airton
366
210
210/804
580
Gargrave
366
210/804

Settle

Lancaster

LANCASTER – LEEDS, DAILY 4/DAY

Keighley–Haworth–Oxenhope
(Keighley & Worth Valley Rwy,
☎ 01535 645214, 🖳 www.kwvr.co.uk)
5-11/day, hol/weekend year-round
+ daily July-Aug

580, 210
580
366
East Marton
280
215
Skipton
80
To York

Thornton-in-Craven
215
Lothersdale
79

Earby
215
20/21/22/23/24/25
Keighley

Cowling/Ickornshaw
500
664
663/720

20/21/22/23/24/25
280
Stanbury
664
Haworth
663/720

Preston
Burnley
Blackshaw Head
D
500
Oxenhope
Bradford
Leeds

PRESTON – LEEDS, MON-SAT 1/HR, SUN @ 2HR
592
Hebden Bridge

Todmorden
591/3/5
590/2/4
Halifax

500, 590/2/4
590
528
562

528
Blackstone Edge
Huddersfield

Rochdale
562
Windy Hill
365

Standedge
365

Oldham
PENNINE WAY

MANCHESTER – LEEDS, MON-SAT 2/HR, SUN 1/HR
MON-SAT 4/HR

Manchester
350
Crowden

Hadfield
Glossop
350

DAILY 2/HR

MANCHESTER – SHEFFIELD, DAILY @ 1~2HR
Sheffield

To London
Edale
To London

★ TRAILBLAZER

Public Transport
MAP 1

PUBLIC TRANSPORT INFORMATION

All rail enquiries: ☎ 08457-484950
Keighley & Worth Valley Railway (☎ 01535-645214, 🖥 www.kwvr.co.uk):
Keighley - Haworth - Oxenhope, 5-11/day, bank holidays & weekends
year-round + daily July-Aug

Countrywide bus/coach enquiries: Traveline (☎ 0870-608 2608,
                                          🖥 www.traveline.org.uk)
Greater Manchester bus enquiries: GMPTE (☎ 0161-228 7811,
                                          🖥 www.gmpte.com)
West Yorkshire bus enquiries: Metroline (☎ 0113-245 7676,
                                          🖥 www.wymetro.com)

Please note:
- Frequency listed thus: 2/hr = 2 buses per hour; @2hr = every two hours
- Only direct services are shown.
- Frequencies are typical of daytime services.
- Bank-holiday services generally follow Sunday timetables.
- Services are year-round except as noted (the choice of
'summer' months varies among operators)

- - - - Burnley & Pendle (☎ 01282-427778)
      20/21/22/23/24/25, Mon-Sat 1/hr, Sun @2hr

— - — First Halifax (see Metroline)
      500, Mon-Sat 5/day, Sun 4/day (Sat 4/day Hebden Bridge -
          Todmorden)
      528, daily 1/hr
      562, Mon-Sat 1/hr, Sun @2hr
      590/592/594, Mon-Sat 4/hr, Sun 2/hr
      591/593/595, Mon-Sat 2/hr (+ Sun 2/hr in summer)
      Hebden Bridger D, daily 1/hr

- - - - First Huddersfield (see GMPTE)
      365, Mon-Sat 1/hr, Sun @2hr

- - - - - Hutchinsons (☎ 07971-427935)
      210/804, Sat-Sun 4/day, Easter-October

·········· Keighley & District (☎ 01535-603284)
      79, Mon-Fri 2/day, Sat 1/day
      80, Mon-Sat 2/day, Sun 1-2/day
      663/720, Mon-Sat 2/hr, Sun 1/hr
      664, Mon-Sat 1/hr

———— National Express (☎ 08705-808080, 🖥 www.nationalexpress.com)
      350, daily 3/day

- - - - - Pennine Motor Services (☎ 01756-795515)
      210, Mon-Fri 2/day
      215, Mon-Sat 1/hr, Sun 7-8/day
      580, Mon-Fri 1/hr, Sat @2hr

·········· Royal Mail Postbus (☎ 08457-740740, 🖥 www.postbus.royalmail.com)
      366, Mon-Fri 2/day

— - - — Tyrer Tours (☎ 01282-611123)
      280, Mon-Sat @2hr

.... Alston Road Garage (☎ 01833-640213)
73, Mon-Sat 3/day (+ Wed 2/day to Barnard Castle)

— --- - Arriva NE (☎ 0870-120 1088, 💻 www.arriva.co.uk/northeast)
27/28/X26/X27, Mon-Sat 3/hr, Sun 2/hr
30, Mon-Fri 2/day, Sat 3/day
75/76, Mon-Sat 2/hr, Sun 1/hr
95/96, Mon-Sat 1/hr, Sun @2hr
85/685, Mon-Sat 1/hr, Sun 4/day (with Stagecoach)
602, Mon-Sat 2/hr, Sun 1/hr (with Stagecoach)

- --- - Buskers (☎ 01896-755808)
223, Sun 2/day (+1/day Kelso–Berwick only)

— --- Clifford Ellis (☎ 01969-667598)
112, meets any train (book by 6pm previous day)

ooooooo Dales & District (☎ 01677-425203, 💻 www.dalesanddistrict.co.uk)
156/157, Mon-Sat 1/hr, Sun 4/day

— -- — Hodgsons Coaches (☎ 01833-637641)
72, Mon-Sat 5/day
574, Mon-Sat 2/day (+ 1/day Barnard Castle–
Bowes only)

.... Munro (☎ 01835-862253)
81, Mon-Sat 7/day, Sun 3/day
131, Mon-Sat 1/day

——— National Express (☎ 08705-808080, 💻 www.nationalexpress.com)
383, daily 1/day

.... Royal Mail Postbus (☎ 08457-740740, 💻 www.postbus.royalmail.com)
277, Mon-Fri 2/day, Sat 1/day
364, Mon-Fri 3/day, Sat 1/day

...... Snaith (☎ 01830-520609)
449, Mon-Fri 1/day (term time only)
808, Mon-Fri 3/day, Sat 1/day
915, Thu-Fri 1/day, Sun 2/day (eve)

——— Stagecoach in Cumbria (see Traveline)
AD122 (Hadrian's Wall Bus Service),
daily 5/day Carlisle–Hexham with one on to
Newcastle (+ 1/day w/o Greenhead, daily
June-Sept & Sun Easter-Oct)
185, Mon-Sat 2/day (+ 1/day w/o Once Brewed)

--- --- Swans Coaches (☎ 01289-306436)
23, Mon-Fri 7/day, Sat 5/day

xxxxxxxxx Thomas Robinson (☎ 01768-351424)
573, Fri 2/day

·········· Tyne Valley Coaches (☎ 01434-602217)
880, Mon-Thu 6/day, Fri-Sat 8/day, Sun 3/day

·— ·— ·· Wright Brothers Coaches (☎ 01434-381200)
680, Mon-Fri 3/day, Sat 2/day (with Caldew Coaches,
☎ 01228 710963; + Sat 1/day Carlisle–Alston
only, Stagecoach)
681, Mon-Sat 1/day
888, from Nenthead Mon-Sat 1/day (+ from Penrith 1/day,
Apr-Sep, but only Fri-Mon in May)

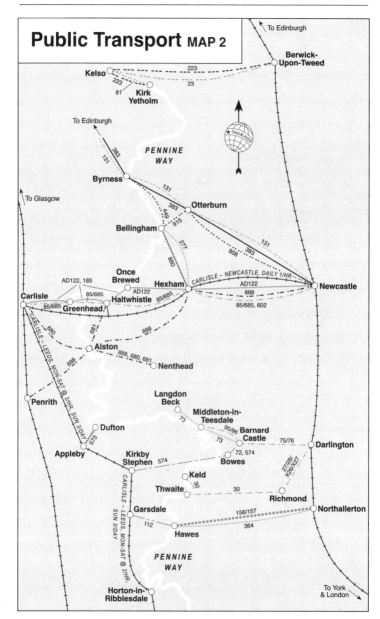

By air

There are cheap tickets available for internal flights from the rest of Britain to Manchester, Newcastle and Edinburgh, but remember that by the time you've checked in, been delayed, landed, got into the city and then out the other side you probably won't have saved any time over the train or coach. You do have to bear in mind, as well, that air travel is by far the least environmentally-sound option (see 🖳 www.chooseclimate.org for the true costs of flying).

LOCAL TRANSPORT

Getting to and from most parts of the Pennine Way is relatively simple due to the comprehensive public transport network including trains, coaches and local bus services. This opens up the potential for linear walks from an hour to several days without the worry of where to park the car and how to get back to it. The public transport map on pp36-9 gives an overview of routes which are of particular use to walkers, approximate frequency of services in both directions and who you should contact for detailed timetable information.

If the regional enquiry lines for bus information prove unsatisfactory contact **Traveline** (☎ 0870-608 2608, 7am-9pm, 🖳 www.traveline.org.uk) or **Public Transport Information** (🖳 www.pti.org.uk) both of which have timetable information for the whole of the UK. Local timetables can also be picked up from tourist information centres along the Way.

PART 2: MINIMUM IMPACT

Walk as if you are kissing the Earth with your feet **Thich Nhat Hanh** *Peace is every step*

Britain has no wilderness, not by the dictionary definition of land that is 'uncultivated and uninhabited'. But what you will walk through on the Pennine Way is the closest we have, and it is a fragile environment. Visitors have come in large numbers for over a century to sample the healing balm that comes from walking in these less touched places and as the world gets increasingly faster, more polluted and urbanized there is an even greater need for wild country where you can go for re-creation in the true sense of the word.

Inevitably this too brings its problems. As more and more people enjoy the freedom of the hills so the land comes under increasing pressure and the potential for conflict with other land-users is heightened. Everyone has a right to this natural heritage but with it comes a responsibility to care for it too.

You can do this while walking the Pennine Way by practising many of the suggestions in this section. Rather than being a restriction, learning how to minimize your impact brings you closer to the land and to those who work it.

ECONOMIC IMPACT

Rural businesses and communities in Britain have been hit hard in recent years by a seemingly endless series of crises. The countryside through which the Pennine Way passes is no exception and there is a lot that the walker can do to help. Playing your part today involves much more than simply closing the gate and not dropping litter; the new watchword is 'local' and with it comes huge social, environmental and psychological benefits.

Buy local
Look and ask for local produce to buy and eat. Not only does this cut down on the amount of pollution and congestion that the transportation of food creates, so-called 'food miles', but also ensures that you are supporting local farmers and producers; the very people who have moulded the countryside you have come to see and who are in the best position to protect it. If you can find local food which is also organic so much the better.

Support local businesses
If you spend £1 in a local business 80p of that pound stays within the local economy where it can be spent again and again to do the most good for that community and landscape. If, on the other hand, you spend your money in a branch of a national or multinational chain store, restaurant or hotel the situation is reversed; only 20% (mainly the staff wages) stays within the local economy and the other 80% is effectively lost to that community as it's siphoned off to pay

---

❏ **Food for thought**
● A supermarket provides one job for every £250,000 spent, compared with a village shop which provides one job for every £50,000 spent.
● A small portion of chicken can cost £3 in a supermarket; farmers get little more than £1 for an entire chicken.
● Sheep can be bought for as little as 25p a head.
● Farm incomes have fallen 90% in the last five years.
● BSE has cost every household in the UK £200.

---

for goods, transport and profit. The more money which circulates locally and is spent on local labour and materials the more power the community has to effect the change it wants to see; a world of difference from the corporatization of the countryside which we are currently witnessing.

Encourage local cultural traditions and skills

No part of the countryside looks the same. Buildings, food, skills and language evolve out of the landscape and are moulded over hundreds of years to suit the locality. Discovering these cultural differences is part of the pleasure of walking in new places. Visitors' enthusiasm for local traditions and skills brings awareness and pride, nurturing a sense of place; an increasingly important role in a world where economic globalization continues to undermine the very things that provide security and a feeling of belonging.

ENVIRONMENTAL IMPACT

By choosing a walking holiday you have already made a positive step towards minimizing your impact on the wider environment. By following these suggestions you can also tread lightly along the Pennine Way.

Use public transport whenever possible

Traffic congestion throughout Great Britain is becoming worse and worse. Public transport is improving, and gets better still with use. Try and use it whenever you can. There are times in the Peak District National Park, particularly after Bank Holidays, when a visible black band of pollution sits on top of the horizon. Once the cars have gone home, so the band disperses.

Noise pollution is also a growing problem. There's nothing more disappointing than sitting on top of a hill for lunch in front of a beautiful view only to have the background hum of traffic intrude on the peace. Nearly all of us contribute to this pollution in some way and the best way to stop it is to stay out of our cars and use public transport instead, becoming part of the solution rather than part of the problem.

Never leave litter

Leaving litter shows a total disrespect for the natural world; if you enjoyed it, show it some respect by keeping it clean. As well as being unsightly litter kills wildlife, pollutes the environment and can be dangerous to farm animals. One good idea is to repackage your food into reusable containers or plastic bags as this not only saves space and weight but also reduces the amount of rubbish you take with you. Also tie a plastic bag to the back of your rucksack so you can pick up other people's litter as you go without worrying about dirtying the inside of your pack. Find a suitable bin for it in the next village you pass.

Is it OK if it's biodegradable? Not really. Apple cores, banana skins, orange peel and the like are unsightly, encourage flies, ants and wasps and ruin a picnic spot for others. In high-use areas such as the Pennine Way it isn't appropriate to leave them behind.

The lasting impact of litter A piece of orange peel left on the ground takes six months to decompose; silver foil 18 months; a plastic bag 10 years; clothes 15 years; and an aluminium drinks can 85 years.

Erosion
Stay on the main trail The effect of your footsteps may seem minuscule but when they are multiplied by several thousand walkers each year they become rather more significant. Avoid taking shortcuts, widening the trail or creating more than one path; your boots will be followed by many others.

Consider walking out of season Maximum disturbance by walkers coincides with the time of year when nature wants to do most of its growth and repair. In high-use areas, like that along much of the Pennine Way, the trail often never recovers. Walking at less busy times eases this pressure while also generating year-round income for the local economy. Not only that, but it may make the walk a more relaxing experience for you as there are fewer people on the path and there's less competition for accommodation.

Respect all wildlife
Care for all wildlife you come across; it has just as much of a right to be there as you. Tempting as it may be to pick wild flowers leave them so the next people who pass can enjoy them too. Don't break branches off or damage trees in any way.

If you come across wildlife keep your distance and don't watch for too long. Your presence can cause considerable stress particularly if the adults are with young or in winter when the weather is harsh and food scarce. Young animals are rarely abandoned. If you come across deer calves or young birds keep away so that their mother can return.

The code of the outdoor loo
'Going' in the outdoors is a lost art worth reclaiming, for your sake and everyone else's. As more and more people discover the joys of the outdoors this is becoming an important issue. In some parts of the world where visitor pressure is higher than in Britain walkers and climbers are required to pack out their excrement. This could soon be necessary here. Human excrement is not only offensive to our senses but, more importantly, can infect water sources.

Where to go Wherever possible **use a toilet**. Public toilets are marked on the trail maps in this guide and you will also find facilities in pubs, cafés and campsites. The Pennine Way is not a wilderness area and the thousands of walkers using it each year mean you need to be as sensitive as possible.

If you do have to go outdoors choose a site at least **30 metres away from running water**. Carry a small trowel and **dig a small hole** about 15cm (6") deep to bury your excrement in. It decomposes quicker when in contact with the top layer of soil or leaf mould. Use a stick to stir loose soil into your deposit as well as this speeds up decomposition even more. Do not squash it under rocks as this slows down the composting process. If you have to use rocks to hide it make sure they are not in contact with your faeces.

Toilet paper and sanitary towels Toilet paper takes a long time to decompose whether buried or not. It is easily dug up by animals and can then blow into water sources or onto the trail. The best method for dealing with it is to **pack it out**. Put the used paper inside a paper bag which you place inside a plastic bag (or two). Then simply empty the contents of the paper bag at the next toilet you come across and throw the bag away. You should also pack out **tampons** and **sanitary towels** in a similar way; they take years to decompose and will be dug up and scattered about by animals.

Wild camping

Wild camping is not generally allowed on the Pennine Way but you may occasionally be able to ask permission from a local landowner. If you do, follow these suggestions for minimizing your impact and encourage others to do likewise.

Be discreet Camp alone or in small groups, spend only one night in each place and pitch your tent late and move off early.

● **Never light a fire** The deep burn caused by camp fires, no matter how small, seriously damages the turf and can take years to recover. Cook on a camp stove instead.

● **Don't use soap or detergent** There is no need to use soap; even biodegradable soaps and detergents pollute streams. You won't be away from a shower for more than a couple of days. Wash up without detergent; use a plastic or metal scourer, or failing that, a handful of fine pebbles from the stream or some bracken or grass.

● **Leave no trace** Enjoy the skill of moving on without leaving any sign of having been there: no moved boulders, ripped up vegetation or dug drainage ditches. Make a final check of your campsite before heading off; pick up any litter that you or anyone else has left, so leaving the place in a better state than you found it.

ACCESS

The Pennine Way, as a designated 'Long Distance Footpath', is a right of way with open access to the public. Walkers have a responsibility to be considerate to those using the land for other purposes such as farming, forestry and field sports. This means following the country code and respecting the lambing and grouse-shooting seasons.

The Country Code

● **Enjoy the countryside and respect its life and work** Access to the countryside depends on being sensitive to the needs and wishes of those who live and work there. Being courteous and friendly to those you meet will ensure a healthy future for all based on partnership and co-operation.

● **Guard against all risk of fire** Accidental fire is a great fear for farmers and foresters. Never make a camp fire and take matches and cigarette butts out with you to dispose of safely.

● **Leave all gates as you found them** If in doubt close a gate to avoid farm animals straying.

● **Keep your dogs under control** Keep them on a lead whenever you cross enclosed land or near livestock so that the farmer knows they are under control.

● **Keep to paths across farmland** Avoid damaging crops by sticking to the waymarked Pennine Way whenever you are crossing arable or pasture land.

● **Use gates and stiles to cross fences, hedges and walls** There are well maintained-stiles and kissing gates all along the Pennine Way. If you have to climb over a gate which you can't open, always do so at the hinged end.

● **Leave livestock, crops and machinery alone** Help farmers by not interfering with their means of livelihood.

● **Take your litter home** (see p42)

● **Help keep all water clean** Leaving litter and going to the toilet near a water source can pollute people's water supplies.

● **Protect wildlife, plants and trees** (see p43)

● **Take special care on country roads** If you travel by car drive with care and reduced speed on country roads. Park your car with consideration of others' needs especially to avoid blocking gateways. Walkers should take special care on country roads. Cars travel dangerously fast on narrow winding lanes. To be safe walk facing the oncoming traffic and carry a torch or wear highly-visible clothing when it's getting dark.

● **Make no unnecessary noise** Enjoy the peace and solitude of the outdoors by staying in small groups and acting unobtrusively. Avoid noisy and disruptive behaviour which might annoy residents and other visitors and frighten farm animals and wildlife.

Lambing

There is little that lifts the spirits more than watching lambs dancing on a warm sunny day. Lambing takes place from mid-March to mid-May and is a critical economic time for farmers. Please do not interfere with livestock farming in any way. If a ewe or lamb seems to be in distress contact the nearest farmer.

Grouse shooting

Grouse shooting is an important part of the rural economy and management of the countryside. Not only is moorland prevented from becoming an overgrown jungle (Britain is home to 20% of the world's moorland, and is under a duty from the Rio Convention of 1992 to look after it), but rare and fantastic birds such as the merlin would not survive without this management. The season runs from 12 August to 10 December but shooting is unlikely to affect your walk.

❏ Your ecological footprint

We modern people think we can just trample on something in our way as you trample on an ant and it will not make the slightest difference to the universe ... Somewhere it has an impact and it does affect us, no matter how small or insignificant ... That is why it is important that we recover this sense of belonging and the responsibility as individuals of being a good neighbour to all forms of life. **Laurens van der Post**

Practical steps for minimizing our impact on the trail are important, but do they go far enough? Walkers, perhaps more than most people, know the real value of 'wild' places where they can go to touch something elemental; where the spirit can be renewed and where physical challenges can be met. They also witness at first hand how many of these places are being destroyed, more so today than at any other time in the history of man. Unfortunately what we often don't see is the link between this exploitation of the countryside and the way we live our everyday lives.

As individuals we all make an impact on the planet. The question facing us today, in these times of high consumerism and population growth, is how much can the earth take? Your ecological footprint is the amount of productive land and water required to produce the resources you consume and the waste you create. It includes for example a little bit of Saudi Arabia for your oil, and a little bit of Costa Rica for your coffee.

If we divide the earth's resources between us equally it is estimated that we each have 1.5 hectares of productive land and water. In Britain, each person is currently using around 5 hectares. Some countries are worse (Americans use 10ha per person), and some, mainly in the developing world, are considerably better. It is estimated that humanity's footprint may soon be 30% bigger than fits the world. There's obviously a huge imbalance here which needs redressing as quickly as possible.

It is important we realize our ecological footprint is far more damaging than the bootprints we leave behind on the trail. Those who value 'the great outdoors' must choose a low-impact lifestyle off the trail as well as on. We can't on the one hand bemoan the loss of the countryside and on the other be a part of this spiral of destruction.

PART 3: THE ENVIRONMENT AND NATURE

An eye to perceive and a heart to feel **William Wordsworth**

For such a small place Great Britain has an extraordinarily wide range of habitats. They include orchid-strewn grasslands, woodland, heathland, moorland, mountains and coastal and freshwater areas. The only major habitat you won't see anything of on the Pennine Way is coastland, which is a remarkable fact.

What follows is a brief description of some of the many plants and animals you may encounter so you can understand what their business is as they scuttle, fly or run past you, or if a plant simply bows its head in the breeze as you walk by. Just as it's good to have some background knowledge before visiting a museum or art gallery, so it is with the glorious displays of the countryside.

There may be times when you feel lonely on the Pennine Way, but rest assured you are not alone; something will be watching and listening to you. The countryside is a community; the birds, animals and insects have evolved to be able to exploit different food sources so they are not in competition with each other. Please try and fit into this community by taking note of the points made in the previous chapter on minimum impact walking.

Conservation issues are also explored in this chapter on the premise that to really learn about a place you need to know more than just the names of all the plants and animals in it. It is just as important to understand the interactions going on between them and man's relationship with this ecological balance.

Conserving the Pennines

Most of us are painfully aware of the destruction of the countryside that went on in the half century since the end of the Second World War. In that time Britain lost some of its most precious habitats: over 150,000 miles of hedgerow, 95% of lowland hay meadows and 80% of chalk and limestone grassland to name but three. The otter which was once common is only now beginning to make a comeback, the large blue butterfly has become extinct, as have ten species of plant; several types of bat are endangered and even the common frog is no longer common. The figures go on and on and are a sad reflection of our once-abundant countryside.

We now live in a time when 'conservation' and 'the environment' are well-used terms and it is tempting to be complacent in the belief that the countryside is in safe hands. While there have been a few significant improvements in the last decade or so, many areas have continued to decline. Populations of wild birds, for instance, are good indicators of biodiversity as they are near the top of the food chain. The State of the Countryside 2001 report showed the serious decline in populations of 41 common farmland and woodland birds because of habitat destruction and pollution. In the Pennines the number of skylark has fallen by 39% in the last decade. The species that remain are increasingly being forced to live in ghettos which limits their chances of breeding successfully and could lead to damaging in-breeding. These trends are extremely worrying and are being mirrored throughout the world. If they continue the world could lose a quarter of its plant and animal species in the next thirty years.

As a nation we have lost touch not only with country matters, but with nature itself. Today most people's only contact with nature is through anthropomorphizing books or wildlife documentaries on television. This is hardly surprising. In the first census in 1801 70% of British people lived in the countryside. In the year 2000 that figure had fallen to a staggering 10%. Even though they may live in the countryside many in that 10% category have no real contact with the land and little interest in rural affairs.

As walkers who frequently spend quality time in the outdoors we are in a privileged position to re-establish our relationship with nature and become interested and active in how it is looked after. It is after all, to some extent, all of our land; we depend on it for physical and spiritual sustenance. It's therefore useful to have some understanding of how it is currently being managed on our behalf.

GOVERNMENT AGENCIES AND SCHEMES

Government responsibility for the countryside is handled in England by the **Countryside Agency**. Their efforts are delegated to a bewildering array of bodies, each with its mnemonic which is supposed to be easy to remember but usually simply confuses and alarms.

National Parks

National Park status is the highest level of landscape protection available in Britain and recognizes the importance of the area in terms of landscape, biodiversity and as a recreational resource. The Pennine Way passes through three of them: the Peak District, Yorkshire Dales and Northumberland. Although they wield a considerable amount of power and can easily quash planning applications from the local council, their management is always a knife-edge balance between conserving the landscape and wildlife, looking after the needs of visitors and protecting the rights and livelihoods of those who live within the park.

Following the Foot and Mouth crisis in 2001 the Association of National Park Authorities suggested to the government that Parks be used as a test bed for rural revival by setting up task forces to explain funding available to small

---

Opposite Top: The view from the glaciated bowl of High Cup (see p183). **Bottom**: A sign at a junction marks the route of the Pennine Way (see p202) north of Alston. (Photos © Bryn Thomas).

❏ **National Parks and the honey-pot issue**

The Peak District was Great Britain's first National Park, set up in 1951. Over a third of the population of England lives within an hour of the Peak District and it is currently the country's most visited park.

There is a constant problem between managing the demands of people and the needs of the environment. This can sometimes be put down to the 'honey-pot' issue. If you give an area a special designation because of its beauty, you are immediately alerting more people to its existence. But the National Parks are extremely skilled in managing this situation and can generally avoid conflict between people and conservation (through effective footpath creation, for example). Their guiding principle comes from the 1974 Sandford Report which states that where there is a conflict between conservation and the recreational demands of people conservation always takes priority.

You can support the work of the National Parks by joining **Friends of National Parks** (☎ 020-7924 4077, 💻 www.cnp.org.uk/Friends), 246 Lavender Hill, London SW11 1LJ.

rural businesses, generating ideas for projects, acting as the public element where necessary (eg in setting up farmers' markets) and advising on how to build on successes. It is hoped that these measures will help the government's stated objective, 'to move environmental and social goals closer to the heart of agricultural policy alongside its economic objectives'.

The existence of the National Parks does however, raise the question of what is being done to conserve and protect the countryside outside their boundaries? The policy of giving special protection to certain areas suggests that those areas not protected tend to be ignored when funding comes to be allocated. Since only 7% of the British Isles has National Park status, the conclusion to be drawn is that vast areas remain neglected and under threat.

Areas of Outstanding Natural Beauty (AONBs)
Land which falls outside the remit of a National Park, but which is nonetheless deemed special enough for protection may be designated as an AONB, the second level of protection after National Park status.

Sites of Special Scientific Interest (SSSIs)
SSSI is another important designation which purports to afford extra protection to unique areas against anything that threatens the habitat or environment. They range in size from a small site where orchids grow, or birds nest, to vast swathes of upland, moorland and wetland. The country through which the Pennine Way passes has its share but they are not given a high profile for the very reason that this would draw unwanted attention when what is wanted is for them to be left undisturbed. They are managed in partnership with the owners and occupiers of

---

Opposite Top: Jacob's Ladder (see p72), the first steep climb you come to on the Way. **Bottom**: The Packhorse Bridge, at the foot of Jacob's Ladder.

❏ **National Trails**
The Pennine Way is one of 15 National Trails in England and Wales. These are Britain's flagship long-distance paths which grew out of the post-war desire to protect the country's special places, a movement which also gave birth to National Parks and AONBs.

National Trails in England are designated and largely funded by the Countryside Agency and are managed on the ground by a National Trail Officer. They co-ordinate the maintenance work undertaken by the local highway authority and landowners to ensure that the trail is kept to nationally agreed standards.

the land but it seems as if this management is not always beneficial. A recent study found evidence of continuing decline in the condition of SSSIs in the region, with 74% being in an 'unfavourable condition'.

The England Rural Development Programme (ERDP)

This was introduced in 2001 by the **Department of Environment, Food and Rural Affairs (DEFRA)** to underpin the Government's New Direction for Agriculture with the intention of making farmers more environmentally responsible. Funding to the tune of £1.6bn will be made available over the next seven years for environmental protection and rural development.

VOLUNTARY ORGANIZATIONS

Voluntary organizations started the conservation movement back in the mid-1800s with the founding of the **Royal Society for the Protection of Birds** (RSPB). The rise of its membership figures accurately reflect public awareness and interest in environmental issues as a whole: it took until the 1960s to reach 10,000, but then rocketed to 200,000 in the 1970s and mushroomed to over one million by the year 2000. A major spur to the movement's metamorphosis came

❏ **Organic farming**
It has taken some time for agriculture to become even a little more environmentally friendly and it's true to say that it's often the policy formers, rather than the farmers, who have been the ones encouraging the destruction of the countryside for purely short-term economic reasons. Organic food production and sales, however, are now on the up, largely due to the public's anxieties about food safety and the use of pesticides on crops. It's hoped that organic agriculture represents a more sustainable approach to food production than the type of farming practised over the last 50 years, particularly in terms of its impact on biodiversity and pollution of the water and soil.

The steadily-increasing conversion of Pennine farms to organic production is a positive sign for the region's environment. We can only hope that the word 'organic' will not be hijacked by profiteering marketers and be applied to food produce that is not grown in the spirit of the Soil Association's original definition and, as a consequence, is little better for us and the environment than traditional intensive agriculture.

Government agencies

- **Countryside Agency** (☎ 01242-521381, ⌨ www.countryside.gov.uk), John Dower House, Crescent Place, Cheltenham, Gloucestershire, GL50 3RA. Resulted from a merger between the Countryside Commission and the Rural Development Commission; its aims are to conserve and enhance the countryside and to help everyone to enjoy it.
- **Department for Environment, Food and Rural Affairs** (☎ 020-7238 6000, ⌨ www.defra.gov.uk), Nobel House, 17 Smith Sq, London, SW1P 3JR. Government ministry responsible for sustainable development in the countryside.
- **English Heritage** (☎ 0870-333 1181, ⌨ www.english-heritage.org.uk), Customer Services Dept, PO Box 569, Swindon, SN2 2YP. Government body responsible for the care and preservation of ancient monuments in England.
- **English Nature** (☎ 01733-455000, ⌨ www.english-nature.org.uk), Northminster House, Peterborough, PE1 1UA. Describes itself as the government agency that 'champions the conservation of wildlife, geology and wild places in England'. Set up the Species Recovery Programme in 1991, which now has 400 species of flora and fauna on its list, and has identified another 250 that need help. Also responsible for the Biodiversity Action Plan, a 20+ year plan to maintain and enhance biodiversity (defined as 'the amazing richness and variety of wildlife and habitats on earth, from snow fields to rain forests and from mountain tops to the deep ocean floor).
- **Forestry Commission** (☎ 0131-334 0303, ⌨ www.forestry.gov.uk), 231 Corstophine Rd, Edinburgh, EH12 7AT. Government department for establishing and managing forests for a variety of uses.
- **Peak District National Park** (☎ 01629-816200, ⌨ www.peakdistrict-npa.gov.uk), Aldern House, Baslow Rd, Bakewell, Derbyshire, DE45 1AC. Responsible for the 555 square miles of the Peak District.
- **Northumberland National Park** (☎ 01434-605555, ⌨ www.nnpa.org.uk), Eastburn, South Park, Hexham, Northumberland, NE46 1BS. Responsible for the 405 square miles of northern England that fall within the Park.
- **Yorkshire Dales National Park** (☎ 01969-650456, ⌨ www.dales.org.uk), Colvend, Hebden Rd, Grassington, Skipton, North Yorkshire, BD23 5LB. Responsible for the 683 square miles of the Dales that fall within the Park.

in 1962 when Rachel Carson published a book called *Silent Spring* documenting the effects of agricultural and industrial chemicals on the environment. It was the long overdue wake-up call needed to bring environmental issues into the public eye.

Voluntary conservation bodies are still at the forefront of developments. Independent of government but reliant on public support, they can concentrate their resources either on acquiring land which can then be managed purely for conservation purposes, or on influencing political decision-makers by lobbying and campaigning.

Managers and owners of land include the well-known bodies such as the RSPB with their 182 nature reserves in the UK and the **Campaign to Protect Rural England** (CPRE) which exists to promote the beauty and diversity of rural England by encouraging the sustainable use of land and other natural resources in town and country.

Action groups such as **Friends of the Earth**, **Greenpeace** and the **World Wide Fund for Nature** (WWF) also play a vital role in environmental protection by raising public awareness with government agencies when policy needs to be formulated. The huge increase in public interest and support during the last 20 years indicates that people are more conscious of environmental issues and believe that it cannot be left to our political representatives to take care of them for us without our voice. We are becoming the most powerful lobbying group of all; an informed electorate.

BEYOND CONSERVATION

When we read about the work of the numerous voluntary and statutory bodies responsible for conservation it is easy to conclude that the countryside is in good hands and that we don't have to worry. But each day we read reports of

---

❑ **Voluntary organizations and campaigns**

● **British Trust for Conservation Volunteers** (BTCV) (☎ 01491-821600, 🖥 www.bctv.org), 36 St Mary's St, Wallingford, Oxfordshire, OX10 0EU. Their vision is of a world where people value their environment and take practical action to improve it.

● **Campaign to Protect Rural England** (CPRE) (☎ 020-7976 6433, 🖥 www.cpre.org.uk), Warwick House, 25 Buckingham Palace Rd, London, SW1W 0PP. Their name says it all.

● **Friends of the Earth** (☎ 020-7490 1555, 🖥 www.foe.co.uk), 26/28 Underwood St, London, N1 7JQ. International organization campaigning for a better environment for all.

● **Greenpeace** (☎ 020-7865 8100, 🖥 www.greenpeace.org), Greenpeace House, Canonbury Villas, London N1 2PN. International organization promoting peaceful activism in defence of the environment worldwide.

● **National Trust** (☎ 020-7222 9252, 🖥 www.nationaltrust.org.uk), 36 Queen Anne's Gate, London, SW1H 9AS. A charity with 2.8 million members which aims to protect, through ownership, threatened coastline, countryside and buildings for everybody to enjoy.

● **Royal Society for Nature Conservation** (RSNC) (☎ 01636-670000, 🖥 www.rsnc.org), The Kiln, Waterside, Mather Rd, Newark, Nottinghamshire, NG24 1WT. Works throughout the UK to effect the strategic protection of wildlife and the environment.

● **Royal Society for the Protection of Birds** (RSPB) (☎ 01767-680551, 🖥 www.rspb.org.uk), The Lodge, Sandy, Bedfordshire, SG19 2DL. The largest voluntary conservation body in Europe. They create and manage nature reserves to help birds and other wildlife.

● **The Land is Ours** (TLIO) (☎ 07961-460171, 🖥 www.tlio.org.uk), 16B Cherwell St, Oxford, OX4 1BG. A campaign, not an organization which aims to highlight the exclusion of ordinary people from the land.

● **Woodland Trust** (☎ 01476-581111, 🖥 www.woodland-trust.org.uk), Autumn Park, Dysart Rd, Grantham, Lincolnshire, NG31 6LL. Their aims are to conserve, restore and re-establish trees, particularly broadleaved, and to secure and enhance the enjoyment of them by the public.

❑ **Sustainability websites**
For lovers of the natural world who have ever asked 'but what can I do?', the following websites are a good place to start:
● **The Ecologist Magazine** (💻 www.theecologist.org)   Britain's longest-running environmental magazine.
● **International Society for Ecology and Culture** (💻 www.isec.org.uk) Promoting locally-based alternatives to the global consumer culture to protect biological and cultural diversity.
● **Permaculture Magazine** (💻 www.permaculture.co.uk) Explains the principles and practice of sustainable living.
● **Resurgence Magazine** (💻 www.gn.apc.org/resurgence) 'The flagship of the green movement'.

how threatened the countryside really is. Walkers are supposed to be environmentally-friendly people, the kind who take their newspapers to the paper bank and recycle their plastic bottles, carefully removing the caps. Yet there is not one among us who cannot examine their own commitment to environmental issues and find him- or her-self wanting.

What is called for is a total change of mind-set in people so that care for their environment is the first consideration, not the last. We all need to take a long, hard look at the way we live now and ask ourselves if we are not contributing to the gradual destruction of the natural world. Who has not seen the contents of a car ash-tray deposited on a car park, the filter tips affronting the very tarmac itself? Who has not walked along a canal and seen plastic wrappers stuffed into the hedgerow, or seen plastic bags festooning the hawthorn bushes alongside roads? We are all guilty. Because for every person who has seen these horrors, how many have cleared them away? Is other people's litter our problem? We think it is. For if there are people irresponsible enough to scatter their waste across the countryside, doesn't it need a balance of people who are willing to pick it up?

Yet this is just the tip of the iceberg. As our materialistic society expands, so the demand for affluence and acquisition increases. Put simply, the more we buy, the more nature we destroy. Consumerism means profligacy and waste, all exerting pressure on the world around us.

Why should we, individually, do more than we are doing to slow down this massive consumption of our natural resources on a global scale? Because, quite simply, we can do more. And we must do more if the world we know is going to be here for our descendants, our great, great grandchildren, not just our children. When we return a book borrowed from a friend, would we send it back tattered and torn and defaced with every evidence of our carelessness and indifference? Of course not. The countryside is the book we borrowed. Let us pass it on in even better condition than we found it so that future generations will say, they knew what it meant to take care.

Flora and fauna

MAMMALS

Roe deer are the smallest of Britain's native deer, and are hard to see. They normally inhabit woodland areas but you may see one in grassland or, if you are very lucky, swimming in a lake. The males (bucks) claim a territory in spring and will chase a female (doe) round and round a tree before she gives in to his pursuit, like a playground game of kiss-chase. This leaves circles of rings round the base of the tree, which are known as 'roe rings'.

Badgers like to live in deciduous woodland. Their black-and-white striped head makes them highly recognizable, but you are most likely to see them at night. They are true omnivores eating almost anything including berries, slugs and dead rabbits. The female (sow) gathers dry grasses and bracken in February for her nest. She then tucks them between her chin and forequarters and shuffles backwards, dragging them into her home (sett). The young are born blind in February and March and stay underground until spring. Badgers are accused of spreading TB to cows and for this unproven allegation 25,000 were summarily executed in the 1980s and 1990s. The jury is still out, but there is no doubt that they do contract and carry the disease. Some conservationists argue that it is more likely that they catch it from cows rather than the other way round. Much hope for a solution is placed in a possible vaccine.

Foxes are common wherever there are animals or birds to be preyed on, or dustbins to scavenge from, which is just about everywhere. Britain is estimated to have forty times the fox population of northern France. They are believed to have been here since before the last Ice Age when the sabre-toothed tiger would have prevented them from enjoying their current supremacy in the food chain. Fox hunting is currently the most emotive countryside issue. A lot of conservationists believe that the fox itself is the best control of its numbers. If an environment is unsuitable they tend not to try and inhabit it and a pregnant vixen will reabsorb her embryos if conditions are unfavourable for raising cubs. Foxes have a suspicious air about them, and tend to slope nervously from place to place looking like they know they should not be where they are. But they do a useful job eating carrion, which sometimes includes dead lambs, and rabbits. If they could learn to leave alone capercaillie and other protected birds they would even get the RSPB firmly on their side.

The **otter** is a sensitive indicator of the state of our rivers. They nearly died out in the last century due to a number of attacks on them, their habitat and their environment, and the law has protected them since 1981. Due to the work of conservationists they are now making a good comeback, but even small amounts of pollution can set back the efforts to give them a strong foothold in the wild. They are shy and reclusive so you will be incredibly lucky if you see one. They not only eat fish, but water voles and small aquatic birds are also on the otter menu. Their most successful hunting tactic is to launch a surprise attack from below as an otter's eyes are set on the top of its head and they have unique muscles that compensate for the visual distortion caused by water.

Mink were introduced from North America and only exist in the wild because they escaped or were set free from mink farms. They are successful predators and one of the most serious pests in the countryside; being an alien species nature has yet to work out how to balance their presence. They spend a lot of time in rivers feeding on aquatic birds and fish and can be distinguished from otters by their considerably smaller size and white chin patch.

The **stoat** is a small but fierce predator. They are native and fairly widespread and can be recognized by their elongated and elegant form, reddy-brown coats and white bellies. They are very adaptable, moving in wherever they can find a den, including old rabbit burrows, and may live for up to ten years. Minks, stoats, polecats, otters, badgers, weasels (the world's smallest carnivores) and pine martens are all from the same family.

The **red squirrel** is native, unlike the grey squirrel, but it is now rare to see one. They are beautiful little animals, smaller than their grey cousins and with a vibrant red coat and fabulously bushy tail (although their coat turns a little browner in winter). Note, too, the tufts that grow at the tips of their ears.

The alien **grey squirrel** has played a big part in the demise of the red squirrel, partly because it is able to eat the red squirrel's food before it ripens. Efforts to reintroduce the red squirrel have not had a great deal of success, partly because they are reluctant to move from tree to tree along the ground and therefore need a dense tree canopy and also because they do not have any traffic sense, which is a big problem in urban areas.

The **common shrew** is a tiny and pretty animal that lives in woodland and hedgerows. It needs to eat every four hours, and in a 24-hour period will eat insects weighing twice its body weight, using its long sensitive nose to sniff them out. It spends a lot of time underground eating earthworms. The mother and babies are sometimes seen covering open ground in a train-like procession, with each shrew holding the tale of the one in front. It is the second most common British mammal.

The **water shrew** is an indicator of clean water. Bigger and fiercer than the common shrew, it is semi-aquatic and normally, but not exclusively, lives by water.

The **mole** is armed with powerful forearms that it uses to burrow a network of underground tunnels that act as traps for unsuspecting earthworms. They patrol these every four hours, either eating all visitors on the spot or gathering them up to save for later after immobilizing them through decapitation.

In woodland or anywhere near buildings you may see the smallest of Britain's 15 resident species of **bat**, the **pipistrelle**. Bats have been here consistently since the ice age and are now a protected species. Even though the pipistrelle weighs a tiny 3-8 grams (about the same as a single clove of garlic, or two sheets of kitchen roll), in one night it may eat as many as 3500 insects. Bats and dormice are the only British mammals to truly hibernate throughout the whole winter from October to April. They will wake, however, if the temperature warms up.

REPTILES

The **adder**, or viper, is Britain's only poisonous snake but is harmless if left alone. It can be recognized by a black ziz-zag down its back and found in woodland and moorland. They hibernate in winter and when possible laze around in the morning and evening sun in spring and summer, eating everything from slugs to small birds. The males fight for females by rearing up and twisting themselves round each other as if trying to climb a tree; victory is often down to length. While this strenuous activity is going on the females are still asleep. They wake to find the victorious male rubbing his body against her and sticking his tongue out. It may sound all too familiar to many.

Although the **slow worm** looks like a snake, it is in fact a lizard, sharing their notched tongue (rather than a snake's forked tongue), moveable eyelids (snakes have no eyelids) and fixed jaw (snakes have a free jaw for devouring large prey). They eat slugs and insects and inhabit thick vegetation and rotting wood. The **common lizard** inhabits grass, in woods, moorland or grassland. They feed on insects and spiders. Snakes and lizards are cold blooded so find it easier to survive winters.

BIRDS

You will see a lot of birds on your walk. Some of them will be common ones that you see in your garden or in city streets, others will be rarer. It is impossible to know everything about birds – scientists are still learning and the more they discover, the more they find there is to discover. And evolution is, of course, an ongoing process. Birds do hybridize, that is cross-breed with other species, but the hybrids cannot themselves reproduce.

The best way of identifying birds is through their song. Each species sings a different tune, and not just for your pleasure. It is their way of letting others know that their territory is still occupied and not up for grabs, as well as a mating song. The dawn chorus is such a cacophony of song because most avian fatalities take place at night, so when they wake and are still alive they have to let opportunist home-hunters know it. They also have a call, or alarm, which is different again from the song.

Birds evolved from reptiles. Their feathers are made from keratin, as are reptiles' scales. Feathers give birds their shape, warmth, courting colour, waterproofing and the ability to fly. All birds moult at least once a year.

A bird's beak is an extension of its upper jaw. It is used for nest building, eating, preening and as a weapon and has evolved to suit individual needs. A wading bird, for instance, will have a probing beak of a length to suit its feeding ground, whether it be mud, sand or shallow water. Different types of waders can therefore feed in the same area without competing. Because its brain is suspended by quasi-ligaments a woodpecker can bang its bill against wood in a way that would leave other birds brain-damaged.

Birds' feet have evolved to particular tasks too, even within the three specific design groups of perching, walking/wading and swimming. Perching birds use a tendon along the back of their legs that tightens the toes as the leg is bent. This keeps it on the perch as it sleeps. Feet have different coverings too, being any one of feathers or bristles, scales or leathery skin. Most birds have four toes, three pointing forwards and one back, but some have less. Owls can turn their outer toe backwards to help them grasp their prey.

Claws help with this too, and they have also evolved to perform different tasks. Birds of prey tend to have stronger, curved talons; short, strong blunt claws are good for scratching the ground; the heron has adapted a comb-like claw for preening.

Some birds perform incredible migrations, navigating thousands of miles each year to exactly the same nest they occupied the previous summer (such as the swallow). Recent research suggests that some birds ingest their own organs to keep themselves fuelled for the flight. Swifts are believed to fly non-stop for up to two years, only coming down at the end of that period to lay eggs. They can also survive cold periods by entering a state of torpor.

Streams, rivers and lakes

Both the **great-crested grebe** and the **little grebe** live on natural lakes and reservoirs. The great-crested grebe's 'penguin dance', where they raise themselves from the water breast to breast by furiously paddling their feet and churning the water into a froth in the process, and then swing their heads from side to side, can be seen in spring. They also have their full plumage, including an elaborate-looking and colourful collar that could well have served as the inspiration for the collars on some Elizabethan outfits. They were nearly made extinct in Britain in the nineteenth century, but are now doing reasonably well again. They have plenty of enemies including pike, rooks, mink and even the wake from boats, which can flood their nests. The **little grebe** is small and dumpy but very well designed for hunting sticklebacks under water.

Yellow wagtails are summer visitors that are as likely to be seen on lakesides as they are in water meadows, pasture and even moors. How to recognize them? They have a yellow underneath, unlike the **grey wagtail** which has a black chin and then a yellow belly. If the bird is by a fast-flowing stream it will almost certainly be a grey wagtail.

Reservoir water tends to be acid and supports little wildlife except wildfowl including **goosanders**, especially in winter, and the similar-looking **red-breasted mergansers**. They are both members of the sawbill family which use serrated bill edges to seize and hold small fish. Trout in the reservoirs will have been introduced by man for anglers.

In streams and rivers you may see **common sandpipers**. Most of them have an annual ticket to Africa for the winter, but about 50 are thought to brave it out in Britain. You might see them stalking insects, their head held slowly and horizontally before a sudden snap marks the end of the hunt. They also inhabit lake edges. **Dippers** are the only songbirds that can 'fly' underwater or walk along streambeds. You may well see them 'curtseying' on rocks in the middle of swift-flowing streams before they dive under the surface. They fly extremely quickly, because their small wings were designed for maximum efficiency in the water and are far too small to keep the huge bodies airborne without enormous amounts of flapping and maintaining momentum.

Woodland

Where you come across areas of broad-leaved woodland (it is rare, and for instance only covers 1% of the Yorkshire Dales National Park) you will find a variety of bird-life. You may see, or more likely hear, a **green woodpecker**, the largest woodpecker in Britain (the size of a jackdaw). They are very shy and often hide behind branches. They feel in holes and cavities with their tongue, which has a sticky tip like a flycatcher to trap insects.

The further north you go the more likely you are to see **pied flycatchers**, summer visitors from Africa. The male can practise bigamy and is known to keep territories well over a mile apart, perhaps to keep his wives from meeting.

Nuthatches are sparrow sized with blue backs, orange breasts and a black eye-stripe, and have the almost unique ability to clamber up and down trunks and branches. Here year-round, in summer they eat insects and in the autumn crack open acorns and hazel nuts with hard whacks of their bill.

Treecreepers cling to trees in the same way as nuthatches and woodpeckers. They have a thin, downward-curved bill that is ideal for picking insects out of holes and crevices. They are brown above and silvery-white underneath, which should help you distinguish them from the similar sized and behaviourally similar **lesser-spotted** woodpecker, which is black and white and not seen on the more northern sections of the Pennine Way. The male woodpecker also has a red crown.

Coniferous woodland (coniferous means cone-bearing) is not home to much wildlife at all, because the tree canopy is too dense. You may, however, see nesting **sparrowhawks**, Britain's second commonest bird of prey. It suffered a big decline in numbers in the 1950s due to the use of pesticides in farming. In all the British raptor (bird of prey) species the female is larger than the male, but the male sparrowhawk is one of the smallest raptors in Britain. It feeds entirely on birds (brightly-coloured plumage may attract mates, but it also makes the wearer easy to spot by predators), and has long legs and a long central toe for catching and holding them. It has a square-ended tail and reasonably short wings for flying between trees.

You may also see **short-eared owls** in young plantations because of the preponderance of their principal prey, the short-tailed vole. It also hunts over open moors, heaths and rough grasslands. This owl is probably the one that is most often seen in daylight. It has two ear-tufts on the top of its head which are, you've guessed it, shorter than the long-eared owl's. They are not always sticking up though.

You may also see a **black grouse**, also known as **black game**. Conifer plantations are providing temporary havens for them while they try to regain some of their numbers. The males, black cocks, perform in mock-fights known as a lek in front of the females, **grey hens**. This happens throughout the year and if you see one fluffing up the white of its tail and cooing like a dove don't necessarily expect to see a female present, because they are quite happy to perform for anyone.

Coniferous woods are also home to the greeny-yellow **goldcrest**, Britain's smallest bird. It weighs less than 10 grams but along with the **coal tit** is possibly the dominant species in coniferous woods. Because it is one of the few species that can exploit conifers it is growing in number.

Moor, bog and grazing

Many birds have developed to live in the wettest, windiest, most barren places in England. On heather moors you will almost certainly see **red-grouse**, for whom the heather is intensively managed to ensure a good supply of young shoots for food. They are reddy brown, slightly smaller than a pheasant and likely to get up at your feet and fly off making a lot of noise. Moorland is also home to Britain's smallest falcon, the **merlin**. The male is slate-grey, the female a reddish brown. They eat small birds, catching them with low dashing flights. Their main threat comes from the expense of maintaining moorland for grouse shooting; as the costs grow so fewer and fewer farmers are doing it and with the disappearance of the moor we will see the disappearance of the merlin.

Bogs are breeding grounds for many species of waders, including the **curlew**, the emblem of the RSPB. Long-legged, brown and buff coloured, they probe for worms and fish with their long, downward-curving bill. The **lapwing** is rela-

CURLEW
L: 600MM/24"

tively common, quite large and can be recognized by its whispy black plume on the back of its head and, in summer, the aerial acrobatics of the male. They fly high to dive steeply down, twisting and turning as if out of control before pulling out at the last minute.

Snipe and **Jack Snipe** live in wet areas. The former is the more common and bigger of the two (but is in itself smaller than a grouse), but they both share very similar plumages. Both have long bills for feeding in water, but the snipe's is particularly long. They rely on being camouflaged rather than escaping predators by flight, and hence often get up right

LAPWING/PEEWIT
L: 320MM/12.5"

at your feet. Once airborne their trajectory is anything but straight, being zigzag and fast.

Golden Plover live in peaty terrain in winter and move to grassland in the summer. They are a little larger than a snipe, have golden spotted upper parts, are generally seen in a flock and can be recognized by their feeding action of running, pausing to look and listen for food (seeds and insects) and bobbing down to eat it. **Dunlins** also live in peaty terrain and are half the size of a golden plover but not dissimilar in colouring to the inexperienced eye. They are a very common wader.

Patches of gorse and juniper scrub are often chosen as a nesting site for **linnets**, which flock together during the winter but operate in small colonies at other times. They are small birds that will also be seen on open farmland, as will the slightly larger **yellow hammer**, recognizable by its yellow head and chest. It too nests in gorse and juniper bushes.

You may also see but are more likely to hear the continuous and rapid song of the **skylark**. They tend to move from moorland to lower agricultural land in the winter. Just bigger than a house sparrow, they have brown upper parts and chin with dark flakes and a white belly.

The **meadow pipit** is an amusing bird to watch. Small, and a classic LBJ (little brown job), they make plenty of noise and on a still day will climb to about 15 metres (50ft) and then open their wings to parachute gently down. They can sometimes be recognized by their white outer tail feathers as they fly away from you.

The **peregrine falcon** had a hard time during the 20th century, being shot during the Second World War to protect carrier pigeons and then finding it hard to rear young after eating insects that had fed on pesticide-soaked plants. Their recent comeback is therefore a sign that things are picking up again in the British countryside.

Buildings and cliffs

Swallows, **house martins** and **swifts** all nest in barns and other buildings. They are hard to tell apart, but as a simple guide: swallows are the largest, are blue-black above and have a white belly and a long-forked tail; swifts are the next down in size, are essentially all black with a shallow forked tail that is usually closed and probably fly the fastest; and house martins are the smallest, have a relatively short tail and a completely white underneath and, most usefully for identification purposes, a white rump (on top, near the tail). As a walker, you may be able to relate to why a non-breeding swift will fly 100 miles to avoid rain. If insects are bugging you, thank nature for swifts. A single one will eat 10,000 pesky buzzers a day, so think how many more bites you would suffer if it were not for them.

Peregrine falcons, **kestrels** and **jackdaws** (similar to a crow but with a whitish back of the head) nest in cliffs. The kestrel, Britain's commonest and most familiar bird of prey, also nests in man-made structures and is sometimes seen in city centres. It can be distinguished from the sparrow hawk, the second commonest raptor, by its pointed wings and hovering when hunting. The male has a blue-grey head and a rich chestnut above, while the female is a duller chestnut both above and on her head. Jackdaws are very common in villages and towns; if you see a crow-like bird sitting on a chimney top, reckon on it being a jackdaw.

Owls may also nest in cliffs and barns. You are most likely to see a **little owl**, which is a non-native resident that will often occupy the same perch day after day. Local knowledge can be useful for finding one of these. **Barn owls** are on the decline but are also one of the most widely-distributed birds in the world. They have been affected by intensive agriculture.

TREES, WOODS AND FORESTS

Woods are part of our natural heritage as reflected in our folklore, Little Red Riding Hood and Robin Hood for example, and also in our history with the hunting grounds of Henry VIII and the timber ships that led to the British 'ruling the waves'. To the west of Edale, at the start of the walk, is the small town of Chapel-en-le-Frith. Translated, its name means 'chapel in the forest' because it used to be a small clearing in an enormous forest that stretched to Edale and beyond.

Ten thousand years ago, before man started to 'manage' the landscape, 90% of the country was wooded. In 1086 when William the Conqueror ordered a survey it had declined to 15% and it then shrank to 4% by the 1870s. Today, just less than 9% of England is wooded with an estimated 1.3 billion trees, making 25 for every person. What these figures disguise is that a huge proportion of the tree cover today, as opposed to 900 years ago or even 100 years ago, is made up of ecologically-damaging plantations of conifers (see below).

It is hoped that by 2020 woodland will cover 20% of England and that a large proportion will be made up of indigenous species, such as oak. Despite this progress England will still be one of the least-wooded countries in Europe where the average wood cover is 36%.

Oak and broadleaf woodlands

The number of **oak** trees has increased by 20% in 20 years. They are now the commonest species in England. There are two native species, the **common** and the **sessile**. Sessile woodlands are generally remnants of the woodland of William the Conqueror's time and before. Broadleaf woods, that is deciduous (annual leaf-shedders) hardwood, including **beech**, **sycamore**, **birch**, **poplar**

❏ **Fungi, micro-organisms and invertebrates**
In the soil below your feet and under the yellow leaves of autumn are millions, possibly billions, of organisms beavering away at recycling anything that has had its day and fallen to decay. One gram of woodland soil contains an estimated 4-5,000 species of bacteria. Almost all of them are unknown to science and the vitally-important role they play in maintaining the natural balance of our ecosystems is only just beginning to be appreciated. Many scientists now believe these organisms actually run the earth. Research into them is at an early stage but as one American academic put it, 'As we walk across leaf litter we are like Godzilla walking over New York City.'

> ### ❏ The Forestry Commission
> The Forestry Commission is the governmental body in charge of Britain's forests. It states its mission to be 'To protect and expand Britain's forests and woodlands and increase their value to society and the environment'. It manages 800,000 hectares of woodland throughout Britain, and although it was largely responsible for encouraging the vast numbers of acres of coniferous woodland, it is now a driving force behind diversification of tree species in woodlands.

and **sweet chestnut**, have grown by 36% since 1980. However, they still only account for 1% of the Yorkshire Dales National Park.

In areas of poorer soil you will also see 'pioneer' species such as **rowan**, **silver birch**, **downy birch** and the much rarer **aspen**. In a natural environment these improve the soil for longer-lasting species such as oak.

Coniferous woodland

The full extent of the demise of our native woodlands was not fully comprehended until the Second World War when politicians realized we had an inadequate strategic reserve of timber. The immediate response was to plant fast growing low-management trees such as the North American **Sitka spruce** across the low-quality land of the British uplands. The mass-planting continued apace into the 1970s and '80s with big grants and tax breaks available to land owners and wealthy investors.

You can see the result of this 'blanket planting' throughout northern England and Scotland; miles upon miles of same-age trees laid out in neat rows that have such a dense canopy that nothing grows underneath. As with all monocultures pests easily build up and have to be controlled with chemicals. The deep ploughing and use of heavy machinery damages soil structure and also leads to a higher incidence of flash floods as drainage patterns are altered. It has also been found that acid rain gets trapped in the trees and is released into the streams during a downpour killing young fish and invertebrates.

What's more, the end product from this environmentally-damaging land-use is a low-grade timber used mainly for paper, a hideous waste of a valuable raw material. Perversely and misleadingly this is often advertised as 'paper from sustainable forestry'. There are now efforts under way to replant felled coniferous timber with a wider range of species and the number of conifer plantations has fallen by 7% in the past 20 years. These new woodlands are not only planted for timber, but also promote recreation, tourism and are good for wildlife.

WILD FLOWERS, GRASSES AND OTHER PLANTS

Many grasses, wild flowers, heather, mosses and liverworts (lichen-type plant with liver-shaped leaves) owe their continued existence to man's management of the land; if left to its own devices much of the land would almost certainly return to the woodland it was 10,000 years ago. Rare breeds of livestock are often excellent grazers for rough grassland because they are hardier and so do not have to be fed extra food that will then over fertilize the ground. They also seem to be more selective in what they eat, and taste better too.

Spring and early summer is generally the best time to see wild flowers. You may be amazed by how many of the plants you walk over are edible. Some examples are given below, but you should seek expert identification before trying any as some plants are poisonous.

Intensive agriculture took its toll on the wild flower population in the same way that it did on the birds and mammals. The flowers are making a comeback now and one of the few silver linings of the Foot and Mouth crisis in 2001 was the sight of hillsides littered with colour, either random specks or great swathes of it 'painting the meadows with delight', as Shakespeare wrote.

It is illegal to pick many types of flowers now and the picking of most others is discouraged. It is always illegal without the landowners' permission, no matter what the type. Cut flowers only die, after all. It is much better to leave them to reseed and spread and hopefully magnify your or someone else's enjoyment another year.

Bogs and wet areas

Look out for **cotton grass** (a type of sedge), **deer-grass**, **cloudberry** (a dwarf blackberry with a light orange berry when ripe that can be used as a substitute for any fruit used in puddings and jams) and the insect-eating **sundew**. Drier areas of peat may be home to **crowberry** (a source of vitamin C) and **bilberry** (see below).

Peat itself is the ages-old remains of vegetation, including **sphagnum mosses**. This type of moss is now rare, but may be found in 'flushes' where water seeps out between gritstone and shale. Also look out for **bog asphodel**, **marsh thistle** and **marsh pennywort**.

Woodlands

Not much grows in coniferous woods because the dense canopy prevents light getting in. But in oak woodlands the floor is often covered with interesting plants such as **bilberries**, whose small, round black fruit is ripe for picking from July to September and is much tastier than the more widely commercially sold American variety. It's recommended in jams, jellies, stews and cheesecake. Bilberry pie is known in Yorkshire as 'mucky-mouth pie', for reasons you can work out, and is eaten at funerals. **Cowberry** (also used in jams and also grows on moors), **wavy hair grass** and **woodrush** are other species you may see. Other shrubs to look out for include **guelder rose** and **bird cherry**.

❏ **Why are flowers the colour they are?**
The vast majority of British wild flowers range in colour from yellow to magenta and do not have red in them. The poppy is the most notable exception. This is because they are largely insect pollinated as opposed to being pollinated by birds. Birds see reds best, insects see yellow to magenta best.

Higher areas

Much is peaty (see bogs and wet areas above) and many types of grass turn brown in winter. Those present include **matgrass**, **heath rush**, **bent**, **fescues** and **wavy hair grass**. Flowers include **tormentil** and **harebell**.

Heather is the main plant of higher areas and is carefully farmed for grouse. It is burnt in strips over the winter to ensure new growth as a food supply for the birds. It has many uses, including as a tea and flavouring beer, and makes a very comfortable impromptu bed on a warm, sunny afternoon. When it flowers around August time it turns the whole view purple in places.

Bracken, large quantities of **gorse** and **tufted hair grass** are all signs that the land is not being intensively managed.

Lower areas

These are where you will see the most flowers, whose fresh and bright colours give the area an inspiring glitter, particularly if you have just descended from the browns and greens of the higher, peaty areas.

On valley sides used for grazing you may see **self heal**, **cowslips** (used to make wine and vinegar), **bloody cranesbill** and **mountain pansy**. **Hawthorn** seeds dropped by birds sprout up energetically and determinedly but are cropped back by sheep and fires. This is a good thing; these shrubs can grow to 8 metres (26ft) and would try to take over the hillsides to the detriment of the rich grasslands. They do, however, have a variety of uses: the young leaves are known as 'bread and cheese' because they used to be such a staple part of a diet; the flowers make a delicious drink and when combined with the fruit make a cure for insomnia. **Rushes** indicate poor drainage. Also look out for **bird's eye primrose**, **white clover** and the grasses such as **crested dog's tail** and **bent**.

❏ Orchids

These highly colourful and prized plants, the occasional object of highly professional thefts, are often thought to only grow in tropical places. They come from one of the largest families in the world and their range is in fact widespread, reaching right up to the Arctic Circle in some places. The only continent they do not grow on is Antarctica. Their name derives from the Latin for testicle and Venus is believed to be a big fan, hence a mediaeval warning not to take them in large quantities. Three types in Australia grow underground. There are over 40 types growing wild in Britain and you would be unlucky not to see any on the Pennine Way. Look especially in quarries and on hillsides. The **Lady's-slipper**, first discovered in Ingleborough in 1640; the **narrow-lipped helleborine**, which grows in Northumberland and the **frog orchid** are just some you may come across. The **early-purple orchid** (see photo opposite) is made into a drink called Saloop, which was popular before coffee became the staple. It was believed to have aphrodisiac properties, probably because the twin tubers' don't look too dissimilar to testicles.

Although they have a tendency to grow on other plants, orchids are not parasites, as many people believe; they simply use them for support. Many growers of orchids say they are no more difficult to grow at home than many other houseplants. With their flowers being generally spectacular and the scent strong and wonderful they are well worth the effort. They usually have one petal longer than the other two.

Foxglove
Digitalis purpurea

Meadow Cranesbill
Geranium pratense

Water Avens
Geum rivale

Common Vetch
Vicia sativa

Heartsease (Wild Pansy)
Viola tricolor

Germander Speedwell
Veronica chamaedrys

Early Purple Orchid
Orchis mascula

Violet
Viola riviniana

Red Campion
Silene dioica

Spear Thistle
Cirsium vulgare

Common Knapweed
Centaurea nigra

Common Fumitory
Fumaria officinalis

Bell Heather
Erica cinerea

Heather (Ling)
Calluna vulgaris

Blackthorn
Prunus spinosa

Devil's-bit Scabious
Succisa pratensis

Harebell
Campanula rotundifolia

Bluebell
Endymion non-scriptus

Cowslip
Primula veris

Marsh Marigold (Kingcup)
Caltha palustris

Meadow Buttercup
Ranunculis acris

Ox-eye Daisy
Leucanthemum vulgare

Tormentil
Potentilla erecta

Birdsfoot-trefoil
Lotus corniculatus

Dandelion
Taraxacum officinale

Common Ragwort
Senecio jacobaea

Primrose
Primula vulgaris

Rosebay Willowherb
Epilobium angustifolium

Rowan tree
Sorbus aucuparia

Gorse
Ulex europaeus

Lousewort
Pedicularis sylvatica

Herb-Robert
Geranium robertianum

Scarlet Pimpernel
Anagallis arvensis

Hemp-nettle
Galeopsis speciosa

Ransoms (Wild Garlic)
Allium ursinum

Yarrow
Achillea millefolium

PART 4: ROUTE GUIDE & MAPS

The trail guide and maps have not been divided into rigid daily stages since people walk at different speeds and have different interests. The **route summaries** below describe the trail between significant places and are written as if walking the Way from south to north. To enable you to plan your own itinerary, **practical information** is presented clearly on the trail maps. This includes walking times for both directions, all places to stay, camp and eat, as well as shops where you can buy supplies. Further service **details** are given in the text under the entry for each place.

For an overview of this information see Itineraries, p21.

TRAIL MAPS

Scale and walking times

The trail maps are to a scale of 1:20,000 (1cm = 200m; $3^1/8$ inches = one mile). Walking times are given along the side of each map and the arrow shows the direction to which the time refers. Black triangles indicate the points between which the times have been taken. **See note below on walking times**.

The time-bars are a tool and are not there to judge your walking ability. There are so many variables that affect walking speed, from the weather conditions to how many beers you drank the previous evening. After the first hour or two of walking you will be able to see how your speed relates to the timings on the maps.

Up or down?

The trail is shown as a dotted line. An arrow across the trail indicates the slope; two arrows show that it is steep. Note that the arrow points towards the higher part of the trail. If, for example, you are walking from A (at 80m) to B (at 200m) and the trail between the two is short and steep it would be shown thus: A— — — >> — — – B. Reversed arrow heads indicate downward gradient.

Accommodation

Apart from in large towns where some selection of places has been necessary, everywhere to stay that is within easy reach of the trail is marked. Details of each place are given in the accompanying text.

❏ **Important note – walking times**
Unless otherwise specified, **all times in this book refer only to the time spent walking**. You will need to add 20-30% to allow for rests, photography, checking the map, drinking water etc. When planning the day's hike count on 5-7 hours actual walking.

Unless otherwise specified **B&B prices** are summer high season prices per person assuming two people sharing a room with a separate bathroom. (See p17 for more information on prices).

The number and type of room is given after each entry: S = single room, T = twin room, D = double room, F = family room (sleeps at least three people).

Other features

Features are marked on the map when they are pertinent to navigation. In order to avoid cluttering the maps and making them unusable not all features have been marked each time they occur.

The route guide

EDALE

For many whose dream it has been to walk the Pennine Way, Edale will have assumed mystical significance. The very name conjures up a vision of grit-stone cottages on the edge of wild moorland, and it does not disappoint. A stone church set against green pastoral hills, a single lane road winding through the middle to a dead end and some beautiful old houses. Edale is a mecca for walkers with fine walks from short rambles to full days all around. It is boot and rucksack city, the campers' capital, the hikers' heaven.

Having arrived by train or car would-be Pennine wayfarers make their way up the lane to the Old Nag's Head for their farewell pint, but they do not linger. They are eager to be off, to break free, to step out on the biggest long distance footpath of them all, the fabled Pennine Way.

Transport

The **train** is by far the easiest way to get to and from Edale. It's about half an hour from Sheffield through beautiful countryside and 15 minutes longer from Manchester (see public transport map, pp36-9).

There are infrequent **bus** services between Castleton and Chapel-en-le-Frith.

If you choose to drive you need to be aware that you can leave your car in the car park for a maximum of only three days (£5). A day's car parking costs £2.50. For

taxis try Michael Rowland (☎ 01433-621924) or Brian Jackson (☎ 01433-620525).

Services

Before leaving, pop into the **Park Information Centre** (☎ 01433-670207, daily 9am-1pm and 2-5pm from Easter to end Oct; at other times Sat 9am-1pm and 2-5pm and Sun 9am-1pm) to see the excellent display on the history of the area, the Peak District National Park and the evolution of walkers' rights. There are maps, guidebooks, snacks and souvenirs for sale and a collection box for the Edale Mountain Rescue Team. Don't tempt fate; make a donation to help these volunteers who have saved many walkers' lives. It is worth repeating here, if you need emergency help at any stage of the Pennine Way, dial ☎ 999 and ask for 'Police *and Mountain Rescue'*.

At the top end of the village there's a **post office** (☎ 01433-670220, open Mon, Tue, Thu 9am-1pm) and a basic village **shop** (open daily 9am-1pm and 2-5pm, but closed Wed afternoon).

Where to stay

If you are coming from any distance it makes sense to spend a night in Edale before starting your walk so that you have a whole day to complete the fairly arduous section to

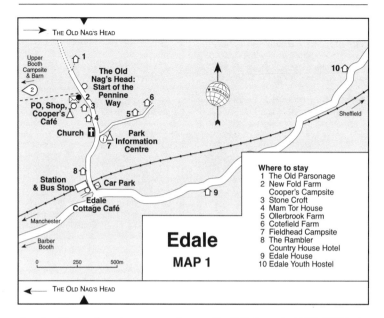

THE OLD NAG'S HEAD

Upper Booth Campsite & Barn

1

The Old Nag's Head: Start of the Pennine Way

2
PO, Shop, Cooper's Café

3

4

5

6

Church

Park Information Centre

7

8

Station & Bus Stop

Car Park

Edale Cottage Café

9

10

Sheffield

Manchester

Barber Booth

0   250   500m

Edale

MAP 1

THE OLD NAG'S HEAD

Where to stay
1 The Old Parsonage
2 New Fold Farm
   Cooper's Campsite
3 Stone Croft
4 Mam Tor House
5 Ollerbrook Farm
6 Cotefield Farm
7 Fieldhead Campsite
8 The Rambler
   Country House Hotel
9 Edale House
10 Edale Youth Hostel

Crowden. Most walkers choose to stay in the centre of the village for its convenience but make sure you have booked ahead as beds fill up quickly at peak times.

There is also a good choice of accommodation in the surrounding settlements, all of which have 'Booth' in their name. This means 'shelter' and stems from the days before farming when the valley would have been forested and reserved for hunting.

Edale There are two **campsites** in the centre of the village both of which are open all year: *Fieldhead* (☎ 01433-670386, 🖳 www.fieldhead-campsite.co.uk) by the Park Information Centre, costs £4 per adult per night and *New Fold Farm Cooper's Camp and Caravan Site* (☎/🖹 01433-670372, 🖳 www.edalevalley.co.uk/coopers .htm), up the hill by the post office, charges £3 per person.

There's a simple **camping barn** with outside toilet, water tap and cooking area ten minutes' walk to the east of the village

at *Cotefield Farm* (☎ 01433-670273, for bookings call the YHA ☎ 0870-770 6113, 🖳 campingbarns@yha.org.uk). It costs £5 per person but you need to bring your own sleeping bag. There's also **bunkhouse** accommodation nearby at *Ollerbrook Farm* (☎ 01433-670235) with a kitchen and two showers costing £8 per person.

Walkers requiring B&B are well catered for. One of the best is *Edale House* (☎ 01433-670399, 🖳 www.sallydog.co.uk/ edalehouse, 1S/2T), a big, old country house just outside the village which charges £30.

In the centre of the village there's the friendly *Mam Tor House* (☎ 01433-670253, 🖳 www.edale-valley.co.uk/mam tor.htm, 2T/1F) just above the church charging £20, the more luxurious *Stone Croft* (☎ 01433-670262, 🖳 www.stone croftguesthouse.co.uk, 2D one en suite), two doors up which costs from £28.50 (£33.50 en suite), or the secluded and good value *Old Parsonage* (☎ 01433-670232,

1S/1T/1D, Apr-Oct) at the very start of the Pennine Way costing from £17 which caters primarily for walkers. *The Rambler Country House Hotel* (☎ 01433-670268, 🖳 therambler@dorbiere.co.uk, 4F/3D/2T), charges £27 (£36 Fri-Sat) with breakfast.

Nether Booth   *Edale Youth Hostel* (bookings ☎ 0870-770 5808, 🖳 edale @yha.org.uk, open all year) is just over a mile to the east of the village in Nether Booth and costs £11.80 for adults, £8.50 for under 18s. You can get there via a network of footpaths from the village or walk along the lane. Unlike most youth hostels which open only at 5pm this is open all day and there's an evening meal available from 5.30pm to 7.15pm.

Upper Booth   Located two miles (3km) into the Pennine Way (see **Map 2**), Upper Booth can make a nice warm up the night before you start your walk proper. There's camping here at *Upper Booth Farm Campsite* (☎ 01433-670250, 🖳 www .edale-valley.co.uk/upbooth.htm) for £3 per person. You will need to bring your own sleeping bag as no sheets are provided. Fresh free-range eggs and milk can be bought at this award-winning farm where conservation and business can be seen

working hand in hand; an excellent example of how hill farming can be a sustainable and integral part of the local economy and community.

If you're really stuck for accommodation **Barber Booth**, a small hamlet just under one mile south-east of Upper Booth, has a couple of options. *Waterside Campsite* (☎ 01433-670215, 🖳 www .edale-valley.co.uk/waterside.htm) offers camping for £2 per person plus £2 per tent and *Brookfield Guesthouse* (☎ 01433-670227, Easter to October, 1D/2T) has B&B for £20.

Where to eat
Being the traditional start of the Pennine Way, most walkers choose to eat at the *Old Nag's Head* (☎ 01433-670291) at the top of the village which serves food in the £5-8 range. It used to be a great country pub, but now both it and *The Rambler Country House Hotel* (see above) are owned by a Manchester company that has applied a money-making formula to them. This has inevitably been at the expense of character. Other places serving food in the village are *Edale Cottage Café* (open daily 9am-5pm, 5.30pm at weekends) near the station and *Cooper's Café* by the post office, both of which have varied and plentiful menus.

EDALE TO CROWDEN   MAPS 1-9

This, the first day on The Pennine Way, is widely held to be one of the two worst sections, the other being the last of all, between Byrness and Kirk Yetholm. It is every step of **16 miles (26km, 5¹/₄–6¹/₂hrs)** and crosses the expanses of wilderness comprising the Kinder plateau and Bleaklow, a moor infamous in fact and fiction.

Until quite recently the going was so bad underfoot that it was said to wipe out half of all those who set out to walk The Pennine Way. A bad first day has discouraged many a walker, for sure. Today the peaty wastes have been subdued by the use of heavy stone slabs, salvaged from demolished cotton mills, and laid end to end to ensure dry feet over the former morass. Since one is effectively walking on a pavement, this takes its toll on the muscles and causes sore feet, blisters and tired ankles and knees. At least there is consolation in the knowledge that however hard the going, it used to be worse.

The path as far as the foot of Jacob's Ladder through the welcoming enclave of **Upper Booth** is a Sunday afternoon stroll, a pleasant introduction to the lower pastures of the Edale Valley and a fine way to warm up, in preparation for the stiff zig-zags of the **Jacob's Ladder** path before open moorland is reached near **Edale Cross**. The route from the top of Jacob's Ladder to Kinder Downfall is an introduction to the famed **Kinder Edges**, a high-level scramble through the boulders on a path that becomes on summer weekends a pedestrian motor-way, thronged with day walkers.

The first triangulation column or trig point of the Pennine Way is encoun-tered at **Kinder Low**, the first of many. How many? Answers on a postcard please. On second thoughts, don't bother since these concrete columns are no longer used now that satellite navigation has replaced the need for them.

Beyond the rather disappointing **Kinder Downfall** there is more of the same terrain, namely boot-scarred peat and slabs, until **Mill Hill**, then it's slabs, slabs and more slabs as far as the **Snake Pass**. If you've already had enough you can walk down the road to **Snake Pass Inn** (see p70) and call a taxi to take you home. If you are made of sterner stuff, it's a further three and a half hours to the bridge at Torside, so buckle down and set your mind on the sunken track known as **Devil's Dike**, with Bleaklow as your next objective.

The route to **Bleaklow Head** is confusing and needs careful navigation. There are hardly any signs or way-marks to see you safely there, and some of the amateur attempts to mark the route are more of a distraction than a help, however well-intentioned. Bleaklow is not so much a mountain, more of a pud-ding that has failed to rise. With luck and some compass work you can reach the summit pile of stones with its stake sticking up at a crazy angle. From this point on it is all downhill to the **Longendale Valley**, aided by more slabs and, in clear weather, the sight of reservoirs below. If you find yourself heading for a valley without reservoirs in it, you're lost. The route skirts the top edge of **Clough**

❏ **Kinder Scout**
The Pennine Way used to go up Grindsbrook Clough to strike across the summit wastes of Kinder Scout, a hazardous and challenging route that usually resulted in walkers becoming muddy and lost in the labyrinthine maze of channels in the peat which seemed to lead nowhere. As the peat became eroded by generations of wan-dering boots, the decision was taken to re-route the Way via the present path known as the Jacob's Ladder route, a much more navigable path which should enable most walkers to find their way without mishap.

Still purists and the ignorant march straight past the Old Nag's Head and up Grinds Brook, seemingly determined to stick their head right into the lions mouth. This is not a good idea. Unless you know the plateau intimately, don't try this yourself.

For those who will not take no for an answer, the best way to cross the wilder-ness and reach Kinder Downfall unscathed is to walk on a grid bearing of 310 degrees from the top of Grindsbrook Clough which should allow you to hit the easier edge path slightly south of the Downfall. It would be important to stick closely to the com-pass and not stray north, even by a few degrees.

Up there, there is nothing to see, no landmarks, misleading piles of stones or stakes indicating nothing. There are no signs. Even the wildlife lays low. The occa-sional golden plover pipes its warning call, a hare may spring up and run off at speed. Otherwise – nothing. Give it a wide berth is my advice.

Edge, a deep heather-clad gully formed by the stream of Torside Grain finding its way to the valley.

Once the road, the **B6105**, is reached there's a meeting of several ways: the Trans Pennine Way and the Longendale Trail. The Pennine Way crosses the road, follows the access road across the dammed end of **Torside Reservoir** and turns east above the shoreline to the frantic main road, the **A628**. **Crowden**, amounting to no more than a campsite and a youth hostel, is a short distance along a track parallel with the Sheffield road bringing you wearily to the end of your first day.

SNAKE PASS   [Map 6]
Once you reach the Snake Pass, the *Snake Pass Inn* (☎ 01433-651480), a lively house with a good choice of beer and tasty home-cooked bar meals, is down the main A57 road to the right or reached by a footpath, the Snake Path from Ashop Head. It's open all day, food is served 12 noon-9pm Mon-Sat, 12 noon-5.30pm on Sunday. It's a pity you're only just into the walk, making a trip down here too soon if you're going to make Crowden tonight, because this is a pub that is full of history and character.

TORSIDE   [Map 9]
Just over a mile from Crowden, the area around the reservoir is known as Torside. *The Old House* (☎ 01457-857527, 🖳 www.oldhouse.torside.co.uk, 1D/1T/1F) is 500m from the Way. There's B&B from £22.50 per person in en suite rooms, packed lunches for £3.50 and it's a walker-friendly place.

You could also try *Windy Harbour Farm Hotel* (☎ 01457-853107, 🖳 www.peakdistrict-hotel.co.uk, Woodhead Rd, Torside, 4S/4D/1T/1F) which is about a mile from the Way. They charge £25 per person for B&B and also offer **camping** for £3 per person.

CROWDEN   [Map 9]
For many walkers Crowden is synonymous with *Crowden Youth Hostel* (☎ 01457-852135, bookings ☎ 0870-770 5784, 🖳 crowden@yha.org.uk, open Apr-Oct, closed Sun May-Aug, Sun-Mon Apr and Sep/Oct), the salvation of many a sufferer over the years. Modernized and comfortable, it has 38 beds in 2-, 4- and 6-bedded rooms and

the charge is £10.60 (under 18s £7.20). The kitchen is well equipped and serves an evening meal, one sitting only at 7.30pm, and breakfast with plain but plentiful helpings.

The only other accommodation at Crowden is for campers in the *Camping and Caravanning Club Site* (☎ 01457-866057, non-members £6.55 July-Aug, £5.55 earlier or later), a site with good facilities including a shop. The site is closed between September and March.

If you are stuck for accommodation you will have to seek it to the west in **Padfield**, 4 miles (6km) away, where you'll find the *Peels Arms* (☎ 01457-852719, 🖳 www.glossop.com/peels, 2T/2D, Temple St, Padfield), the nearest pub, which charges £22.50 for single occupancy, £40 for a double/twin and serves bar meals.

Also in Padfield is *White House Farm* (☎ 01457-854695, 🖳 www.thepennineway.co.uk/whitehousefarm, Main Rd, 2T/1D), with B&B from £20.

Glossop has plentiful B&B accommodation. *Birds Nest Cottage* (☎ 01457-853478, 🖳 www.birdsnestcottage.co.uk, 40-42 Primrose Lane, 2S/3T/1F) does B&B from £17.50 per person. It's run by helpful walker-friendly people who will collect you from the Way (a 10-minute drive) and take you back next morning.

The National Express **coach** between Manchester and Sheffield comes through Crowden three times a day (see public transport map, pp36-9).

If you need to call a **taxi**, try Goldline Taxis (☎ 01457-857777 or ☎ 01457-853333).

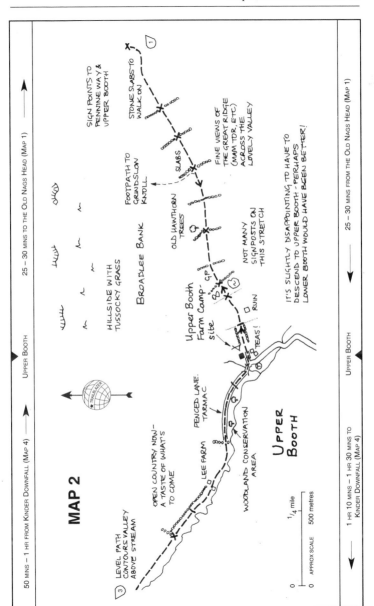

MAP 2

25 – 30 MINS TO THE OLD NAGS HEAD (MAP 1) →

25 – 30 MINS FROM THE OLD NAGS HEAD (MAP 1)

SIGN POINTS TO PENNINE WAY & UPPER BOOTH

STONE SLABS TO WALK ON

①

FINE VIEWS OF THE GREAT RIDGE (MAM TOR, ETC) ACROSS THE LOVELY VALLEY

SLABS

FOOTPATH TO GRINDSLOW KNOLL

OLD HAWTHORN TREES

NOT MANY SIGNPOSTS ON THIS STRETCH

HILLSIDE WITH TUSSOCKY GRASS

BROADLEE BANK

Upper Booth Farm Campsite

GP

②

B

TEAS!

RUIN

IT'S SLIGHTLY DISAPPOINTING TO HAVE TO DESCEND TO UPPER BOOTH – PERHAPS LOWER BOOTH WOULD HAVE BEEN BETTER!

UPPER BOOTH

← TRUE MAG →

OPEN COUNTRY NOW – A TASTE OF WHAT'S TO COME

LEE FARM

FENCED LANE. TARMAC

WOODLANDS CONSERVATION AREA

UPPER BOOTH

③ LEVEL PATH CONTOURS VALLEY ABOVE STREAM

¼ mile

500 metres

0

0

APPROX SCALE

1 HR 10 MINS – 1 HR 30 MINS TO KINDER DOWNFALL (MAP 4)

50 MINS – 1 HR FROM KINDER DOWNFALL (MAP 4) →

UPPER BOOTH

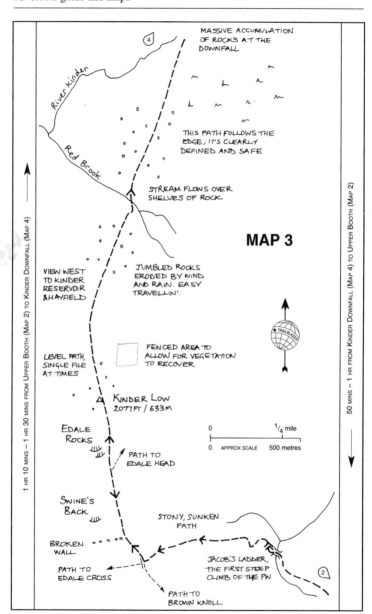

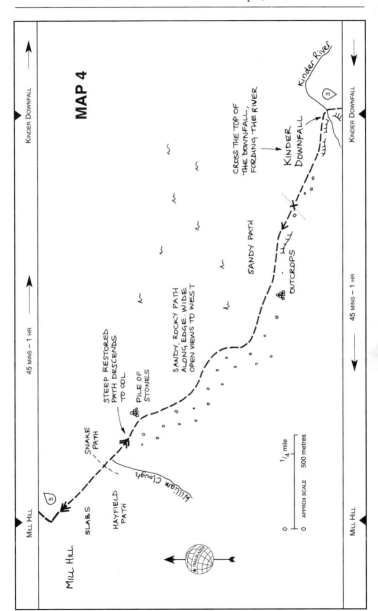

Peat

The Way has not become synonymous with hard going through seemingly endless miles of bogs for nothing. New paving stones have alleviated a lot of the misery this can cause the walker, but why is it so wet?

Peat is normally the cause. England used to be covered with trees. Everywhere except a few places such as the highest moorland and sandy beaches was wooded. Lions and tigers hunted and lived in the forests, alongside elephants and rhinoceros. Sadly you won't see much evidence of the ancient woodlands on your walk, and you'll be relieved to know that you won't have large wild carnivores bouncing up behind you (although wolves did live in the Pennines until the 16th century). The reason for the disappearance of this beautiful and iconic species is not a natural phenomenon, such as an ice-age, but the farming habits of man.

When the trees were cut for farming by Britain's earliest occupants the land was laid to waste. Rotting vegetation formed into peat. Sitting on top of impervious rock it became saturated and has remained so to this day. So when your boots next fill with black peaty water, don't curse nature because it is not what she intended. Curse your forebears instead.

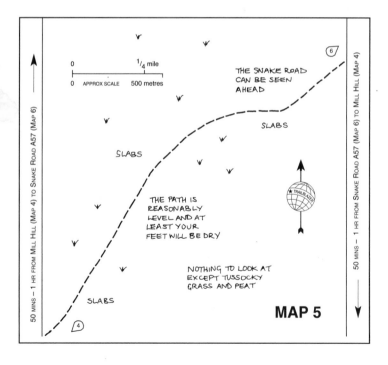

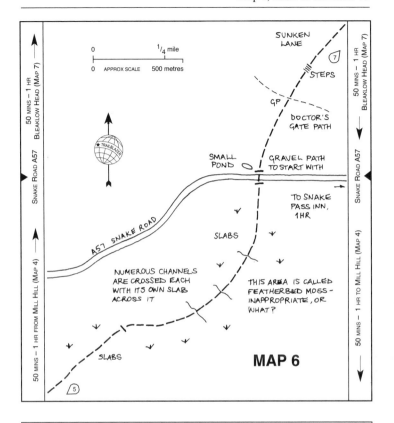

❏ Trans Pennine Trail

Walkers may wonder what the TPT is as signs appear at Crowden (Map 9). It's a trail linking the Irish Sea with the North Sea, coast to coast, using disused railway lines, canal towpaths and bridleways. Much of it wends its way through urban landscape but it offers scope for cyclists and horse riders as well as walkers. Much of it is accessible for the disabled and for people with young families with pushchairs.

Three official route guides are available covering the western, central and eastern sections in detail using OS mapping. Further information can be obtained from the Trans Pennine Trail Office (☎ 01226-772574, 💻 www.transpenninetrail.org), Barnsley MBC, Central Offices, Kendray St, Barnsley, S70 2TN.

The TPT will eventually form part of a much longer route known as the E8, Atlantic to Istanbul, a distance of 2750 miles (4390km), which, when complete will offer a huge challenge for those with the time and the feet to tackle it.

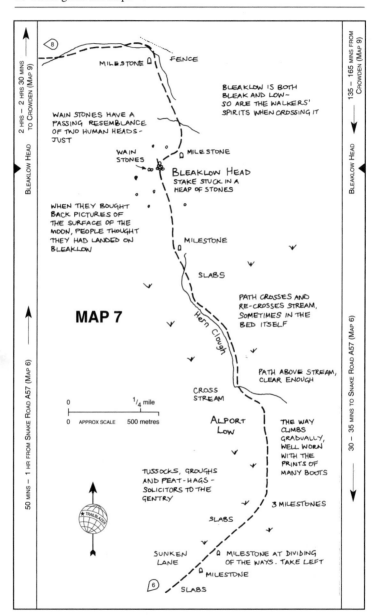

8

MILESTONE

FENCE

BLEAKLOW IS BOTH
BLEAK AND LOW ~
SO ARE THE WALKERS'
SPIRITS WHEN CROSSING IT

WAIN STONES HAVE A
PASSING RESEMBLANCE
OF TWO HUMAN HEADS -
JUST

WAIN
STONES

MILESTONE

BLEAKLOW HEAD
STAKE STUCK IN A
HEAP OF STONES

WHEN THEY BOUGHT
BACK PICTURES OF
THE SURFACE OF THE
MOON, PEOPLE THOUGHT
THEY HAD LANDED ON
BLEAKLOW

MILESTONE

SLABS

MAP 7

Hern Clough

PATH CROSSES AND
RE-CROSSES STREAM,
SOMETIMES IN THE
BED ITSELF

PATH ABOVE STREAM,
CLEAR ENOUGH

CROSS
STREAM

ALPORT
LOW

THE WAY
CLIMBS
GRADUALLY,
WELL WORN
WITH THE
PRINTS OF
MANY BOOTS

TUSSOCKS, GROUGHS
AND PEAT-HAGS -
SOLICITORS TO THE
GENTRY

3 MILESTONES

SLABS

SUNKEN
LANE

MILESTONE AT DIVIDING
OF THE WAYS. TAKE LEFT

MILESTONE

6

SLABS

0   1/4 mile
0   APPROX SCALE   500 metres

★ TRAILBLAZER

2 HRS - 2 HRS 30 MINS
TO CROWDEN (MAP 9)

BLEAKLOW HEAD

50 MINS - 1 HR FROM SNAKE ROAD A57 (MAP 6)

135 - 165 MINS FROM CROWDEN (MAP 9)

BLEAKLOW HEAD

30 - 35 MINS TO SNAKE ROAD A57 (MAP 6)

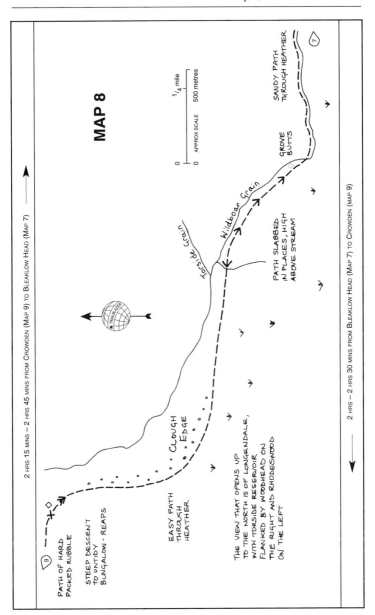

2 HRS 15 MINS – 2 HRS 45 MINS FROM CROWDEN (MAP 9) TO BLEAKLOW HEAD (MAP 7) →

MAP 8

¼ mile

0

0   500 metres

APPROX SCALE

SANDY PATH THROUGH HEATHER

⑦

GROVE BUTTS

Wildboar Grain

Torside Grain

PATH SLABBED IN PLACES, HIGH ABOVE STREAM

TRAIL BLAZER

CLOUGH EDGE

EASY PATH THROUGH HEATHER

THE VIEW THAT OPENS UP TO THE NORTH IS OF LONGENDALE, WITH TORSIDE RESERVOIR FLANKED BY WOODHEAD ON THE RIGHT AND RHODESWOOD ON THE LEFT

PATH OF HARD PACKED RUBBLE

STEEP DESCENT TO UNTIDY BUNGALOW - REAPS

⑨

2 HRS – 2 HRS 30 MINS FROM BLEAKLOW HEAD (MAP 7) TO CROWDEN (MAP 9) →

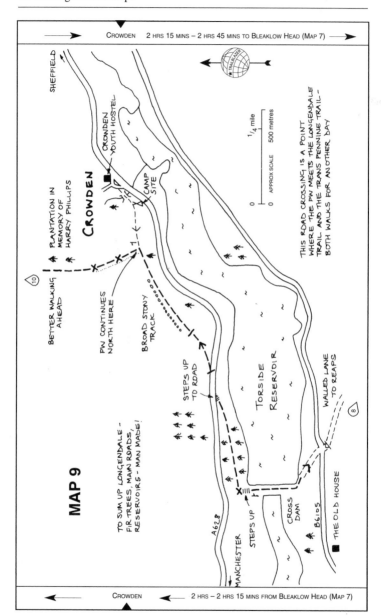

MAP 9

SHEFFIELD

CROWDEN YOUTH HOSTEL

CROWDEN

CAMP SITE

PLANTATION IN MEMORY OF HARRY PHILLIPS

BETTER WALKING AHEAD

(10)

PW CONTINUES NORTH HERE

BROAD STONY TRACK

THIS ROAD CROSSING IS A POINT WHERE THE PW MEETS THE LONGDENDALE TRAIL AND THE TRANS PENNINE TRAIL – BOTH WALKS FOR ANOTHER DAY

¼ mile

0   500 metres

0

APPROX SCALE

STEPS UP TO ROAD

TORSIDE RESERVOIR

WALLED LANE TO REAPS

(8)

TO SUM UP LONGDENDALE – FIR TREES, MAIN ROADS, RESERVOIRS – MAN MADE!

A628

MANCHESTER

STEPS UP

CROSS DAM

B6105

THE OLD HOUSE

CROWDEN TO STANDEDGE   MAPS 9-15

This section is a modest **11 miles (18km, 5-6¼hrs)**, one of the shortest days on the trail and possibly one of the least distinguished. The early gritstone outcrops of the Crowden Great Brook valley characterize an area of classic south Pennine country where wet feet are averted by the ubiquitous slabs all the way to the uninspiring summit of **Black Hill**. Here the white triangulation column stands an isolated guard over an expanse of peaty morass, now crossed by a causeway of slabs laid with painstaking care by the Peak National Park staff using nothing but a few crowbars and a kind of pallet-truck with caterpillar tracks, very slow and cumbersome to handle.

It has been remarked that this area is bisected by east/west roads which carve the wilderness into bite-size chunks, making the going at least progressive. **Wessenden Head** is the first, the A635 carving out its course across the moors. Another easy hour uses the access roads of the reservoirs which are great holding tanks for the seemingly endless rainfall in the area. Wessenden, Blakely, Swellands – the eye will be drawn to these successive stretches of water, scanning the surface for birdlife and rewarded, probably, by some Canada geese, a species of fowl that has a huge capacity for leaving its mark on the landscape, and which many birdwatchers dismiss as having no charm. They were introduced in the 17th century and have adapted to life in public parks in towns as well as in the countryside.

The approach to **Standedge Cutting** aims directly for the pub, the Great Western, raising hopes too soon because it turns sharp left along an old pack-horse route before reaching the road by the last reservoir, Redbrook. Standedge is a nothing kind of place. Even the few houses along the fast A62 offer no relief for the visitor and it's a dispiriting trudge to the accompaniment of heavy traffic to the nearest B&B, Globe Farm (see below).

STANDEDGE   [Map 15]

There are two B&Bs within half a mile of Standedge Cutting of which the best known is *Globe Farm Guest House* (☎ 01457-873040, 🖳 www.globefarm.co.uk, 1S/3D/2T/1F en suite), an establishment that has become part of the legend of the Way with its stories of walkers arriving with bleeding feet and broken hearts.

Although you can get a top breakfast and generous pack lunches (advisable for the next section which is not over-provided with places of refreshment), they have stopped doing evening meals. You can't blame them. Walkers would arrive hours late and wonder where the meal they booked for 7pm was. The cost per night is £22.50 per person.

If Globe Farm is full, try *New Barn* (☎ 01457-873937, Harrop Green Farm, Diggle, 1S/1T/1D/1F), at £20-25 per person.

At one time there was a choice of pubs at Standedge but they are now closed and returned to use as private not public houses. The nearest pub is the *Great Western* (☎ 01484-844315), east along the A62; bar meals are available.

The best bet for eating however, would be *Diggle Hotel* (☎ 01457-872741, 3D), a family-run free house with a loyal local clientele, good food and several real ales including Timothy Taylor's Landlord bitter. Accommodation is also available here at £35 for singles or £45 for the room if two are sharing.

Standedge is served by **buses** to Huddersfield and Oldham (see public transport map, pp36-9).

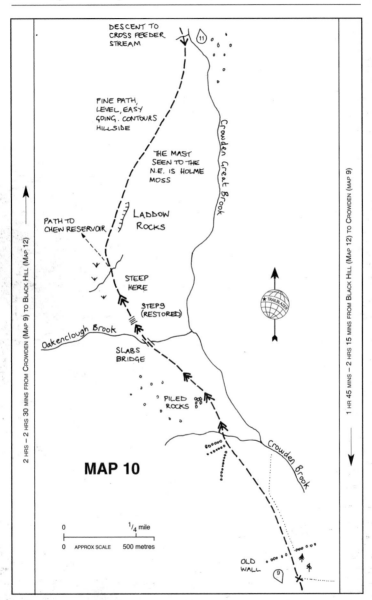

DESCENT TO
CROSS FEEDER
STREAM

11

FINE PATH,
LEVEL, EASY
GOING. CONTOURS
HILLSIDE

THE MAST
SEEN TO THE
N.E. IS HOLME
MOSS

Crowden Great Brook

PATH TO
CHEW RESERVOIR

LADDOW
ROCKS

STEEP
HERE

STEPS
(RESTORED)

Oakenclough Brook

SLABS
BRIDGE

PILED
ROCKS

Crowden Brook

MAP 10

TRAILBLAZER

2 HRS – 2 HRS 30 MINS FROM CROWDEN (MAP 9) TO BLACK HILL (MAP 12)

1 HR 45 MINS – 2 HRS 15 MINS FROM BLACK HILL (MAP 12) TO CROWDEN (MAP 9)

0   1/4 mile

0   APPROX SCALE   500 metres

OLD
WALL

9

Opposite Top: Laddow Rocks (see map above). **Bottom**: Trig point, Blackstone Edge (see p92).

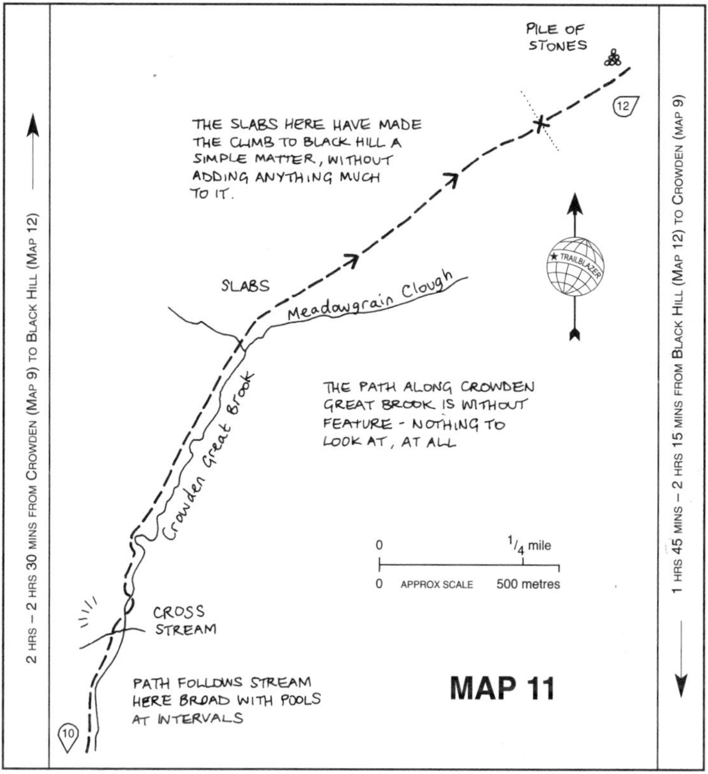

PILE OF STONES

THE SLABS HERE HAVE MADE THE CLIMB TO BLACK HILL A SIMPLE MATTER, WITHOUT ADDING ANYTHING MUCH TO IT.

SLABS

Meadowgrain Clough

★ TRAILBLAZER

THE PATH ALONG CROWDEN GREAT BROOK IS WITHOUT FEATURE - NOTHING TO LOOK AT, AT ALL

Crowden Great Brook

0   1/4 mile

0   APPROX SCALE   500 metres

CROSS STREAM

MAP 11

PATH FOLLOWS STREAM HERE BROAD WITH POOLS AT INTERVALS

2 HRS – 2 HRS 30 MINS FROM CROWDEN (MAP 9) TO BLACK HILL (MAP 12)

1 HRS 45 MINS – 2 HRS 15 MINS FROM BLACK HILL (MAP 12) TO CROWDEN (MAP 9)

Opposite Top: The Parsonage where the Brontës lived and wrote (see p98), is now a museum that's well worth the detour to Haworth. **Bottom left**: The cobbled streets of Haworth. **Bottom right**: Stoodley Pike (see p95).

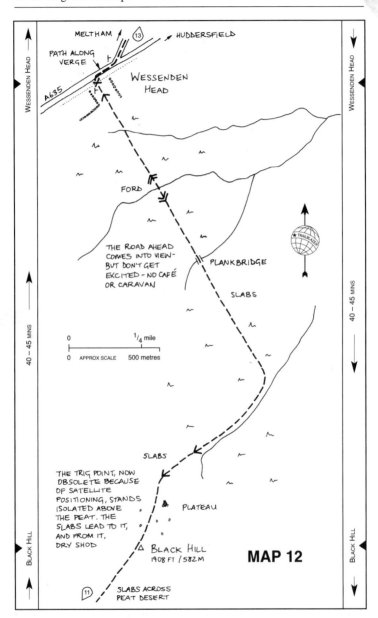

MELTHAM ⑬ HUDDERSFIELD

PATH ALONG VERGE

A635

WESSENDEN HEAD

FORD

WESSENDEN HEAD

WESSENDEN HEAD

THE ROAD AHEAD COMES INTO VIEW - BUT DON'T GET EXCITED - NO CAFÉ OR CARAVAN

PLANKBRIDGE

SLABS

40 – 45 MINS

40 – 45 MINS

0   ¼ mile
0   APPROX SCALE   500 metres

SLABS

SLABS

THE TRIG POINT, NOW OBSOLETE BECAUSE OF SATELLITE POSITIONING, STANDS ISOLATED ABOVE THE PEAT. THE SLABS LEAD TO IT, AND FROM IT, DRY SHOD

PLATEAU

△ BLACK HILL
1908 FT / 582 M

MAP 12

BLACK HILL

BLACK HILL

⑪ SLABS ACROSS PEAT DESERT

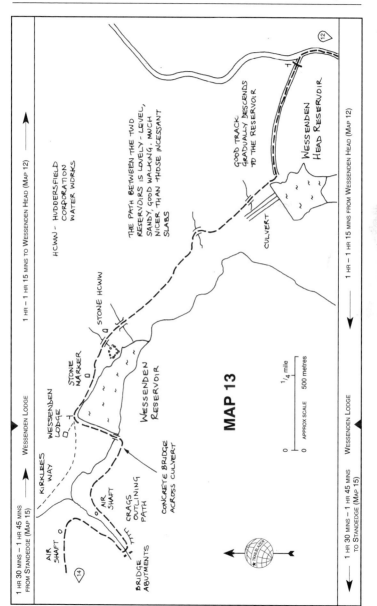

1 HR 30 MINS – 1 HR 45 MINS FROM STANDEDGE (MAP 15) ←——— WESSENDEN LODGE ———→ 1 HR – 1 HR 15 MINS TO WESSENDEN HEAD (MAP 12)

HCWW – HUDDERSFIELD CORPORATION WATER WORKS

THE PATH BETWEEN THE TWO RESERVOIRS IS LOVELY – LEVEL, SANDY, GOOD WALKING. MUCH NICER THAN THOSE INCESSANT SLABS

GOOD TRACK GRADUALLY DESCENDS TO THE RESERVOIR

WESSENDEN HEAD RESERVOIR

STONE HCWW

STONE MARKER

WESSENDEN LODGE

KIRKLEES WAY

CULVERT

WESSENDEN RESERVOIR

MAP 13

0 APPROX SCALE
0 500 metres
¼ mile

AIR SHAFT

CRAGS OUTLINING PATH

CONCRETE BRIDGE ACROSS CULVERT

AIR SHAFT

BRIDGE ABUTMENTS

← 1 HR 30 MINS – 1 HR 45 MINS TO STANDEDGE (MAP 15) ———— WESSENDEN LODGE ———→ 1 HR – 1 HR 15 MINS FROM WESSENDEN HEAD (MAP 12)

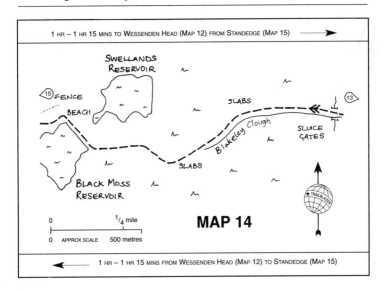

1 HR – 1 HR 15 MINS TO WESSENDEN HEAD (MAP 12) FROM STANDEDGE (MAP 15) ⟶

SWELLANDS RESERVOIR

15 FENCE

BEACH

SLABS

Blakeley Clough

SLUICE GATES

13

BLACK MOSS RESERVOIR

SLABS

MAP 14

0   ¼ mile

0   APPROX SCALE   500 metres

★ TRAILBLAZER

1 HR – 1 HR 15 MINS FROM WESSENDEN HEAD (MAP 12) TO STANDEDGE (MAP 15)

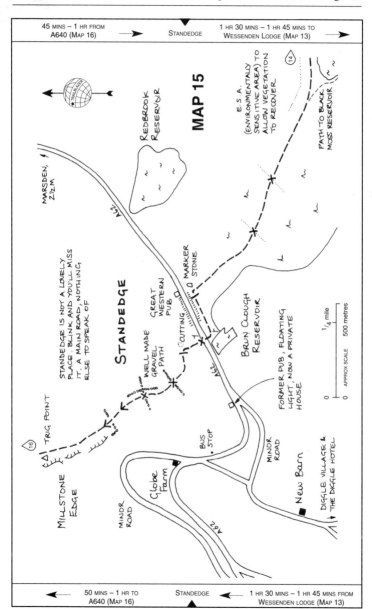

MAP 15

REDBROOK RESERVOIR

MARSDEN, 2½M

A62

E.S.A. (ENVIRONMENTALLY SENSITIVE AREA) TO ALLOW VEGETATION TO RECOVER

14

PATH TO BLACK MOSS RESERVOIR

STANDEDGE

STANDEDGE IS NOT A LOVELY PLACE. BLINK AND YOU'LL MISS IT. A MAIN ROAD, NOTHING ELSE TO SPEAK OF

GREAT WESTERN PUB

MARKER STONE

CUTTING

WELL MADE GRAVEL PATH

A62

BRUN CLOUGH RESERVOIR

FORMER PUB, FLOATING LIGHT, NOW A PRIVATE HOUSE

16 TRIG POINT

MILLSTONE EDGE

BUS STOP

MINOR ROAD

GLOBE FARM

MINOR ROAD

A62

NEW BARN

MINOR ROAD

DIGGLE VILLAGE & THE DIGGLE HOTEL

¼ mile

500 metres

0   APPROX SCALE

STANDEDGE TO THE CALDER VALLEY (FOR HEBDEN BRIDGE)
MAPS 15-22

The day, which covers **14 miles (23kms, 5-6¹/₂hrs)**, starts enthusiastically with the crossing of **Millstone Edge**, the first of several edges we shall encounter today, an exciting rock-hop which unfortunately soon deteriorates into more soggy moorland, good only as water catchment as the numerous reservoirs testify. Near **Windy Hill** we meet main roads again. First the A672 and then the M62 motorway which has to be crossed on a pencil-slim bridge which travellers from west to east by road may have often passed beneath. It looks fine from the motorway but induces vertigo when you're on it.

Beyond the M62, the wastes of **Redmires** used to demand their annual tribute of walkers' boots but now lie quiescent under the mighty flagstones. Time will tell if Redmires will swallow these whole as it used to swallow whole troops of walkers.

It is topped by **Blackstone Edge**, an airy rampart along which the pace can pick up, giving more opportunity for the nimble of foot. The other reason for quickening the pace is to reach the White House pub (see below) in good time in preparation for the afternoon's hard-pounding along the reservoirs where for an hour or so tarmac is the surface underfoot.

Soon afterwards, the needle-pointed monument of Stoodley Pike is visible long before we get to it, the climb up **Coldwell Hill** being mostly on slabs which wend their way through stunted heather and grass, the way designated intermittently with piles of stones, to the crossroads known as **Withen's Gate**. If you're booked into the youth hostel (see p87), take the left-hand path down to **Mankinholes**, the way here forming part of the Calderdale Way.

If the Calder Valley, or Hebden Bridge is your objective, carry on the short distance to the prominent monument of **Stoodley Pike** where a short rest is called for, to admire the view if the day is clear, or inspect your blisters if it is not.

From here on it is downhill by a good path and adequate signposting to the Rochdale Canal and the River Calder where a decision has to be made whether to plod the extra mile into **Hebden Bridge** or carry on for two miles (3km) to the next possible accommodation at **Colden**.

WINDY HILL/A672   [Map 17]

There's usually a **snack caravan** (or 'roach coach' as these invaluable establishments are scurrilously known in some quarters) in the lay-by on the A672 where the words sandwiches and bacon can be combined to create a culinary delicacy enjoyed the length and breadth of the land. Get one down you.

You can also catch the regular **bus** between Oldham and Halifax from here (see public transport map, pp36-9).

BLACKSTONE EDGE/A58   [Map 19]

The *White House* (☎ 01706-378456), a former packhorse inn on the A58 near Blackstone Edge Reservoir, is a perfectly serviceable place for a pint or a meal. Admittedly it caters mostly for motorists but who would be in business if they relied solely on Pennine Way walkers? It serves food 12 noon-2pm and 6.30-9pm Mon-Sat, and all day on Sunday.

The hourly **bus** between Rochdale and Halifax will stop here if requested (see public transport map, pp36-9).

MANKINHOLES [Map 20]

The accommodation between Standedge and the Calder Valley is to be found around Mankinholes, often the day's destination for those walkers who are unable to break away from the established division of the route into set-piece days.

There's the basic *Mankinholes Youth Hostel* (☎ 01706-812340, bookings ☎ 0870-770 5952, 🖳 mankinholes@yha.org .uk, open mid-Apr to Oct, closed Sun-Mon) which charges £10.60 (under 18s £7.20) but does not provide meals, so you'll have to cook your own or go to the pub.

Those preferring B&B can get it locally at *Cross Farm* (☎ 01706-813481, 2D/2T) from £20 per person; basic camping (facilities in barn) costs £3.50.

Other than using the youth hostel, there is no real need to spend the night at Mankinholes. It means a diversion off the route and unless you retrace your steps to Withen's Gate to rejoin the trail proper, you'll have missed out part of the Pennine Way, a crime too reprehensible to contemplate. It makes more sense to reach the Calder Valley and divert to Hebden Bridge.

HEBDEN BRIDGE [see map overleaf]

This small former mill town attractively-located in the steep-sided Calder Valley is well worth the short detour from the Way. Since the mills closed it's attracted a large 'alternative' population and now has an alternative technology centre, plenty of lively pubs, lots of good restaurants, interesting shops and a budding arts scene.

Hebden Bridge is a 30-40 minute stroll east of the Pennine Way, from where it crosses the busy and noisy A646. The most pleasant route into the town is along the canal towpath. Alternatively, you could come via the picturesque village of **Heptonstall** with its cobbled streets, local museum and old churches.

Services

There are frequent **trains** from Leeds, Bradford, Manchester and Preston. There are no direct **buses** from any major cities, but regular local services operate to Burnley, Rochdale, Todmorden, Haworth and Halifax (see public transport map, pp36-9). The **tourist information centre** (☎ 01422-843831, 🖳 www.hebdenbridge .co.uk/tourist-info) is on the A646 and in the middle of the town. It's open Apr-Oct: Mon-Fri 9.30am-5.30pm, Sat/Sun 10.30am- 5pm; Nov-Mar: Mon-Fri 10am-5pm, Sat/Sun 10.30am-4.15pm.

There are Lloyds, NatWest and Barclays **banks**, all with cash machines. Valet Stores (Mon-Sat 9.30am-5pm, Sun 12.30-4.30pm) is a reliable **gear shop** in Crown St. There's a small Spar **supermarket** (Mon-Sat 8am-11pm, Sun 8am-10.30pm) opposite, where you'll find a good selection of alcohol and snacks but not much else. Alternatively try the Co-op (Mon-Sat 8am-9pm, Sun 10am-4pm) on the A646 which is well stocked.

The Picture House **cinema** (☎ 01422-842807) shows matinées at 3pm at the weekend and the main programme at 7.45pm daily. There are regular performances at the **Little Theatre**, beside the Holme St Arts Centre.

The **Alternative Technology Centre** is worth visiting and open daily.

At Java Lounge.co.uk **internet café** (see p88) access is £2 per hour.

Where to stay

There are no campsites in town, but several B&Bs and hotels. On the western edge there's **Prospect End** (☎ 01422-843 586, 🖳 prospect.end@tesco.net, 8 Prospect Tce, Savile Rd, 1D/1T en suite, 1S,) which has rooms from £23 per person. In order to reach it from the Way you'll have to walk in on the A646, not the canal towpath.

More central is *1 Primrose Terrace* (☎/🖳 01422-844 747, 1S/1D, £17 per person) which has friendly owners. Neither of the rooms is en suite but the bathroom is next door.

Angeldale Guest House (☎ 01422-847321, 🖳 www.angeldale.co.uk, 2D/2T/1F), at the top of Hangingroyd Lane, is also fairly central and has beds from £23 per person, two rooms are en suite.

Myrtle Grove B&B (☎ 01422-846078, 🖳 www.myrtlegrove.btinternet.co.uk, Old

Hebden Bridge (MAP 22a)

Pennine Way & Todmorden

SAVILE RD

Pennine Way & Todmorden

St George's Sq

Where to stay
1 To Myrtle Grove B&B (300m)
2 Angeldale Guest House
3 The White Lion
28 Prospect End
29 1, Primrose Terrace

Where to eat
4 Innovation Café Bar
5 Shoulder of Mutton
6 Hole In The Wall Pub
7 The White Swan
9 Watergate Tea Rooms
10 Theo's Greek Feast
11 Brian's Farm Fayre
14 Pennine Wine & Cheese Co
21 Organic House
22 Java Lounge
23 The Swiss Connection
26 Canal Café Bar

Other
8 Chemist
12 Valet Stores
13 Spar Supermarket
15 Nat West Bank
16 Lloyds Bank
17 TIC
18 Picture House Cinema
19 Post Office
20 Holme St Arts Centre & Little Theatre
24 Barclays Bank
25 Co-op Supermarket
27 HB Alternative Technology Centre

Station

Halifax

Rochdale Canal

River Calder

Lees Rd, 1D en suite), is off the A6033 just north of the town centre up the hill. It's a good place; they charge £25 per person for B&B.

The White Lion Hotel (☎ 01422-842197, 🖥 www.whitelionhotelhb.co.uk, Bridge Gate, 2T/5D/3F) has double rooms from £55 en suite.

Where to eat
There are so many places to eat in Hebden Bridge that you'll be spoilt for choice and variety. There are some particularly good cafés along Market St. *Organic House* does what it says and serves a range of dishes including great avocado hummus with pitta bread and salad for £3.50. Across the street, *Java Lounge* is an internet café

which, as well as offering a wide range of coffees and comfy sofas to lounge in, has good organic dishes such as goat's cheese pancakes with caramelized onions (£2.90). Nearby is *The Swiss Connection* (☎ 01422-845524, open Tue-Sun 9am-5pm) which offers an interesting menu including salmon and broccoli pie (£5.25), a salad bar (£3.25) and an excellent range of home-made cakes.

Near the Alternative Technology Centre, the *Canal Café Bar* is also recommended. The menu includes mouthwatering dishes such as spicy peanut and corn soup with chickpea salsa, seasoned roast potatoes and salad (£4).

As well as stocking a well-chosen selection of wines and cheeses, the *Pennine Wine and Cheese Co* will make up filled rolls (ciabatta, baguettes etc).

Innovation Café Bar (☎ 01422-844094) in Hebden Bridge Mill does home-made soups and crêpes, as well as tradition-al dishes. Corned beef hash with salad is £4.50. It's open daily until 5pm.

On Bridge Gate, which runs off the square, the *Shoulder of Mutton* is open all day and serves pub grub from £4. Just down the road on the left is the *White Swan*, with similarly-priced food. *Brian's Farm Fayre*, almost next door, serves quiches and bacon sandwiches 'all done with the best possible taste'. Opposite is the licensed *Watergate Tea Rooms* (☎ 01422-842978, daily 10.30am-4.30pm) which won a Roy Castle Clean Air Award and is pleasantly smoke free. It does great home-made food such as salmon and asparagus quiche. 'The Works' breakfast is £5.70; veggie version also available. Set into a little recess opposite and down the road a few metres is *Theo's Greek Feast* (☎ 01422-845337), a BYO wine restaurant with main courses at around £9 and the 'Greek Feast' for £15.50.

Just across the pedestrian bridge over Hebden Water is the *Hole in the Wall*, a locals' pub which does rump steaks for £4.95 and 16oz T-bones for £7.45. *The White Lion* (see p88) does pub food for around £6.

❏ **Stoodley Pike** [see Map 21]

This needle-shaped monument above the Calderdale Valley was erected on a site where there had been an ancient burial cairn, assumed to be that of a chieftain. It seems plausible, the height being a commanding one and the ideal spot to erect a memorial.

It was also an ideal site for a beacon since the chain that warned of the approach of the Spanish Armada included Halifax's Beacon Hill and Pendle Hill above Clitheroe, Stoodley being the link between the two.

Be that as it may, in 1814 it was decided to celebrate the defeat of Napoleon by erecting a monument by public subscription and local bigwigs were quick to put their name down. Then as now a chance to appear influential was not to be missed. Unfortunately Napoleon escaped from Elba, raised his armies and overthrew the restored monarchy, cutting short the erection of the monument. After Wellington finally put paid to Bonaparte at Waterloo, the work began again and it was complet-ed before the end of 1815.

Disaster struck in 1854 when the tower collapsed as the country was going to war again, this time in the Crimea, an evil omen indeed. Rebuilt, it has survived to this day although they do say it wobbled a bit on the eve of the Falklands War.

For walkers along the Pennine Way the 37 metre (120ft) high spire is a landmark that beckons them from afar. Roughly at the 40-mile (60km) mark from Edale, it marks a change in the countryside. The peat moors are largely behind us and ahead lie more pastoral scenes as the gritstone gives way to limestone.

Tomorrow to fresh woods and pastures new.

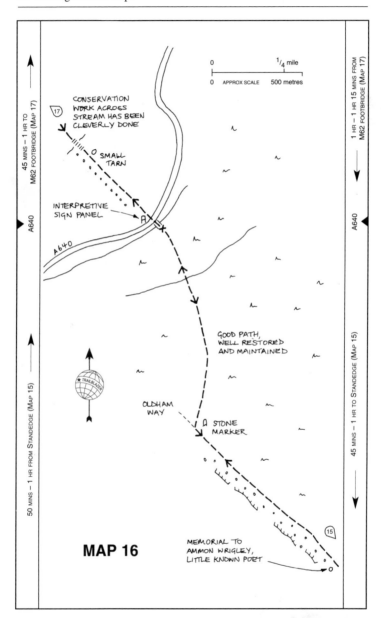

MAP 16

0 ___ 1/4 mile
0 APPROX SCALE 500 metres

17

CONSERVATION WORK ACROSS STREAM HAS BEEN CLEVERLY DONE

SMALL TARN

INTERPRETIVE SIGN PANEL

A640

GOOD PATH, WELL RESTORED AND MAINTAINED

OLDHAM WAY

STONE MARKER

MEMORIAL TO AMMON WRIGLEY, LITTLE KNOWN POET

15

★ TRAILBLAZER

45 MINS – 1 HR TO M62 FOOTBRIDGE (MAP 17)

A640

50 MINS – 1 HR FROM STANDEDGE (MAP 15)

1 HR – 1 HR 15 MINS FROM M62 FOOTBRIDGE (MAP 17)

A640

45 MINS – 1 HR TO STANDEDGE (MAP 15)

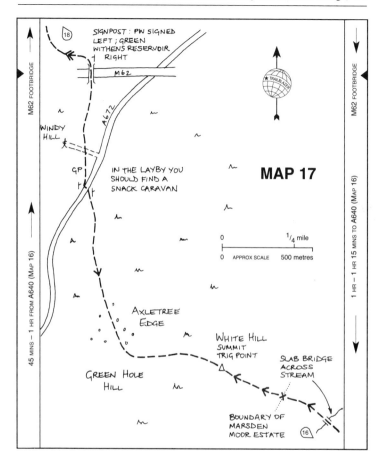

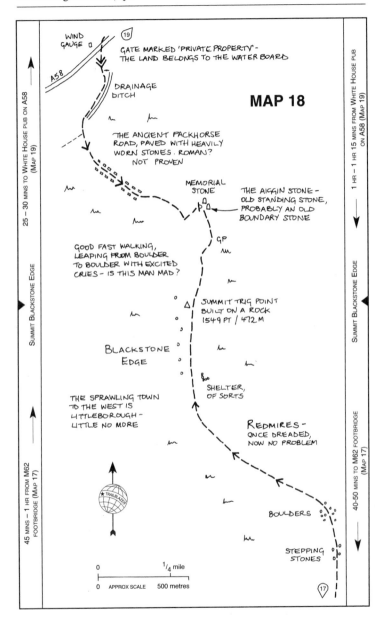

WIND GAUGE □

GATE MARKED 'PRIVATE PROPERTY' –
THE LAND BELONGS TO THE WATER BOARD

A58

DRAINAGE
DITCH

MAP 18

THE ANCIENT PACKHORSE
ROAD, PAVED WITH HEAVILY
WORN STONES. ROMAN?
NOT PROVEN

MEMORIAL
STONE

THE AIGGIN STONE –
OLD STANDING STONE,
PROBABLY AN OLD
BOUNDARY STONE

GP

GOOD FAST WALKING,
LEAPING FROM BOULDER
TO BOULDER WITH EXCITED
CRIES – IS THIS MAN MAD?

SUMMIT TRIG POINT
BUILT ON A ROCK
1549 PT / 472 M

BLACKSTONE
EDGE

SHELTER,
OF SORTS

THE SPRAWLING TOWN
TO THE WEST IS
LITTLEBOROUGH –
LITTLE NO MORE

REDMIRES –
ONCE DREADED,
NOW NO PROBLEM

★ TRAILBLAZER

BOULDERS

STEPPING
STONES

0   ¼ mile

0   APPROX SCALE   500 metres

25 – 30 MINS TO WHITE HOUSE PUB ON A58 (MAP 19)

SUMMIT BLACKSTONE EDGE

45 MINS – 1 HR FROM M62 FOOTBRIDGE (MAP 17)

1 HR – 1 HR 15 MINS FROM WHITE HOUSE PUB ON A58 (MAP 19)

SUMMIT BLACKSTONE EDGE

40-50 MINS TO M62 FOOTBRIDGE (MAP 17)

19

17

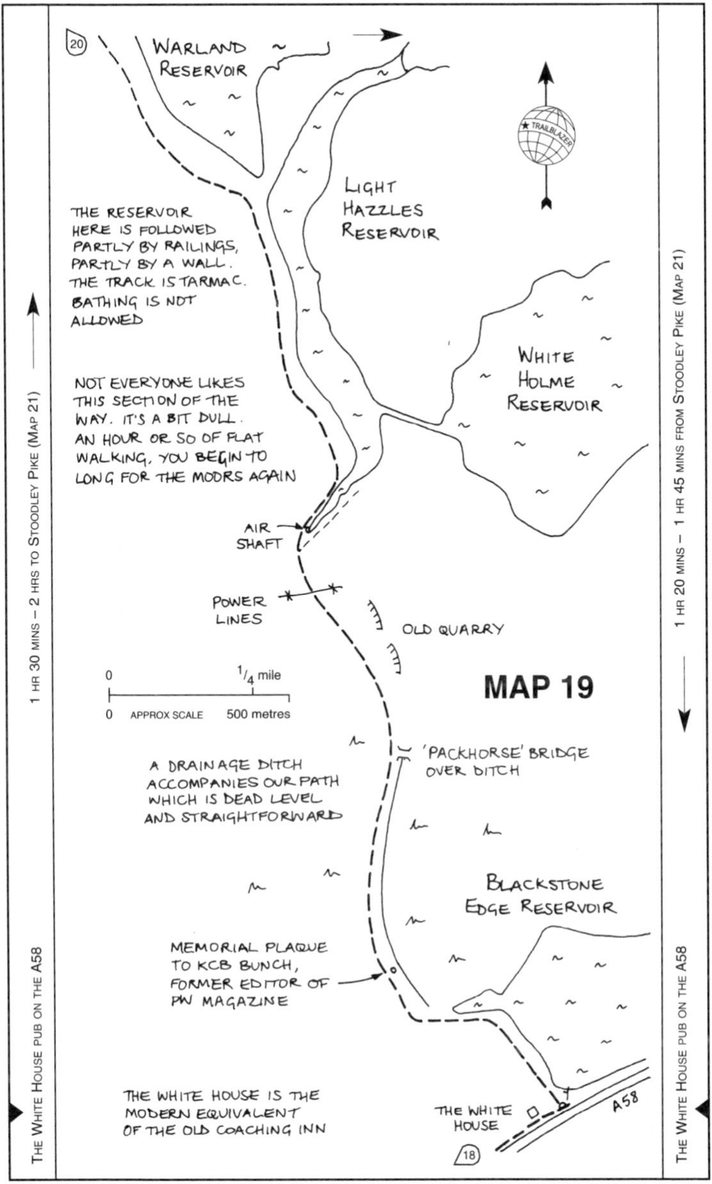

20

WARLAND
RESERVOIR

LIGHT
HAZZLES
RESERVOIR

WHITE
HOLME
RESERVOIR

★ TRAILBLAZER

THE RESERVOIR
HERE IS FOLLOWED
PARTLY BY RAILINGS,
PARTLY BY A WALL.
THE TRACK IS TARMAC.
BATHING IS NOT
ALLOWED

NOT EVERYONE LIKES
THIS SECTION OF THE
WAY. IT'S A BIT DULL.
AN HOUR OR SO OF FLAT
WALKING, YOU BEGIN TO
LONG FOR THE MOORS AGAIN

AIR
SHAFT

POWER
LINES

OLD QUARRY

MAP 19

0   1/4 mile

0   APPROX SCALE   500 metres

'PACKHORSE' BRIDGE
OVER DITCH

A DRAINAGE DITCH
ACCOMPANIES OUR PATH
WHICH IS DEAD LEVEL
AND STRAIGHTFORWARD

BLACKSTONE
EDGE RESERVOIR

MEMORIAL PLAQUE
TO KGB BUNCH,
FORMER EDITOR OF
PW MAGAZINE

THE WHITE HOUSE IS THE
MODERN EQUIVALENT
OF THE OLD COACHING INN

THE WHITE
HOUSE

A58

18

1 HR 30 MINS – 2 HRS TO STOODLEY PIKE (MAP 21)

THE WHITE HOUSE PUB ON THE A58

1 HR 20 MINS – 1 HR 45 MINS FROM STOODLEY PIKE (MAP 21)

THE WHITE HOUSE PUB ON THE A58

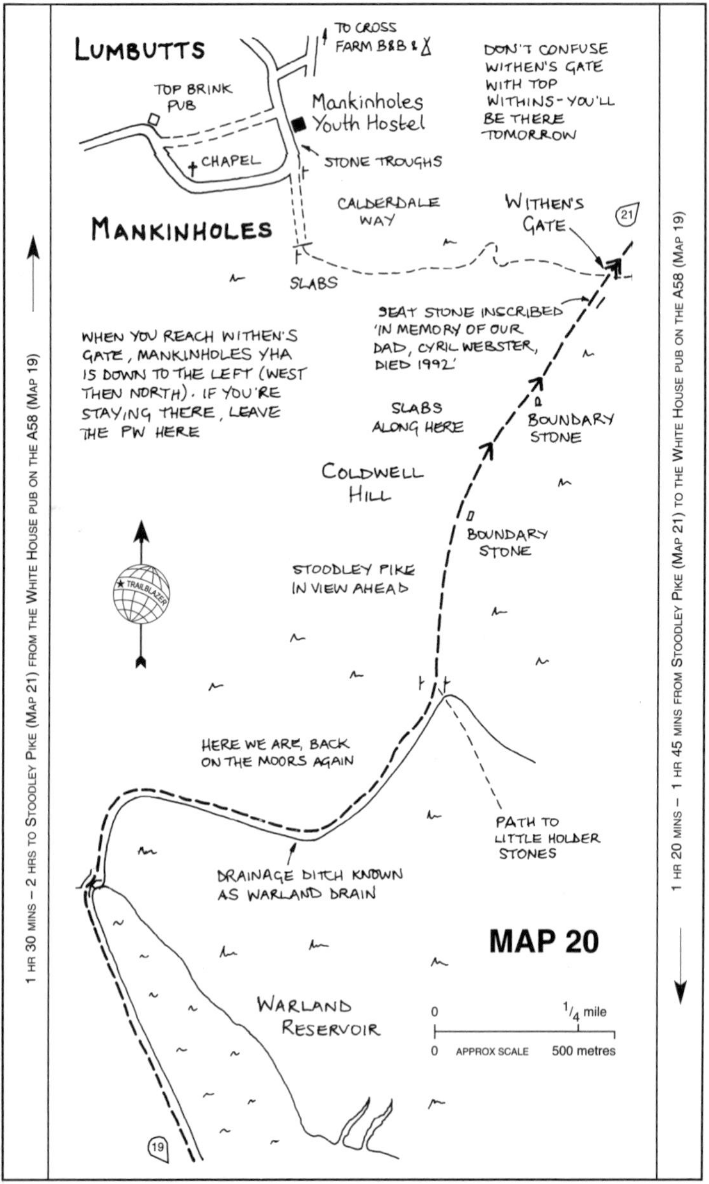

LUMBUTTS

TOP BRINK PUB

TO CROSS FARM B&B & ⚞

Mankinholes Youth Hostel

DON'T CONFUSE WITHEN'S GATE WITH TOP WITHINS - YOU'LL BE THERE TOMORROW

✝ CHAPEL

STONE TROUGHS

MANKINHOLES

CALDERDALE WAY

WITHEN'S GATE

㉑

SLABS

SEAT STONE INSCRIBED 'IN MEMORY OF OUR DAD, CYRIL WEBSTER, DIED 1992'

WHEN YOU REACH WITHEN'S GATE, MANKINHOLES YHA IS DOWN TO THE LEFT (WEST THEN NORTH). IF YOU'RE STAYING THERE, LEAVE THE PW HERE

SLABS ALONG HERE

BOUNDARY STONE

COLDWELL HILL

★ TRAILBLAZER

BOUNDARY STONE

STOODLEY PIKE IN VIEW AHEAD

HERE WE ARE, BACK ON THE MOORS AGAIN

PATH TO LITTLE HOLDER STONES

DRAINAGE DITCH KNOWN AS WARLAND DRAIN

MAP 20

0 — ¼ mile

0 — 500 metres

APPROX SCALE

WARLAND RESERVOIR

⑲

1 HR 30 MINS – 2 HRS TO STOODLEY PIKE (MAP 21) FROM THE WHITE HOUSE PUB ON THE A58 (MAP 19)

1 HR 20 MINS – 1 HR 45 MINS FROM STOODLEY PIKE (MAP 21) TO THE WHITE HOUSE PUB ON THE A58 (MAP 19)

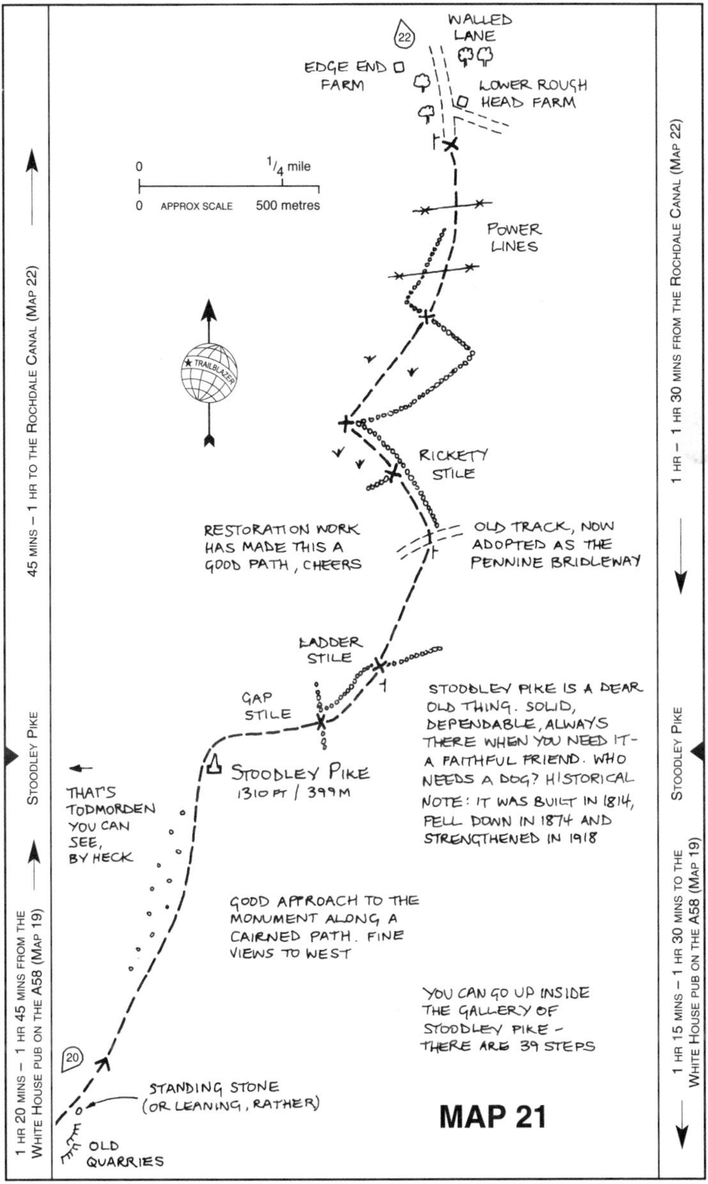

WALLED LANE

EDGE END FARM

LOWER ROUGH HEAD FARM

(22)

POWER LINES

0   1/4 mile
0   APPROX SCALE   500 metres

★ TRAILBLAZER

RICKETY STILE

RESTORATION WORK HAS MADE THIS A GOOD PATH, CHEERS

OLD TRACK, NOW ADOPTED AS THE PENNINE BRIDLEWAY

LADDER STILE

GAP STILE

△ STOODLEY PIKE
1310 FT / 399 M

THAT'S TODMORDEN YOU CAN SEE, BY HECK

STOODLEY PIKE IS A DEAR OLD THING. SOLID, DEPENDABLE, ALWAYS THERE WHEN YOU NEED IT- A FAITHFUL FRIEND. WHO NEEDS A DOG? HISTORICAL NOTE: IT WAS BUILT IN 1814, FELL DOWN IN 1874 AND STRENGTHENED IN 1918

GOOD APPROACH TO THE MONUMENT ALONG A CAIRNED PATH. FINE VIEWS TO WEST

YOU CAN GO UP INSIDE THE GALLERY OF STOODLEY PIKE - THERE ARE 39 STEPS

STANDING STONE (OR LEANING, RATHER)

OLD QUARRIES

(20)

MAP 21

45 MINS – 1 HR TO THE ROCHDALE CANAL (MAP 22)

◀ STOODLEY PIKE

1 HR 20 MINS – 1 HR 45 MINS FROM THE WHITE HOUSE PUB ON THE A58 (MAP 19)

1 HR – 1 HR 30 MINS FROM THE ROCHDALE CANAL (MAP 22)

STOODLEY PIKE

1 HR 15 MINS – 1 HR 30 MINS TO THE WHITE HOUSE PUB ON THE A58 (MAP 19)

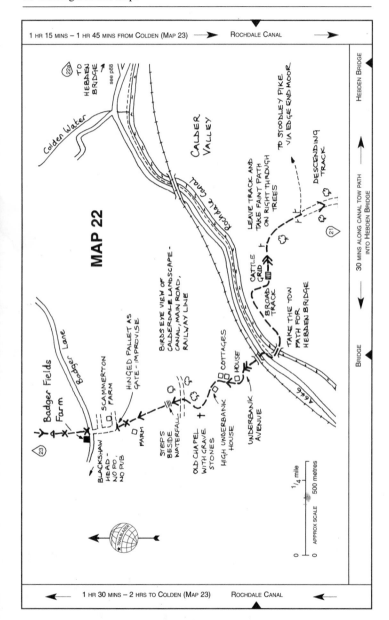

MAP 22

To Hebden Bridge

see p88

Colden Water

Calder Valley

Rochdale Canal

Badger Fields Farm

Badger Lane

Scammerton Farm

Hinged pallet as gate – improvise

Bird's eye view of Calderdale landscape – canal, main road, railway line

Blackshaw Head – no PO, no pub

Steps beside waterfall

Old Chapel with grave stones

High Underbank House

Underbank Avenue

Farm

Cottages

House

Cattle Grid

Broad Track

Take the tow path for Hebden Bridge

Leave track and take faint path on right through trees

To Stoodley Pike via Edge End Moor

Descending track

A646

Approx scale

0   ¼ mile
0   500 metres

CALDER VALLEY TO PONDEN   MAPS 22-28

This is a **12-mile (19km, 3³/₄-5hrs)** stretch and involves a similar decision as on the previous day, whether or not to go down off the moors to visit the village of Haworth, famous in the annals of English literature as the home of the Brontës but also a pleasant place to stop with some good pubs.

As you leave the industrial clutter of the Calder Valley route-finding becomes a little difficult and may induce some gnashing of teeth. Once clear of **Colden** the trail improves and open moorland with the accompanying cotton grass and tussocks lead to one of the best picnic spots on the whole walk, at Graining Water where two streams join under some craggy outcrops.

Lovers of reservoirs will be amply rewarded today with the **Walshaw Dean** three, then it's up onto the slabbed moorland again to reach the isolated ruin of **Top Withens**, said to be the inspiration for the house in *Wuthering Heights*. This is where you must decide whether or not you want to visit **Haworth** since a 3¹/₂-mile (6km) walk will lead there by angling down to the famous Bronte Bridge.

The path from Top Withens to **Ponden Reservoir** has been laid and surfaced with quarry-bottom ensuring a gentle, dry-shod stroll down off the moor with the reservoirs glinting in the sun – or invisible owing to the almost perpetual mist that obscures these hills.

BLACKSHAW HEAD   [Map 22]
Where the trail crosses Badger Lane at Blackshaw Head there is *Badger Fields Farm* (☎ 01422-845161, 🖳 www.badger fields.com, 2T/1D, Map 22) where Mrs Whitaker offers comfortable B&B for £26 or you can **camp** for £2 using the shower in the house.

Blackshaw Head is the place that time forgot and has no services, but **buses** run hourly to Hebden Bridge (see public transport map, pp36-9).

COLDEN   [Map 23]
Within a mile of leaving the valley, we come upon signs pointing the way to Aladdin's Cave, promising untold excesses such as sweets, cakes, groceries and drinks. This is *Highgate Farm* (☎ 01422-842897, Map 23) run by the redoubtable May Stocks who has a natural instinct for what wayfarers want and has provided for them accordingly. Beside the shop which is open daily 9am-8pm, May allows **camping** for free. The amenities are minimal with a cold water tap and a chemical loo.

Further north and just over a mile off the Way, there's camping for £3.50 per per-

son at *Pennine Camp and Caravan Site* (☎ 01422-842287, approx Apr-Oct), High Greenwood House. To reach it take the path for Clough Hole Bridge (see **Map 24**). Turn left at the road which you follow for ³/₄ mile to the campsite.

The New Delight Inn (**Map 23**) at Jack Bridge has now reopened and once again provides a haven for Pennine Way walkers. They do food Tues-Fri 12-1.45pm and 6-7.45pm; Sat 12-2.45pm and 6-7.45pm; Sun 12-4.45pm.

The next pub north is the *Packhorse Inn* (☎ 01422-842803, **Map 25**, food is served Tue-Sun 12 noon-2pm and 7-9.30pm; they close in the afternoon when the last lunchers have left) on the Brierfield–Hebden Bridge road, a few hundred yards off-route. Although it declares itself to be a 'chip free zone' the portions are giant and tasty and will provide ample carbohydrate.

HAWORTH   [see map p100]
The Pennine Way does not go through Haworth, but there are good reasons for taking the path down via the Bronte Bridge and Falls to seek whatever solace may be

❏ **The Brontës of Haworth**

Haworth cannot be separated from the Brontës. Their home, the Parsonage, still stands and is open to the public, attracting tens of thousands of visitors every year from all over the world. A shop sells the complete works in book form, on disc and on tape plus lavender-scented pot-pourris.

The churchyard above which the Parsonage stands can be a haunting and gloomy place on a wet evening, calling to mind Mrs Gaskell's account of life in Haworth. The graveyard, standing at the top of the village, poisoned the water springs which fed the pumps from which the villagers drew their water. Small wonder that typhoid and fever often afflicted the community.

Mrs Gaskell's description sums up the oppressive nature of Haworth in Victorian times, an echo of which can be heard even today:

The rain ceased, and the day was just suited to the scenery – wild and chill – with great masses of cloud, glooming over the moors, and here and there a ray of sunshine...darting down into some deep glen, lighting up the tall chimney, or glistening on the windows and wet roof of the mill which lies couching at the bottom. The country got wilder and wilder as we approached Haworth; for the last four miles we were ascending a huge moor at the very top of which lies the dreary, black-looking village. The clergyman's house was at the top of the churchyard. So through that we went – a dreary, dreary place, literally paved with rain-blackened tombstones, and all on the slope. **Mrs Gaskell** *The Life of Charlotte Brontë*, 1857

The three Brontë sisters, Emily (*Wuthering Heights*, 1847) Charlotte (*Jane Eyre*, 1847) and Anne (*The Tenant of Wildfell Hall*, 1848) were brought up by their father and an aunt in the Parsonage where Rev Brontë had taken a living in 1820. Two older sisters had died through catching typhoid at the school to which they were sent as boarders at Cowan Bridge. The only boy in the family, Branwell, had every hope and expectation lavished on him, taking precedence over his more talented sisters as the son, but squandered his life in drink and drugs, dying in 1848.

The fame of the modest and unassuming sisters was slow to be recognized and they all in turn died comparatively young from the unhealthy conditions in which they lived. Today they live on in their books, known and read throughout the world. Yes, Haworth **is** the Brontës.

required: refreshment, accommodation, literary inspiration, all are there in abundance but the extra 3½ miles (6km) down also involve 3½ miles back up!

This gritstone town has its charms but there is no denying its appeal as a tourist destination on the strength of its association with the Brontë sisters. All year round the streets are thronged with visitors, many of whom would probably not read the works of Emily, Charlotte and Anne if their lives depended on it. However, such is the romantic appeal of the family whose home can be visited that the crowds continue to be drawn here from all over the world.

Haworth has long been a major destination on the UK tour circuit for Japanese visitors; some signs are even in Japanese – directing tourists up the picturesque cobbled Main St and sending dedicated pilgrims up onto the moor to visit Top Withens, supposedly the inspiration for the house in *Wuthering Heights*.

Transport

The **train station** is a stop on the Keighley and Worth Valley Railway Line (☎ 01535-645214, 🖳 www.kwvr.co.uk), a preserved line which runs steam trips at weekends throughout the year and also daily during

July and August between Keighley (where it links up with the main Leeds–Settle–Carlisle line) and Oxenhope.

Bus transport from Haworth connects with Keighley, Stanbury and Hebden Bridge (see public transport map, pp36-9). **Taxi** firms include Bronte Taxis (☎ 01535-644442) and Crown Taxis (☎ 01535-662020).

Services

Haworth has services aplenty including two **post offices**, a Spar **supermarket** (7am-10.30pm daily), souvenir shops, a bookshop, newsagents' and numerous souvenir shops.

The **tourist information centre** (☎ 01535-642329, 💻 www.visithaworth.com) is open daily Apr-Oct 9.30am-5.30pm, Nov-Mar 9.30am-5pm and is situated at the top of the cobbled Main St in a commanding position that's hard to miss.

There are no banks in Haworth but there is a **cash machine** in the Spar supermarket near the station. There's also one in the back porch of the Kings Arms pub but a charge may be made when using this machine. When you include the cost of a pint, inevitable really, the decision to draw cash proves an expensive one.

Halfway up the cobbled Main St, on the corner of 'Purvs Lane', is **Spooks**, an interesting 'alternative' bookshop. If your walk isn't going quite as well as you'd planned you could have a tarot reading (£20) but perhaps the money would be better spent on an aromatherapy massage, also available here for £20.

The **Brontë Parsonage Museum** (☎ 01535-642323, 💻 www.bronte.info, open daily 10am-5pm Apr-Sep and 11am-4.30pm Oct-Mar, admission £4.80 adult, £1.50 child) is at the top of the town. It tells the fascinating story of the family and their tragic life including the only son, Branwell, who gave his life up to riotous living. With such talented sisters, who could blame him?

Where to stay

Haworth Youth Hostel (☎ 01535-642234, bookings ☎ 0870-770 5858, 💻 haworth@ yha.org.uk, Longlands Drive, open mid-Feb to Oct, plus Fri-Sat Nov to mid-Dec) is on the other side of town, 1¹/₂ miles (2km) up a long hill, passing most of the other services on the way. This grand Victorian mansion has 100 beds but the popularity of the town means that it gets very busy at peak times. Adults are charged £11.80, under 18s £8.50. The hostel is open all day and there's an evening meal at 6.30pm.

One of the best B&Bs, *The Apothecary Guest House* (☎ 01535-643642, 💻 www.bronte-country.com/acc omm/apothecary, 86 Main St, 2S/3D/1T/ 1F en suite), is ideally located right in the heart of town, surrounded by places to eat and happy to welcome walkers. Their prices are reasonable at £22.50 per person.

Rookery Nook (☎ 01535-643374, 6 Church St, 3D/2F) offers accommodation with or without breakfast. B&B will cost £20 each for doubles or £22.50 for singles. Without breakfast the charge ranges from £12.50 to £22.50 per person; continental breakfast costs £2.50; cooked breakfast £3.50. Mrs Ross and her son have set about providing a friendly and cheerful service to visitors and you would go a long way before finding anything nicer. What's more, it's literally a stone's throw from the Parsonage.

At the bottom of Main St among a succession of attractive terraced cottages, *The Old Registry* (☎ 01535-646503, 💻 www.oldregistry.com, 2-4 Main St, 9D/1T en suite, from £30) is furnished with an eye for detail and an emphasis on homely luxury and pampering. The beds are four posters and they certainly deserve top marks for marketing.

If you're looking for a really bijou establishment, *Rosebud Cottage* (☎ 01535-640321, 💻 www.rosebudcottage.co.uk, 1 Belle Isle Rd, 1S/2D/1F en suite) has an olde worlde charm that will appeal to some. It is a well-run establishment with rooms at £30 for single and £50 for double, with an evening meal for £14. You'll know it by the Union Jack flying outside.

The *Bronte Hotel* (☎ 01535-644112, 💻 www.bronte-hotel.co.uk, Lees Lane,

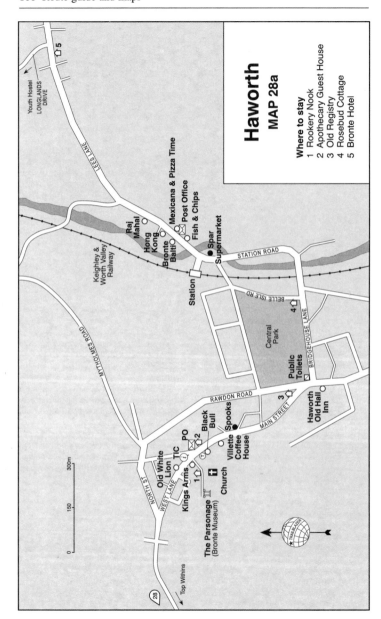

Haworth
MAP 28a

Where to stay
1 Rookery Nook
2 Apothecary Guest House
3 Old Registry
4 Rosebud Cottage
5 Bronte Hotel

3S/2T/3D/3F) is a larger establishment not far from the youth hostel and might be just the ticket for a group of walkers wanting accommodation under the same roof. It's geared for over-nighters with good clean rooms, most en suite and with ample scope for eating and drinking downstairs. You can expect to pay £23 for a single (£33 en suite), £45 for a double room (£55 en suite) and £60 for an en suite family room.

Where to eat

Three of Haworth's pubs, the *Old White Lion*, *Kings Arms*, and *Black Bull*, are clustered together at the top of the cobbled street. However, one of the best, *Haworth Old Hall Inn* (☎ 01535-642709, Sun St), stands apart and is particularly recommended for real ales. They are open all day and a range of bar meals in generous portions is served Mon-Sat 12 noon-2pm and 5.30-9pm, Sunday 12 noon-4pm and 5-8pm. They have a non-smoking room.

The cobbled Main St has a plethora of eating places. For lunches and afternoon teas you can't do better than *Villette Coffee House* (☎ 01535-644967) where such delights as Yorkshire curd tarts, large flat Yorkshire Parkins, delicious sticky ginger buns and a rich spicy scone known as a Fat Rascal can all be savoured. Cream teas are £2.20 and their all-day breakfast is a feast for £3.30. They are open daily 8am-5/6pm – until the last customer leaves.

In the eastern, non-tourist, part of the town is a collection of takeaways and restaurants. *Raj Mahal* (☎ 01535-643890, 51 Mill Hey) is a notable Indian restaurant with dishes reputedly as good as anything Bradford has to offer but you might want to eat at the nearby *Bronte Balti*, just for the name.

There's also the *Hong Kong* Chinese takeaway, a *fish and chip* shop, *Pizza Time* and, for a change of cuisine, *Mexicana*, with nachos, fajitas, burritos, enchiladas, tacos and chimichangas to take away.

PONDEN AND STANBURY   [Map 28]

With **Ponden** in sight, you can **camp** at *Upper Heights Farm* (☎ 01535-644592, 💻 www.brontemoor-breaks.co.uk) for £3.50 and there is self-catering accommodation available if you're likely to stay more than one night; the accommodation is open Apr-Sep only. An evening meal can be arranged and is probably necessary: the pubs in Stanbury are a fair walk away.

Ponden is now much smaller than it was when weaving was dominant in the area. Ponden Mill has been turned into a 'retail experience' and the houses along the Haworth road have been gentrified. Ponden belongs with the parish of Stanbury, a village a mile towards Haworth where there are two pubs, a telephone kiosk but no post office. It is a suburb of Haworth and walkers with no intention of visiting Haworth itself can find accommodation here.

Ponden House (☎ 01535-644154, 💻 www.pondenhouse.co.uk, 1T/2D) would be the first choice because it is right on the trail and is signposted from the point where the Pennine Way meets the reservoir road. B&B costs from £23 or you can camp for £3 per person although the facilities are basic. You can order an evening meal for £15, probably a good idea unless you want to walk the mile to the nearest pub. Campers can get breakfast indoors for £6.

If they are full, a walk down the road towards **Stanbury** will bring you first to *The Old Silent Inn* (☎ 01535 647437, 💻 www.old-silent-inn.co.uk, 2S/1T/5D/1F), an upmarket hostelry where you can get a bed for the night for £38 for singles, £58 twins or doubles, with breakfast. Meals are from a fairly standard bar menu.

In the village itself and, for some, irresistible because of its name (although it has nothing to do with the Brontës), stands the *Wuthering Heights* (☎ 01535-643332, 💻 robinhaworth@aol.com, 2D/1F), a friendly local that's actually not too obsessed with the Brontës. You'll pay a reasonable £25 per head with breakfast. The rooms aren't en suite but are nicely modernized.

If none of these suits jump on the hourly **bus** from Stanbury (see public transport map, pp36-9) or call one of the taxi companies (see p99) and get taken into Haworth where there's plenty of choice.

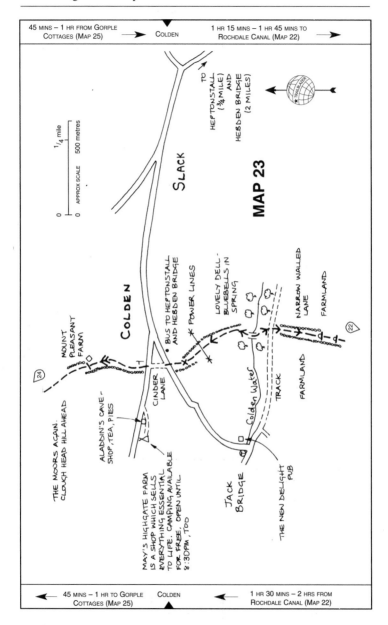

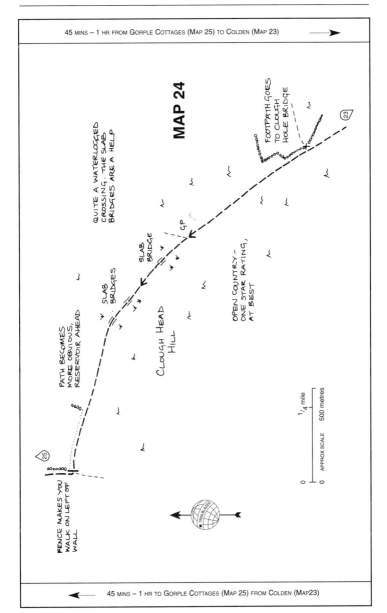

45 MINS – 1 HR FROM GORPLE COTTAGES (MAP 25) TO COLDEN (MAP 23)

MAP 24

FOOTPATH GOES TO CLOUGH HOLE BRIDGE

23

QUITE A WATERLOGGED CROSSING. THE SLAB BRIDGES ARE A HELP

CP

SLAB BRIDGE

SLAB BRIDGES

OPEN COUNTRY – ONE STAR RATING, AT BEST

CLOUGH HEAD HILL

PATH BECOMES MORE OBVIOUS, RESERVOIR AHEAD

25

1/4 mile

500 metres

0   APPROX SCALE

0

TRAILBLAZER

FENCE MAKES YOU WALK ON LEFT OF WALL

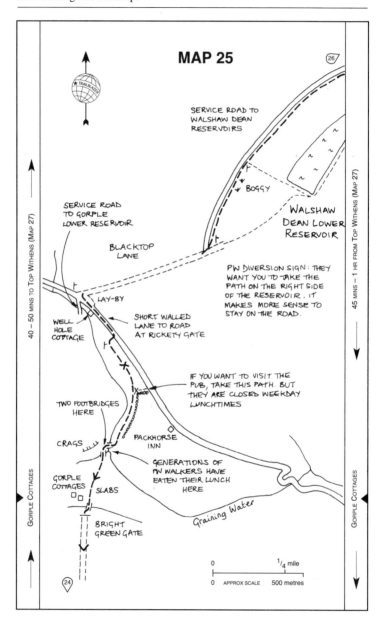

MAP 25

26

SERVICE ROAD TO WALSHAW DEAN RESERVOIRS

SERVICE ROAD TO GORPLE LOWER RESERVOIR

BLACKTOP LANE

↓ BOGGY

WALSHAW DEAN LOWER RESERVOIR

40 – 50 MINS TO TOP WITHENS (MAP 27)

45 MINS – 1 HR FROM TOP WITHENS (MAP 27)

LAY-BY

WELL HOLE COTTAGE

SHORT WALLED LANE TO ROAD AT RICKETY GATE

PW DIVERSION SIGN: THEY WANT YOU TO TAKE THE PATH ON THE RIGHT SIDE OF THE RESERVOIR. IT MAKES MORE SENSE TO STAY ON THE ROAD.

IF YOU WANT TO VISIT THE PUB, TAKE THIS PATH. BUT THEY ARE CLOSED WEEKDAY LUNCHTIMES

TWO FOOTBRIDGES HERE

CRAGS

PACKHORSE INN

GORPLE COTTAGES

SLABS

GENERATIONS OF PW WALKERS HAVE EATEN THEIR LUNCH HERE

Graining Water

BRIGHT GREEN GATE

GORPLE COTTAGES

GORPLE COTTAGES

24

0   ¼ mile

0   APPROX SCALE   500 metres

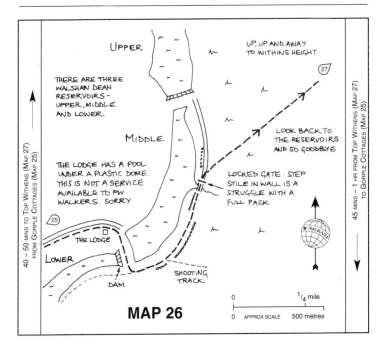

UPPER

UP, UP AND AWAY
TO WITHINS HEIGHT

27

THERE ARE THREE
WALSHAN DEAN
RESERVOIRS —
UPPER, MIDDLE
AND LOWER

MIDDLE

LOOK BACK TO
THE RESERVOIRS
AND SO GOODBYE

THE LODGE HAS A POOL
UNDER A PLASTIC DOME.
THIS IS NOT A SERVICE
AVAILABLE TO PW
WALKERS. SORRY

LOCKED GATE. STEP
STILE IN WALL IS A
STRUGGLE WITH A
FULL PACK

25

THE LODGE

★ TRAILBLAZER

LOWER

SHOOTING
TRACK

DAM

MAP 26

0   1/4 mile

0   APPROX SCALE   500 metres

40 – 50 MINS TO TOP WITHINS (MAP 27)
FROM GORPLE COTTAGES (MAP 25)

45 MINS – 1 HR FROM TOP WITHINS (MAP 27)
TO GORPLE COTTAGES (MAP 25)

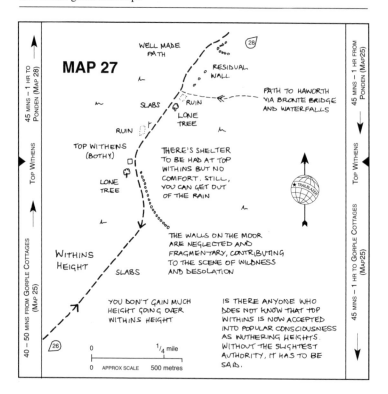

MAP 27

WELL MADE PATH

28

RESIDUAL WALL

PATH TO HAWORTH VIA BRONTE BRIDGE AND WATERFALLS

SLABS

RUIN

LONE TREE

RUIN

TOP WITHENS (BOTHY)

LONE TREE

THERE'S SHELTER TO BE HAD AT TOP WITHINS BUT NO COMFORT. STILL, YOU CAN GET OUT OF THE RAIN

★ TRAILBLAZER

THE WALLS ON THE MOOR ARE NEGLECTED AND FRAGMENTARY, CONTRIBUTING TO THE SCENE OF WILDNESS AND DESOLATION

WITHINS HEIGHT

SLABS

YOU DON'T GAIN MUCH HEIGHT GOING OVER WITHINS HEIGHT

IS THERE ANYONE WHO DOES NOT KNOW THAT TOP WITHINS IS NOW ACCEPTED INTO POPULAR CONSCIOUSNESS AS NUTHERING HEIGHTS. WITHOUT THE SLIGHTEST AUTHORITY, IT HAS TO BE SAID.

26

0   1/4 mile

0   APPROX SCALE   500 metres

45 MINS – 1 HR TO PONDEN (MAP 28)

TOP WITHENS

40 – 50 MINS FROM GORPLE COTTAGES (MAP 25)

45 MINS – 1 HR FROM PONDEN (MAP25)

TOP WITHENS

45 MINS – 1 HR TO GORPLE COTTAGES (MAP25)

PONDEN TO THORNTON-IN-CRAVEN   MAPS 28-34

This **10-mile (16km)** section takes 4^{1}/$_{2}$-5^{3}/$_{4}$**hrs**. The Way has turned its back on the peat hags and groughs of the Haworth Moors and now climbs over two further chunks of deserted moorland before rewarding the wayfarer with a prize, **Lothersdale**, a delightful village with a classic country pub, B&B accommodation, camping and a lovely ambience. It's worth including it in your itinerary if you can.

The country begins to change. Cattle and sheep watch your progress with patient eyes, sometimes crowding together for a glimpse of this strange apparition 'so withered and wild in its attire', invading their space.

At **Pinhaw Beacon** a remarkable view opens up, presenting a panorama that contains some of the big boys: Pendle Hill of witches' fame and Pen y Ghent, one of the three giants of the limestone country and a challenge to come. Then it's downhill through more agricultural pastures to the decorous charm of **Thornton-in-Craven**.

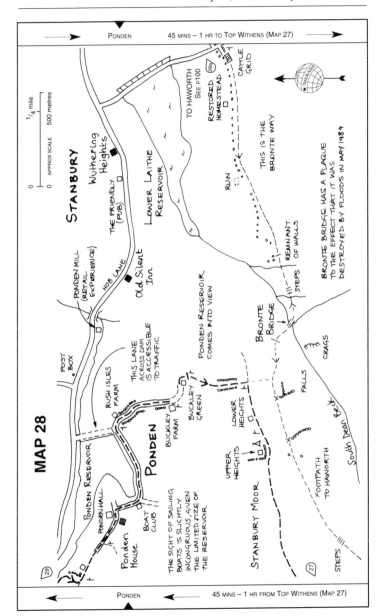

MAP 28

¼ mile

500 metres

0

0   APPROX SCALE

CATTLE GRID

28a

TO HAWORTH SEE P100

RESTORED HOMESTEAD

STANBURY

Wuthering Heights

THE FRIENDLY (PUB)

LOWER LAITHE RESERVOIR

THIS IS THE BRONTE WAY

RUIN

PONDEN MILL (RETAIL-EXPERIENCE)

HOB LANE

Old Silent Inn

REMNANT OF WALLS

STEPS

BRONTE BRIDGE HAS A PLAQUE TO THE EFFECT THAT IT WAS DESTROYED BY FLOODS IN MAY 1989

POST BOX

THIS LANE ACROSS DAM IS ACCESSIBLE TO TRAFFIC

RUSH ISLES FARM

PONDEN RESERVOIR COMES INTO VIEW

BRONTE BRIDGE

CRAGS

PONDEN

BUCKLEY FARM

BUCKLEY GREEN

LOWER HEIGHTS

FALLS

South Dean Beck

PONDEN RESERVOIR

UPPER HEIGHTS

FOOTPATH TO HAWORTH

PONDEN HALL

BOAT CLUB

Ponden House

THE SIGHT OF SAILING BOATS IS SLIGHTLY INCONGRUOUS, GIVEN THE LIMITED SIZE OF THE RESERVOIR.

STANBURY MOOR

STEPS

29

27

ICKORNSHAW & COWLING [Map 31]

The Pennine Way crosses the A6068 between Colne and Keighley at the small settlement of Ickornshaw. If you want to avoid being taken as a stranger, say 'Ick-corn-sher', with the emphasis on the 'corn'.

The nearest B&B is *Winterhouse Barn* (☎ 01535-632234, 🖳 www.thepennine way.co.uk/winterhousebarn, Colne Rd, 2T/1D), a no-frills sort of place where you'll pay an economical £18 with breakfast, or £2.50 for camping. The pub, *The Black Bull* (☎ 01535-637770) is nearby and they have a wide choice of bar meals; food is served from 5pm to 8.30pm.

Ickornshaw is an off-shoot of **Cowling** which is a quarter of mile off-route to the right (east) and has a **post office** (early closing Wed), two general **grocery shops**, a pub, an arms dealer, a Chinese takeaway (*Mei Mei*) and a remarkable, reasonably-priced gourmet restaurant, *The Harlequin* (☎ 01535-633277) that makes a wonderful change from takeaways and pub fare. How about confit of Yorkshire lamb with caramelized red cabbage, rosemary and redcurrant jus (£10.50)? Food is served in the restaurant and in the bar 12 noon-2pm and 6.30-9.30pm (to 8.30pm on Sunday); they're closed on Monday and Tuesday.

For B&B, *Woodland House* (☎ 01535-637886, 🖳 www.woodland-house.co.uk, 2 Woodland St, 2T/1D, some en suite) is a well-run place where a comfortable night is assured (£20 per person).

If you have the energy, however, a better bet might be to walk on to Lothersdale. The villages are served by **buses** to Skipton, Burnley and Keighley (see public transport map, pp36-9).

LOTHERSDALE [Map 32]

The friendly *Hare and Hounds* (☎ 01535-630977) does good pub food for £6-7 (12 noon-2pm and 6-9pm daily; the pub closes during the afternoon), and there are two serviceable B&Bs: *Burlington House* (☎ 01535-634635, 1T/1D, can put an extra bed in each room), an elegant building next to the pub costing £17 (must be booked in advance); and *Lynmouth* (☎ 01535-632744, 1D/2F en suite) maintaining the local aver-

age of £17.50. You can **camp** here for £5. Go into the courtyard and follow the stream up to get to this modern setup. Note that there's no camping at Earby or Thornton-in-Craven.

There's an infrequent **bus** service to Skipton (see public transport map pp36-9).

EARBY [Map 34]

The only hostel accommodation round these parts is *Earby Youth Hostel* (☎ 01629-592707, bookings ☎ 0870-770 5802, 🖳 earby@yha.org.uk, open Apr-Oct), a small cottage in Earby, 1½ miles (2km) off the trail. Adults are charged £10.60, under 18s £7.20. It opens at 5pm and is self-catering only.

Earby is quite a large community. There's a pub, *The Red Lion*, near the hostel, a good Indian restaurant, the *Ashiana* (☎ 01282-843943, open 5.30-11pm daily), *Aspendos* (pizzas and kebabs to take away), a *fish and chip* shop, **post office** and Co-op **supermarket**. There's an hourly **bus** service to Thornton (see public transport map, pp36-9).

THORNTON-IN-CRAVEN [Map 34]

Thornton-in-Craven offers little choice for accommodation seekers. The story goes that a walker arriving in Thornton was told by a resident 'That's your path there. There's nothing here for you.' Evidently this is a local village for local people apart from *The Old Post Office* (☎ 01282-843482, 1S/1T/1D) located just opposite where the Way meets the main road. The cost is £22 per person for an en suite room and £20 for a single with an adjacent bathroom. An evening meal can be had for £11.50 by prior arrangement.

There's also *The Fold* (☎ 01282-843272) but single-night accommodation here can't be booked in advance. There are six cottages sleeping up to four people each and if they're not full they accept passing walkers for £19 to £25 per person, including a basket of food for you to prepare for breakfast. (Each cottage has a kitchen.)

There are regular **buses** along the A56 to Burnley and Skipton (see public transport map, pp36-9).

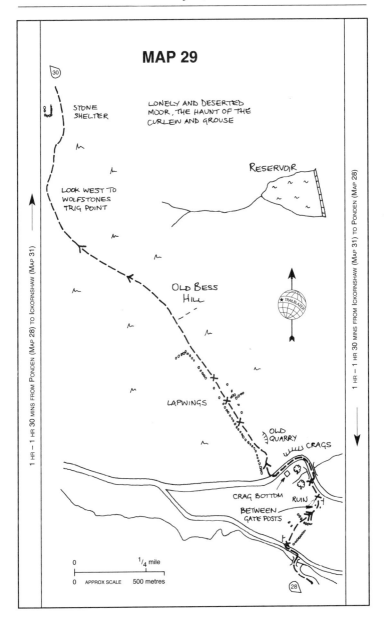

MAP 29

30

STONE
SHELTER

LONELY AND DESERTED
MOOR, THE HAUNT OF THE
CURLEW AND GROUSE

RESERVOIR

LOOK WEST TO
WOLFSTONES
TRIG POINT

OLD BESS
HILL

★ TRAILBLAZER

LAPWINGS

OLD
QUARRY

CRAGS

CRAG BOTTOM

RUIN

BETWEEN
GATE POSTS

28

0   1/4 mile

0   APPROX SCALE   500 metres

1 HR – 1 HR 30 MINS FROM PONDEN (MAP 28) TO ICKORNSHAW (MAP 31)

1 HR – 1 HR 30 MINS FROM ICKORNSHAW (MAP 31) TO PONDEN (MAP 28)

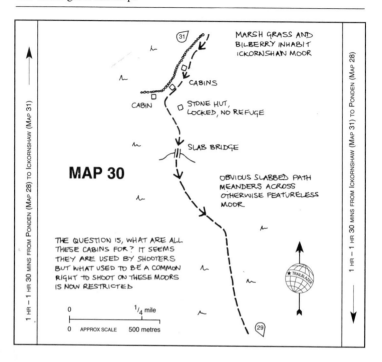

MARSH GRASS AND
BILBERRY INHABIT
ICKORNSHAN MOOR

31

CABINS

CABIN

STONE HUT,
LOCKED, NO REFUGE

SLAB BRIDGE

MAP 30

OBVIOUS SLABBED PATH
MEANDERS ACROSS
OTHERWISE FEATURELESS
MOOR

THE QUESTION IS, WHAT ARE ALL
THESE CABINS FOR? IT SEEMS
THEY ARE USED BY SHOOTERS
BUT WHAT USED TO BE A COMMON
RIGHT TO SHOOT ON THESE MOORS
IS NOW RESTRICTED

★ TRAILBLAZER

0   ¼ mile
0   APPROX SCALE   500 metres

29

1 HR – 1 HR 30 MINS FROM PONDEN (MAP 28) TO ICKORNSHAW (MAP 31)

1 HR – 1 HR 30 MINS FROM ICKORNSHAW (MAP 31) TO PONDEN (MAP 28)

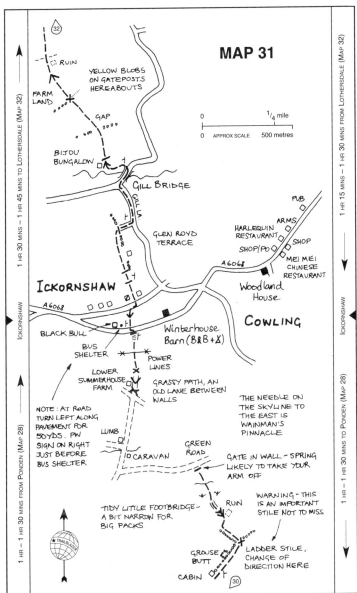

MAP 31

YELLOW BLOBS ON GATEPOSTS HEREABOUTS

RUIN

FARM LAND

GAP

BIJOU BUNGALOW

0   ¼ mile

0   APPROX SCALE   500 metres

GILL BRIDGE

GILL LA

GLEN ROYD TERRACE

PUB

ARMS

HARLEQUIN RESTAURANT

SHOP

SHOP/PO

A6068

MEI MEI CHINESE RESTAURANT

ICKORNSHAW

A6068

Woodland House

COWLING

BLACK BULL

BUS SHELTER

POWER LINES

Winterhouse Barn (B&B + Å)

LOWER SUMMERHOUSE FARM

GRASSY PATH, AN OLD LANE BETWEEN WALLS

THE NEEDLE ON THE SKYLINE TO THE EAST IS WAINMAN'S PINNACLE

NOTE: AT ROAD TURN LEFT ALONG PAVEMENT FOR 50YDS. PW SIGN ON RIGHT JUST BEFORE BUS SHELTER

LUMB

CARAVAN

GREEN ROAD

GATE IN WALL - SPRING LIKELY TO TAKE YOUR ARM OFF

TIDY LITTLE FOOTBRIDGE - A BIT NARROW FOR BIG PACKS

RUIN

WARNING - THIS IS AN IMPORTANT STILE NOT TO MISS

GROUSE BUTT

CABIN

LADDER STILE, CHANGE OF DIRECTION HERE

★ TRAILBLAZER

1 HR 30 MINS – 1 HR 45 MINS TO LOTHERSDALE (MAP 32)

ICKORNSHAW

1 HR – 1 HR 30 MINS FROM PONDEN (MAP 28)

1 HR 15 MINS – 1 HR 30 MINS FROM LOTHERSDALE (MAP 32)

ICKORNSHAW

1 HR – 1 HR 30 MINS TO PONDEN (MAP 28)

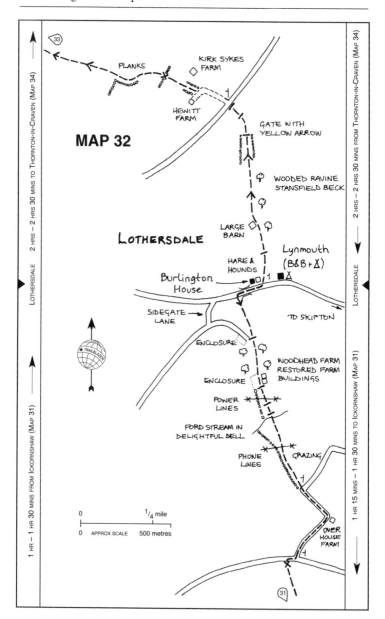

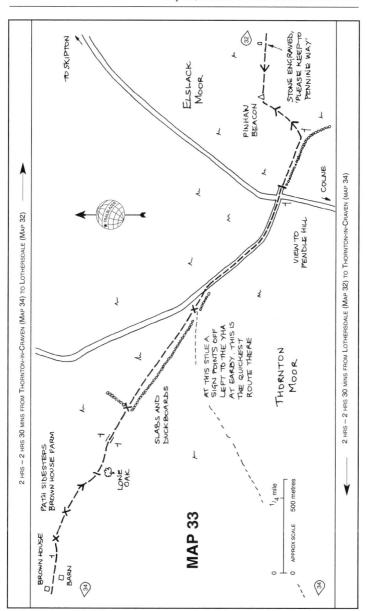

MAP 33

TO SKIPTON

ELSLACK MOOR

PINHAW BEACON

STONE ENGRAVED, 'PLEASE KEEP TO PENNINE WAY'

COLNE

VIEW TO PENDLE HILL

THORNTON MOOR

AT THIS STILE A SIGN POINTS OFF LEFT TO THE YHA AT EARBY. THIS IS THE QUICKEST ROUTE THERE

SLABS AND DUCKBOARDS

PATH SIDESTEPS BROWN HOUSE FARM

LONE OAK

BROWN HOUSE

BARN

0   ¼ mile
0   500 metres
APPROX SCALE

2 HRS – 2 HRS 30 MINS FROM THORNTON-IN-CRAVEN (MAP 34) TO LOTHERSDALE (MAP 32)

2 HRS – 2 HRS 30 MINS FROM LOTHERSDALE (MAP 32) TO THORNTON-IN-CRAVEN (MAP 34)

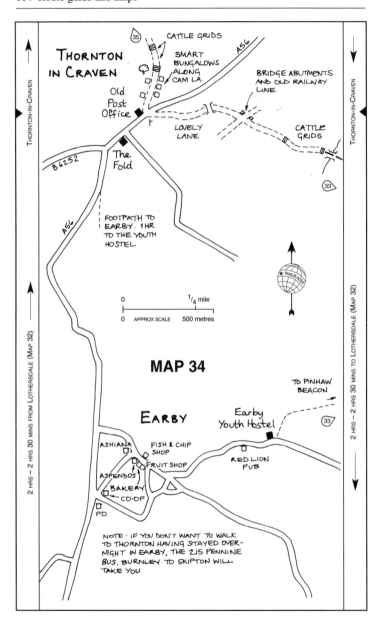

35

CATTLE GRIDS

THORNTON IN CRAVEN

SMART BUNGALOWS ALONG CAM LA.

A56

BRIDGE ABUTMENTS AND OLD RAILWAY LINE

Old Post Office

LOVELY LANE

CATTLE GRIDS

33

B6252

The Fold

A56

FOOTPATH TO EARBY. 1HR TO THE YOUTH HOSTEL

TRAILBLAZER

0   1/4 mile

0   APPROX SCALE   500 metres

MAP 34

TO PINHAW BEACON

EARBY

Earby Youth Hostel

33

ASHIANA

FISH & CHIP SHOP

FRUIT SHOP

RED LION PUB

ASPENDOS

BAKERY

CO-OP

P.O.

NOTE: IF YOU DON'T WANT TO WALK TO THORNTON HAVING STAYED OVER-NIGHT IN EARBY, THE 215 PENNINE BUS, BURNLEY TO SKIPTON WILL TAKE YOU

THORNTON-IN-CRAVEN TO MALHAM   MAPS 34-41

This stretch is only just over **10 miles (16km, 4¹/₄-5¹/₂hrs)** but is as pleasant a walk as you will find on a summer's day, with canal and riverside walking, an excellent café at East Marton and another in Gargrave, lots to look at and no great feats of endurance for your feet.

The Way leaves the rather buttoned-up community of Thornton-in-Craven past prettified bungalows and barn conversions to cross a series of fields to reach the towpath of the **Leeds–Liverpool Canal** near the unusual 'piggy-back' bridge taking the A59 over the canal. Beyond the moorings for the narrow boats and just over the Williamson Bridge is the charming Abbots Harbour Restaurant, a super place where Pennine Way walkers are welcomed with enthusiasm (see below).

Beyond **East Marton** the Way departs from the canal and takes to the green, green fields again, climbing gradually over **Scaleber Hill** from whence the tower of Gargrave church shows us the way down to this compact and cosy little town, the gateway to the Dales.

Gargrave is an interlude worth prolonging and most walkers will avail themselves of the services there, if only to buy a bag of sweets from the Dalesman Café (see p117), more 'caffay' than 'caff'. The long uphill road-walk out of the town branches off to cross **Eshton Moor**, no great challenge, more of a comfortable ramble to meet the delightful River Aire for the second time, it was the Aire we crossed in Gargrave. Riverside walking is on the agenda for the remaining two hours or so until you reach the renowned settlement of **Malham**, venue for a thousand field trips and school visits and the end of this day's section for Pennine Wayfarers.

Not an arduous day, this, but one with perhaps an excess of distractions. Never mind. It's the changing scene which we crave and the scene has certainly changed, with the stark white of the limestone walls dividing the landscape into parcels of green.

EAST MARTON   [Map 35]

There are two B&Bs of note in the enclave of East Marton, set astride the fiendish A59 road that carries heavy traffic to Harrogate and Leeds and hardly a stopping-off place for motorized traffic. It is only canal users and walkers that know it for what it is, a secretive little mooring or a milestone on the Pennine Way.

Just off Church Lane, recognizable by the fact that it leads to the church, is a neat cul-de-sac of bungalows including *Drumlins* (☎ 01282-843521, Herber Drive, 1D en suite, 1T) where a single is £28 or a double £23; Mrs Moran provides comfortable and homely accommodation.

Nearer the trail, in fact next to Abbots Harbour and run by the invaluable Joan Pilling, is *Sawley House* (☎ 01282-843207, 1T/1D) where for £22 you can enjoy the atmosphere of a farmhouse that dates back to the 12th century. For those who prefer to **camp**, £4 will see you securely ensconced, with showers at your disposal, too, and the restaurant nearby.

Abbots Harbour (☎ 01282-843207, open daily 10am-4.30pm) deserves an accolade for its welcome, atmosphere and food. This is a cracking good place to eat, one of the best along the trail and just in case you were wondering, no, I didn't get a free meal. A bacon sandwich is £2.60, all-day breakfast £6.50 and the lunch menu includes home-cooked favourites such as shepherd's pie (£8.20).

The *Cross Keys* is the nearest pub, up the lane facing the main road and open most of the time during the summer for meals and the ever-reliable Black Sheep Bitter.

Should you need a **taxi** ring SD Cars on ☎ 01282-814310. There are also **buses** to Preston and Skipton (see public transport map, pp36-9).

GARGRAVE

This small attractive town has most things you will want, but is spoilt by the busy A65 running through the middle. The beautiful river does compensate to some extent.

Services

Gargrave is on the Leeds to Carlisle railway but **trains** north and south are infrequent.

There are **buses** to Malham, Airton and Skipton (see public transport map, pp36-9).

All shops are on the main road and fairly close together. There is a **pharmacy**, a well stocked Co-op **supermarket** (Mon-Sat 8am-8pm, Sun 10am-6pm). The **post office** (early closing Tue) offers a fax service. There is a **cash machine** at the Co-op. If one person in your party looks as if they may not make it then it may be worth reserving some turf at the **florist**: they claim it to be 'top quality – suitable for graves.'

Where to stay

The Old Swan Inn (☎ 01756-749232, 1S/2D/1T/1F) has en suite rooms costing £50 for a double and £60 for the family room (£30 single). These prices do not include breakfast.

Lavender House (☎ 01756-748600, 1D en suite/1T) at 33 Skipton Rd offers B&B for £20, £22 en suite, an evening meal (by prior arrangement) costs £10.

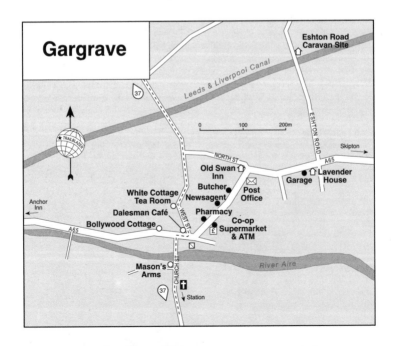

Just north of the town, *Eshton Road Caravan Site* (☎ 01756-749229, 🖂 01756-748060) has **camping** for £3 per person.

If all else fails there is the *Anchor Inn* (☎ 01756-749666), but it's half a mile out of town to the west.

Where to eat
There's a variety of places. As you cross the bridge over the River Aire you will be opposite the *Dalesman Café* (Tue-Sun 9am-5pm, also open on bank holiday Mondays), an excellent place for a break. Run by a couple of ex-teachers, it's been awarded a Roy Castle Clean Air Award and offers a range of good-value food (ham, eggs and chips, £4.95) as well as indulgences such as quality ice cream and sweets sold loose in the old-fashioned way. They claim to have 200 different varieties, some of which have been artistically arranged into a mosaic in the window.

Nearby is a very good Indian restaurant, *Bollywood Cottage* (☎ 01756-749252), open daily from 5.30pm to 11.30pm. There are balti dishes from £4.90, tandoori items from £5.90 and a 10% discount for takeaways.

Just up West St is the *White Cottage Tea Room* (Easter to Oct, Tue-Sun 10am-5.30pm, Nov to Easter 10am-5pm/dusk, also open on bank holiday Mondays) which dishes up delicious triple-decker sandwiches – try their ham with Wensleydale cheese and chutney (£4.65) – and other meals such as home-made soup or ploughman's lunches. Watch your head as you go in through the extremely low door.

The *Mason's Arms*, close to the church, is friendly; their interesting pub food costs around £6 and is served from 12 noon to 2pm and 6pm to 9pm every day, except Sunday evenings when times are 7-9pm.

The *Old Swan Inn* (see above), on the main road, serves pub food between 12 noon and 2pm Mon-Sat (to 4pm on Sun) and daily 6-9pm and has a variety of traditionally-themed rooms such as a flagstone floor 'Snug' and a 'Parlour' with a rocking chair. The staff are very helpful.

AIRTON [Map 39]
For a village which turns its back on the Pennine Way it is a surprise to find an intriguing independent hostel and a top-of-the-range B&B. *Airton Quaker Hostel* (☎ 01729-830263, 14 bunks) is attached to a Quaker Meeting House. It's clean, cheap at £6 and has cooking facilities; of its kind you can't do better than this along the entire trail. Remember to bring sleeping bags though; linen is not provided.

Lindon House (☎ 01729-830418, 1T/3D) is a little way out of the village along the Malham road. The oak beams may be of a fairly recent vintage but nobody can say the stone-layers haven't done their job judging by the ample exposed stonework throughout. The house is licensed and may be rather better appointed than the average Pennine Way walker warrants. The prices are fair enough at £29 per person sharing a double. A tip-top establishment, one to pass on to your friends when they visit the area.

KIRKBY MALHAM [Map 39]
Standing back from the river by 500 yards the village is another gem, carefully preserved by its inhabitants and unspoilt by anything as common as a shop. The church, St Michael the Archangel, has a set of stocks into which I imagine anyone putting up a satellite dish will be clapped and pelted with rotting fruit.

The Victoria Inn (☎ 01729-830499, 1T/2D) charges £22.50 per person and does bar meals indistinguishable from the usual pub fare. Winter opening times are limited so don't count on a lunchtime pint off-season mid-week without checking first.

Yeoman's Barn (☎ 01729-830639, 🖳 www.yeomansbarn.co.uk, 2D) is a small, well-run B&B nearly opposite costing £30 a head. It's a welcoming place with open fire, music, books and a very relaxed ambience.

MALHAM [see map p118]
This little stone village is surrounded by dry stonewalling and farmland and has a clean and pretty river flowing through the middle of it. It looks and feels perfect,

providing a feast for the eyes, stomach and soul.

Services

The **Yorkshire Dales National Park Information Centre** (☎ 01729-830363, 🖥 www.malhamdale.com, Apr-Oct daily 10am-5pm, Nov-Mar Fri-Sun only 10am-4pm) is just to the south of the village and is worth a visit for its interactive displays about the geology and history of the area. It has a 24-hour information screen at the back.

Buses run from Airton, Gargrave and Skipton but are limited (see public transport map, pp36-9). **Skipton Taxis** (☎ 01756-794994/701122) operate to the village and are open 24 hours.

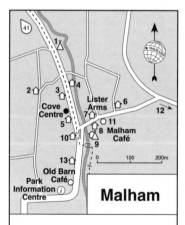

Where to stay
1 Townhead Farm Campsite
2 Hill Top Farm Bunkhouse
3 Ghyll Stones
4 Beck Hall B&B
5 Dale House B&B
6 Malham Youth Hostel
7 Lister Arms
8 Eastwood House
9 Miresfield Farm (B&B & Camping)
10 The Buck Inn
11 Malham Café B&B
12 Gordale Scar House (Camping)
13 River House Hotel

For **shops** there's the Cove Centre (Mon-Sat 10am-4.30pm, Sun 11.30am-5.30pm), fork left at the small triangular green in the centre of the village, where you will get everything you need for your trip, including essentials such as camping fuel and clotted cream fudge. There is also a small village shop on the green.

Places to stay

If it's B&B accommodation you want, note that some places will accept bookings only for a **two-day stay at weekends** at peak times, such is the popularity of short breaks in Malham.

If you want to **camp** in an awesome setting walk one mile east to *Gordale Scar House* (☎ 01729-830333), where they charge £2 per person, £2 per tent. Showers are 10p.

The most central place to camp is at *Miresfield Farm* (☎ 01729-830414, 🖥 www.miresfield-farm.com) right on the Way as you enter the village; charges are £4.50 per person.

North of the village there's camping at *Townhead Farm* (☎ 01729-830287) where a pitch costs £3 per person, £1 per tent.

There's **bunkhouse** accommodation opposite at *Hill Top Farm* (☎ 01729-830320, 🖥 www.malhamdale.com/bunk barn.htm); there are 32 spaces in rooms for 2-11 people (the smaller rooms can be booked), showers, drying room and a fully-equipped kitchen and it costs £8 per person.

In the centre of the village there's the very popular *Malham Youth Hostel* (☎ 01729-830321, bookings ☎ 0870-770 5946, 🖥 malham@yha.org.uk, open mid-Feb to mid-Nov, plus Fri-Sat late Jan to mid-Feb and mid-Nov to mid-Dec), fork right at the green and take a left just after the Lister Arms Hotel. The hostel opens at 5pm and an evening meal is served at 7pm. Adults are charged £11.80, under 18s £8.50.

B&B is available at *Miresfield Farm* (see above, 1S/3T/4D/3F en suite) for £28. *Dale House* (☎ 01729-830664, 🖥 www.yorkshirenet.co.uk/stayat/dalehouse) charges £30 per person in a double or twin

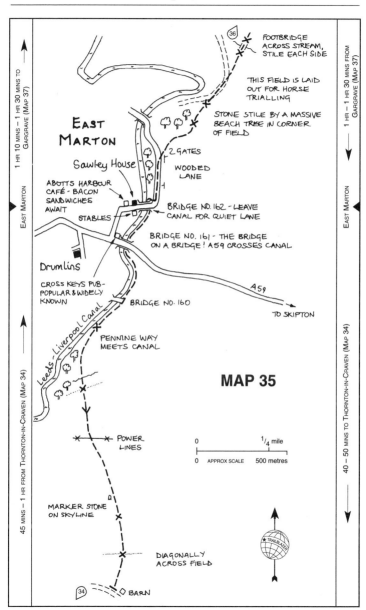

FOOTBRIDGE ACROSS STREAM, STILE EACH SIDE

THIS FIELD IS LAID OUT FOR HORSE TRIALLING

STONE STILE BY A MASSIVE BEACH TREE IN CORNER OF FIELD

EAST MARTON

Sawley House

ABBOTS HARBOUR CAFÉ - BACON SANDWICHES AWAIT

STABLES

2 GATES

WOODED LANE

BRIDGE NO. 162 - LEAVE CANAL FOR QUIET LANE

BRIDGE NO. 161 - THE BRIDGE ON A BRIDGE! A59 CROSSES CANAL

Drumlins

CROSS KEYS PUB - POPULAR & WIDELY KNOWN

BRIDGE NO. 160

A59

TO SKIPTON

Leeds - Liverpool Canal

PENNINE WAY MEETS CANAL

MAP 35

POWER LINES

0   ¼ mile

0   APPROX SCALE   500 metres

MARKER STONE ON SKYLINE

DIAGONALLY ACROSS FIELD

BARN

1 HR 10 MINS – 1 HR 30 MINS TO GARGRAVE (MAP 37)

EAST MARTON

45 MINS – 1 HR FROM THORNTON-IN-CRAVEN (MAP 34)

1 HR – 1 HR 30 MINS FROM GARGRAVE (MAP 37)

EAST MARTON

40 – 50 MINS TO THORNTON-IN-CRAVEN (MAP 34)

room with en-suite facilities or private bathroom, or £25 in a standard double/twin (£40 for single occupancy). The house is currently changing hands but it's likely that they will continue to offer B&B.

Beck Hall (☎ 01729-830332, 🖳 www .beckhallmalham.com, 11 rooms 3T/7D/1F en suite) is in a dream-like setting across a footbridge by the river and costs from £25 per person midweek, £28 Fri-Sat.

In addition there is the centrally located *Eastwood House* (☎ 01729-830409, 🖳 eastwood_house@hotmail.com, 1D/2F en suite) at £25 midweek, £27.50 at the weekend, *Ghyll Stones* (☎ 01729-830487, 1D en suite) by the Cove Centre at £30 for the room and *Malham Café B&B* (☎ 01729-830348, 🖳 www.malhamdale.com/stayat/malham_cafe, 2D/1F en suite) which offers no-smoking accommodation from £25.

If you're looking for more luxury try *The Buck Inn* (☎ 01729-830317, 🖹 01729-830670, 2T/6D/2F) on your left as you come into the village. The rooms are all en suite and cost from £30 to £35 per person. They can do an early breakfast if you are keen to head off promptly the next day. There's also the *Lister Arms* (☎ 01729-830330, 🖳 www.listerarms.co.uk, 5D/1T/3F en suite) which costs £25 (£30 Fri-Sun, minimum two nights) with breakfast.

The *River House Hotel* (☎ 01729-830315, 🖳 www.riverhousehotel.co.uk, 2T/4D/1F en suite) costs from £30 per person.

Places to eat

Lister Arms (see above) has a great restaurant menu and is open Thursday to Sunday 7.30-9pm. Main courses are around £9. They also have a bar menu (12-2pm and 7-9pm) with dishes for about £6. Pub grub is also served at *The Buck Inn* (see above, 12-2pm and 7-9pm) and at *Beck Hall* (see above) where they also do cream teas.

For something simpler try *The Cove Centre* (see p118) where you can get a bowl of soup, a packed lunch or a baked potato. There's also the *Old Barn Café* near the Park Information Centre. An all-day breakfast costs £4.50, jacket potatoes are £3 and they also serve teas and cakes. They're open daily until 5.30pm.

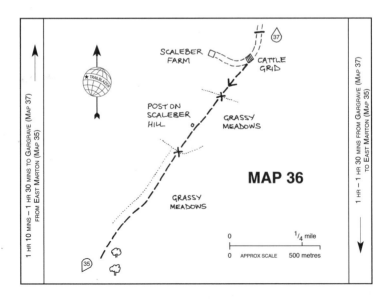

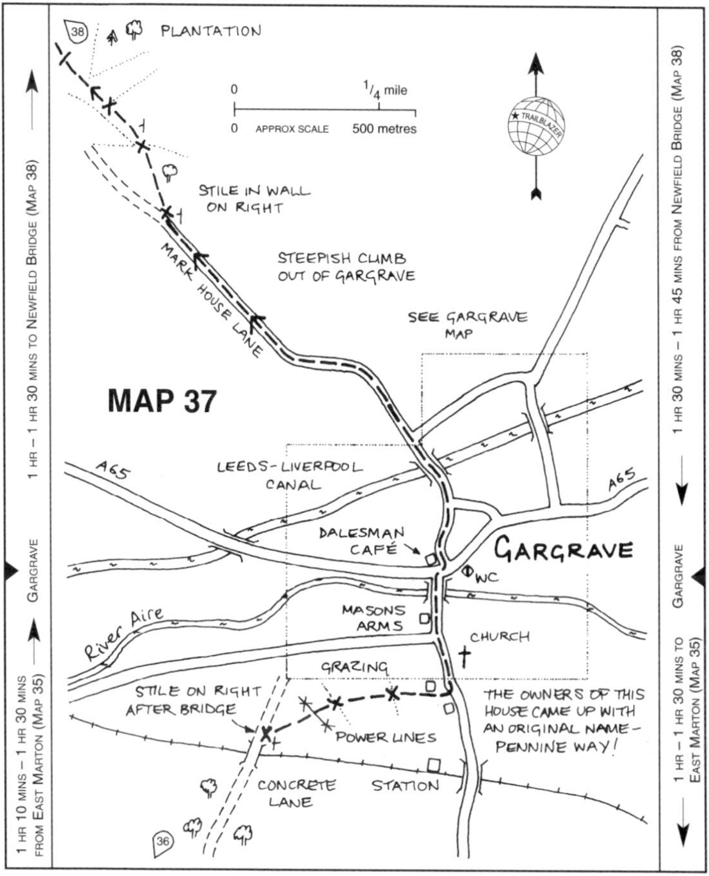
MAP 37
PLANTATION
0 1/4 mile
0 APPROX SCALE 500 metres
TRAILBLAZER
STILE IN WALL ON RIGHT
STEEPISH CLIMB OUT OF GARGRAVE
MARK HOUSE LANE
SEE GARGRAVE MAP
A65
LEEDS-LIVERPOOL CANAL
DALESMAN CAFÉ
GARGRAVE
WC
MASONS ARMS
CHURCH
River Aire
GRAZING
STILE ON RIGHT AFTER BRIDGE
POWER LINES
THE OWNERS OF THIS HOUSE CAME UP WITH AN ORIGINAL NAME - PENNINE WAY!
CONCRETE LANE
STATION
38
36
1 HR – 1 HR 30 MINS TO NEWFIELD BRIDGE (MAP 38)
GARGRAVE
1 HR 10 MINS – 1 HR 30 MINS FROM EAST MARTON (MAP 35)
1 HR 30 MINS – 1 HR 45 MINS FROM NEWFIELD BRIDGE (MAP 38)
1 HR – 1 HR 30 MINS TO EAST MARTON (MAP 35)

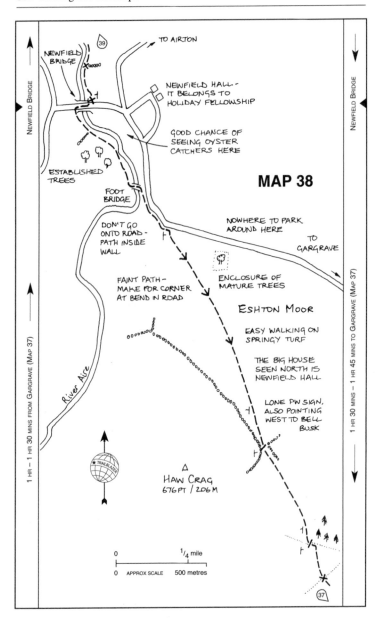

MAP 38

NEWFIELD BRIDGE

NEWFIELD BRIDGE

39

TO AIRTON

NEWFIELD BRIDGE

NEWFIELD HALL - IT BELONGS TO HOLIDAY FELLOWSHIP

GOOD CHANCE OF SEEING OYSTER CATCHERS HERE

ESTABLISHED TREES

FOOT BRIDGE

DON'T GO ONTO ROAD - PATH INSIDE WALL

NOWHERE TO PARK AROUND HERE

TO GARGRAVE

FAINT PATH - MAKE FOR CORNER AT BEND IN ROAD

ENCLOSURE OF MATURE TREES

ESHTON MOOR

EASY WALKING ON SPRINGY TURF

THE BIG HOUSE SEEN NORTH IS NEWFIELD HALL

LONE PW SIGN, ALSO POINTING WEST TO BELL BUSK

River Aire

★ TRAILBLAZER

△
HAW CRAG
676FT / 206M

1 HR - 1 HR 30 MINS FROM GARGRAVE (MAP 37)

1 HR 30 MINS - 1 HR 45 MINS TO GARGRAVE (MAP 37)

0   ¼ mile
0   APPROX SCALE   500 metres

37

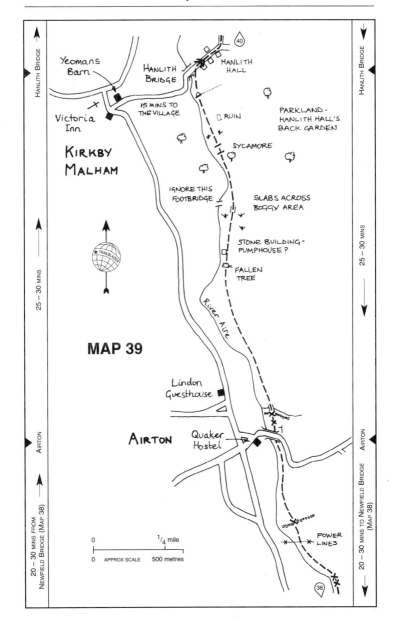

HANLITH BRIDGE

Yeomans Barn

HANLITH BRIDGE

HANLITH HALL

40

15 MINS TO THE VILLAGE

Victoria Inn

PARKLAND - HANLITH HALL'S BACK GARDEN

RUIN

KIRKBY MALHAM

SYCAMORE

IGNORE THIS FOOTBRIDGE

SLABS ACROSS BOGGY AREA

25 – 30 MINS

★ TRAILBLAZER

STONE BUILDING - PUMPHOUSE ?

FALLEN TREE

River Aire

MAP 39

25 – 30 MINS

Lindon Guesthouse

AIRTON

Quaker Hostel

AIRTON

0   ¼ mile

0   APPROX SCALE   500 metres

POWER LINES

38

20 – 30 MINS FROM NEWFIELD BRIDGE (MAP 38)

20 – 30 MINS TO NEWFIELD BRIDGE (MAP 38)

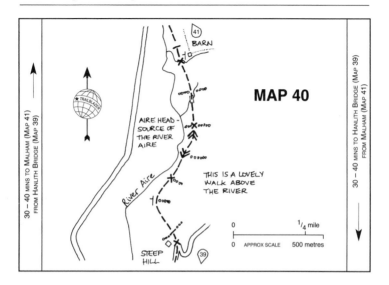

MAP 40

41
BARN

30 – 40 MINS TO MALHAM (MAP 41)
FROM HANLITH BRIDGE (MAP 39)

★ TRAILBLAZER

AIRE HEAD -
SOURCE OF
THE RIVER
AIRE

THIS IS A LOVELY
WALK ABOVE
THE RIVER

River Aire

0   1/4 mile

0   APPROX SCALE   500 metres

STEEP
HILL

39

30 – 40 MINS TO HANLITH BRIDGE (MAP 41)
FROM MALHAM (MAP 39)

❑ **Fountains Fell**   **[see Map 44]**
Named after the great Cistercian monastery of Fountains Abbey near Ripon, its original owner, Fountains Fell had extensive coal deposits beneath its cap of millstone
grit. It probably still has but the coal is not there in sufficient quantity to make it
worth extracting now that demand for coal has fallen so dramatically.

The most active period of coal extraction was the early 1800s when a road was
constructed to the summit plateau where the shafts were sunk. The remnants of this
road are now the Pennine Way.

The output of coal was reckoned to be around 1000 tons a year which would
require something like 10,000 packhorse loads to carry it away.

Very little now remains of the coal industry on Fountains Fell and the shafts have
mostly been filled in. The ruins of the colliery building are in evidence but give no
real idea of what was at one time a flourishing industry. We can spare a thought for
the miners who had to work in this inhospitable place, presumably spending the week
in makeshift accommodation within yards of their work or getting up in the small
hours to trudge to work in all weathers.

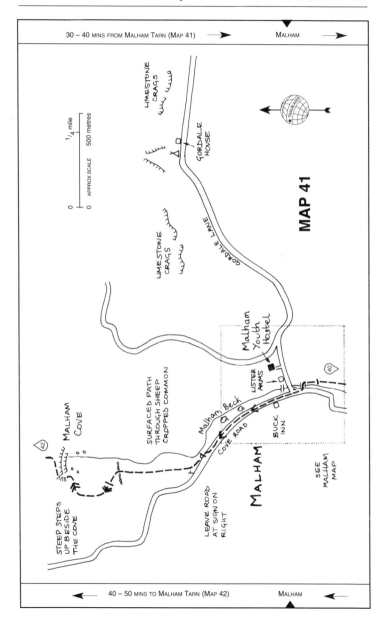

LIMESTONE CRAGS

GORDALE HOUSE

GORDALE LANE

LIMESTONE CRAGS

MAP 41

¼ mile

500 metres

0

0 APPROX SCALE

Malham Youth Hostel

LISTER ARMS

40

Malham Beck

Cove Road

BUCK INN

MALHAM COVE

42

SURFACED PATH THROUGH SHEEP CROPPED COMMON

MALHAM

SEE MALHAM MAP

STEEP STEPS UP BESIDE THE COVE

LEAVE ROAD AT SIGN ON RIGHT

MALHAM TO HORTON-IN-RIBBLESDALE   MAPS 41-48

This is a sensational day's walk, a full **15 miles (24kms, 6-8hrs)** of striding that lifts the Pennine Way into another gear, into the realm on a fine day of the sublime – its apotheosis. For the first time, limestone country opens its arms to the walker, its springy turf and expansive views giving back the investment made so far in weary legs and sore feet.

Gone are the blackened grit-stone walls and hunched farmsteads of Calderdale and the Worth Valley. At last you're in what can really be called walking country. The green roads and stony tracks are made for walking.

The hills, too, are majestic. The massive bulk of **Fountains Fell** (see box on p124) and Pen-y-Ghent are real mountains, challenges worthy of your effort and determination. Limestone, we salute you!

Towards the end of this section, the ascent of **Pen-y-Ghent**, the 'hill of the winds', is the job in hand, and what a job for tired legs! A steep climb from Dale Head Farm, first an almost vertical series of rocky steps followed by an easing of the gradient then another stiff scramble, you at last emerge onto the summit plateau in the knowledge that all that remains is the long downhill stretch on good, well-made paths, to your goal, the 'settlement on muddy ground', **Horton-in-Ribblesdale**.

STAINFORTH

There are no services between Malham and Horton. Two roads are crossed, both of which will eventually lead westwards to Stainforth where there's a shop, a pub and *Stainforth Youth Hostel*, (☎ 01729-823577, bookings ☎ 0870-770 6046, 🖳 stainforth@yha.org,uk, open Fri-Sat, plus daily during school holidays) charging £11.80 for adults (£8.50 under 18s).

The hostel opens at 3pm and an evening meal is served at 7pm. However, it will involve a walk of 3½ miles (6km) from Dale Head to get here which is unlikely to appeal to many.

Taxis can be called out from Settle; try Settle Taxis (☎ 01729-822219 or 824824) .

HORTON-IN-RIBBLESDALE [Map 48]

This is a famous landmark on the Pennine Way, as much for the presence of the Pen-y-Ghent café as for the charm of the village itself.

Services

Horton is on the Leeds–Carlisle railway and **trains** are frequent, making it an ideal place to begin or end a walk along the Way (see public transport map, pp36-9).

If you need a **taxi** call Settle Taxis (☎ 01729-824824/822219, 🖳 www.settle taxi.co.uk).

There is a **post office** (Mon, Tues, Thurs, Sat 9am-1pm) where you can buy basic groceries and the Pen-y-Ghent café (☎ 01729-860333, Mon and Wed-Fri 9am-6pm, Sat-Sun 8am-6pm, closed Tue), doubles as the **tourist information centre** and also sells **camping supplies**, **snacks** – including Kendal Mint Cake, **maps** and **books**.

Where to stay

Holme Farm Camping (☎ 01729-860281) costs £1 per tent plus £2 per person and is conveniently situated in the centre of the village next to the Golden Lion Hotel.

There's a nice **bunkhouse** at *Dub-Cote Farm* (☎ 01729-860238, 🖳 www.three peaksbarn.co.uk), ¾ mile south from Pen-y-Ghent café and up a small road on the left, which costs £8.50 and has a kitchen, drying room, dryers and showers. It's open approximately from April to October. If you're

❏ **Fell running**

Whilst puffing up a hill, with each step feeling as hard as the last one to the summit of Everest, you will probably have been ignominiously overtaken by a wiry person in brief shorts, the scantiest of vests and strange-looking lightly-studded shoes. He or she is a fell runner, participant in a sport that is taken very seriously by an increasing number of people. The routes involve the muddiest tracks and the steepest hills, the sort of terrain that most people would dismiss as un-runnable. It goes to extremes too, and the **Three Peak Challenge** is one of them. People have to run 26 miles (42km) from the Pen-y-Ghent Café up Pen-y-Ghent, Whernside and Ingleborough and back in less than 12 hours. Fancy a challenge?

good with a map you can take a shortcut straight there just after passing Dale Head Farm.

The Willows (☎/🖳 01729-860373, 1D/1T/1F), is a walker-friendly place which charges £25 per person.

The modern *Waltergarth* (☎ 01729-860221, 1D/1T) has en suite rooms at £20 per person.

The Knoll (☎ 01729-860283, 🖳 www.thepennineway.co.uk/theknoll, 1S/1D/2T) is near the post office. B&B costs from £22 per person.

Unfortunately not open for the 2004 season, *The Rowe House* (☎ 01729-860212, 🖳 www.therowehouse.co.uk, 2D/3T) was a B&B that was very popular with walkers. It is hoped that it will reopen in 2005.

Of the two pubs most walkers seem to prefer *The Crown Hotel* (☎ 01729-860209, 🖳 www.crown-hotel.co.uk, 2S/5D/4T/1F) with rooms at £22.50 per person, £25 for a single person, en suite £27.50. They have two cottages which can be booked by large parties of walkers.

The *Golden Lion Hotel* (☎ 01729-860206, 🖳 www.goldenlionhotel.co.uk, 2D/3T) has rooms from £19.95 a head with breakfast, and 15 bunk beds at £8 (bring your own sleeping bag), as well as space outside to pitch tents (but no facilities).

If all these are full try *Middle Studfold Farm* (☎ 01729-860236, 2S/2F) about 1³/₄ miles south of the village towards Settle which does B&B for £25 en suite.

Where to eat

The legendary *Pen-y-Ghent café* is the obvious port of call being a 'One Stop Shop' for the walker with basic kit as well as home-made cakes and filling meals. The Bayes family who run it are very helpful and friendly and provide a superb service for the walker. They are immensely knowledgeable about the area.

As well as operating a check-in/check-out service for day-walkers in the area, since the Pennine Way was opened they've been keeping a **Pennine Way book** for Wayfarers to sign as they pass. There are so many volumes there's now quite a library but it's a wonderful record of everyone who's passed along the Way. Be sure to sign it.

Food on offer here includes filling staples such as beans on toast, vegetable chowder soup with a roll, and chilli con carne (£3.30). They also offer takeaway sandwiches – boiled ham or strong cheese (£1.65).

The Crown Hotel (see above) does pub grub 12-2pm and 6-8.30pm, and *The Golden Lion* (see above) does the same type of fare at similar prices; there's not much to choose between them.

Just outside the village at its northern end is the *Blind Beck Tea Room* (☎ 01729-860396) which serves home-made cakes and scones as well as hot and cold snacks. Blind Beck is open 10am-6pm Mon-Fri and usually 9am-6pm at the weekends.

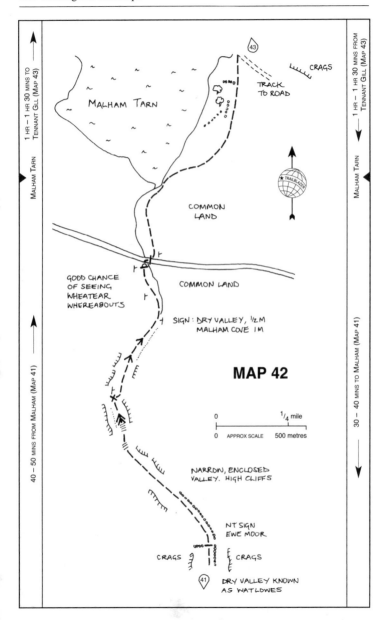

43

CRAGS

TRACK TO ROAD

MALHAM TARN

COMMON LAND

1 HR – 1 HR 30 MINS TO TENNANT GILL (MAP 43)

MALHAM TARN

1 HR – 1 HR 30 MINS FROM TENNANT GILL (MAP 43)

MALHAM TARN

★ TRAILBLAZER

COMMON LAND

GOOD CHANCE OF SEEING WHEATEAR WHEREABOUTS

SIGN: DRY VALLEY, ½M MALHAM COVE 1M

MAP 42

0   ¼ mile

0   APPROX SCALE   500 metres

40 – 50 MINS FROM MALHAM (MAP 41)

30 – 40 MINS TO MALHAM (MAP 41)

NARROW, ENCLOSED VALLEY. HIGH CLIFFS

NT SIGN EWE MOOR

CRAGS   CRAGS

41   DRY VALLEY KNOWN AS WATLOWES

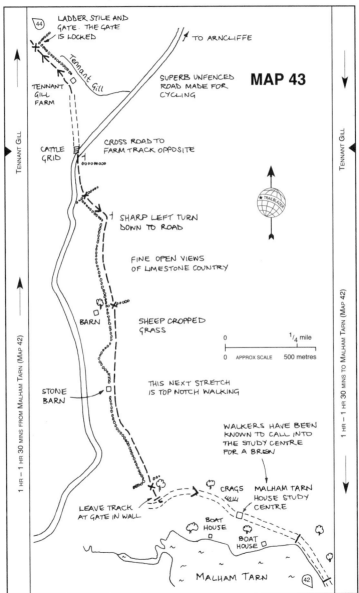

44 LADDER STILE AND GATE. THE GATE IS LOCKED

TO ARNCLIFFE

Tennant Gill

TENNANT GILL FARM

SUPERB UNFENCED ROAD MADE FOR CYCLING

MAP 43

CATTLE GRID

CROSS ROAD TO FARM TRACK OPPOSITE

TENNANT GILL

TENNANT GILL

TRAILBLAZER

SHARP LEFT TURN DOWN TO ROAD

FINE OPEN VIEWS OF LIMESTONE COUNTRY

BARN

SHEEP CROPPED GRASS

0   1/4 mile

0   APPROX SCALE   500 metres

STONE BARN

THIS NEXT STRETCH IS TOP NOTCH WALKING

WALKERS HAVE BEEN KNOWN TO CALL INTO THE STUDY CENTRE FOR A BREW

LEAVE TRACK AT GATE IN WALL

CRAGS

MALHAM TARN HOUSE STUDY CENTRE

BOAT HOUSE

BOAT HOUSE

MALHAM TARN

42

1 HR – 1 HR 30 MINS FROM MALHAM TARN (MAP 42)

1 HR – 1 HR 30 MINS TO MALHAM TARN (MAP 42)

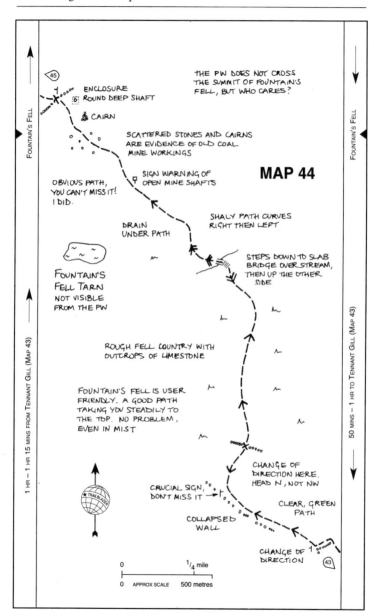

FOUNTAIN'S FELL

45

ENCLOSURE
ROUND DEEP SHAFT

CAIRN

SCATTERED STONES AND CAIRNS
ARE EVIDENCE OF OLD COAL
MINE WORKINGS

SIGN WARNING OF
OPEN MINE SHAFTS

THE PW DOES NOT CROSS
THE SUMMIT OF FOUNTAIN'S
FELL, BUT WHO CARES?

MAP 44

OBVIOUS PATH,
YOU CAN'T MISS IT!
I DID.

DRAIN
UNDER PATH

SHALY PATH CURVES
RIGHT THEN LEFT

FOUNTAIN'S
FELL TARN
NOT VISIBLE
FROM THE PW

STEPS DOWN TO SLAB
BRIDGE OVER STREAM,
THEN UP THE OTHER
SIDE

ROUGH FELL COUNTRY WITH
OUTCROPS OF LIMESTONE

FOUNTAIN'S FELL IS USER
FRIENDLY. A GOOD PATH
TAKING YOU STEADILY TO
THE TOP. NO PROBLEM,
EVEN IN MIST

TRAILBLAZER

CRUCIAL SIGN,
DON'T MISS IT

CHANGE OF
DIRECTION HERE.
HEAD N, NOT NW

CLEAR, GREEN
PATH

COLLAPSED
WALL

CHANGE OF
DIRECTION

43

0   1/4 mile

0   APPROX SCALE   500 metres

FOUNTAIN'S FELL

FOUNTAIN'S FELL

1 HR – 1 HR 15 MINS FROM TENNANT GILL (MAP 43)

50 MINS – 1 HR TO TENNANT GILL (MAP 43)

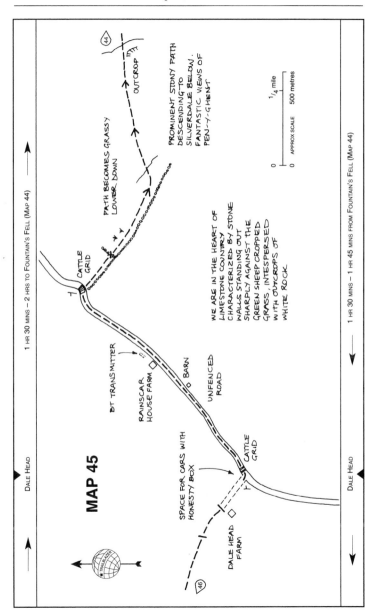

DALE HEAD

1 HR 30 MINS – 2 HRS TO FOUNTAIN'S FELL (MAP 44)

1 HR 30 MINS – 1 HR 45 MINS FROM FOUNTAIN'S FELL (MAP 44)

DALE HEAD

MAP 45

44

PROMINENT STONY PATH DESCENDING TO SILVERDALE BELOW. FANTASTIC VIEWS OF PEN-Y-GHENT

OUTCROP

PATH BECOMES GRASSY LOWER DOWN

CATTLE GRID

WE ARE IN THE HEART OF LIMESTONE COUNTRY CHARACTERIZED BY STONE WALLS STANDING OUT SHARPLY AGAINST THE GREEN SHEEP CROPPED GRASS, INTERSPERSED WITH OUTCROPS OF WHITE ROCK

BT TRANSMITTER

RAINSCAR HOUSE FARM

BARN

UNFENCED ROAD

SPACE FOR CARS WITH HONESTY BOX

CATTLE GRID

DALE HEAD FARM

46

0   1/4 mile
APPROX SCALE
0   500 metres

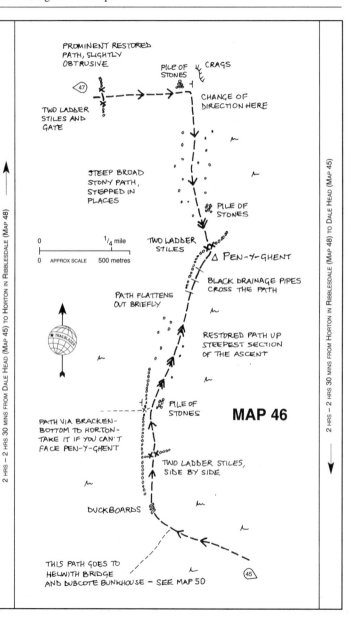

PROMINENT RESTORED PATH, SLIGHTLY OBTRUSIVE

PILE OF STONES

CRAGS

CHANGE OF DIRECTION HERE

⟨47⟩

TWO LADDER STILES AND GATE

STEEP BROAD STONY PATH, STEPPED IN PLACES

PILE OF STONES

TWO LADDER STILES

0   1/4 mile

0   500 metres

APPROX SCALE

△ PEN-Y-GHENT

BLACK DRAINAGE PIPES CROSS THE PATH

PATH FLATTENS OUT BRIEFLY

TRAILBLAZER

RESTORED PATH UP STEEPEST SECTION OF THE ASCENT

PILE OF STONES

MAP 46

PATH VIA BRACKEN-BOTTOM TO HORTON - TAKE IT IF YOU CAN'T FACE PEN-Y-GHENT

TWO LADDER STILES, SIDE BY SIDE

DUCKBOARDS

THIS PATH GOES TO HELWITH BRIDGE AND DUBCOTE BUNKHOUSE - SEE MAP 50

⟨45⟩

2 HRS – 2 HRS 30 MINS FROM DALE HEAD (MAP 45) TO HORTON IN RIBBLESDALE (MAP 48)

2 HRS – 2 HRS 30 MINS FROM HORTON IN RIBBLESDALE (MAP 48) TO DALE HEAD (MAP 45)

2 HRS – 2 HRS 30 MINS FROM DALE HEAD (MAP 45) TO HORTON IN RIBBLESDALE (MAP 48) ⟶

1 HR 45 MINS – 2 HRS 15 MINS FROM LING GILL BRIDGE (MAP 50) TO HORTON IN RIBBLESDALE (MAP 48) ⟶

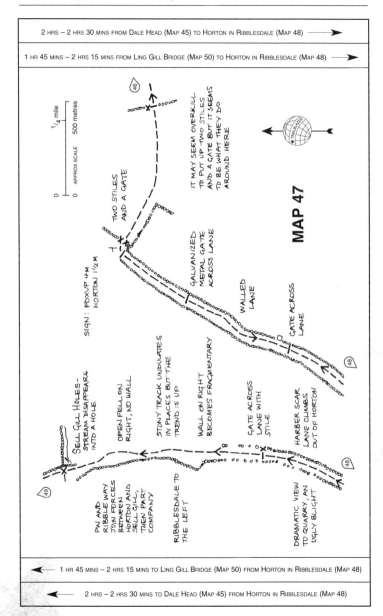

46

¼ mile

500 metres

0 APPROX SCALE

0

TWO STILES AND A GATE

IT MAY SEEM OVERKILL TO PUT UP TWO STILES AND A GATE BUT IT SEEMS TO BE WHAT THEY DO AROUND HERE

MAP 47

SIGN: FOXUP 4M HORTON 1½M

GALVANIZED METAL GATE ACROSS LANE

WALLED LANE

GATE ACROSS LANE

48

SELL GILL HOLES – STREAM DISAPPEARS INTO A HOLE

OPEN FELL ON RIGHT, NO WALL

STONY TRACK UNDULATES IN PLACES BUT THE TREND IS UP

WALL ON RIGHT BECOMES FRAGMENTARY

GATE ACROSS LANE WITH STILE

HARBER SCAR LANE CLIMBS OUT OF HORTON

49

PW AND RIBBLE WAY JOIN FORCES BETWEEN HORTON AND SELL GILL, THEN PART COMPANY

RIBBLESDALE TO THE LEFT

DRAMATIC VIEW TO QUARRY, AN UGLY BLIGHT

48

⟵ 1 HR 45 MINS – 2 HRS 15 MINS TO LING GILL BRIDGE (MAP 50) FROM HORTON IN RIBBLESDALE (MAP 48)

⟵ 2 HRS – 2 HRS 30 MINS TO DALE HEAD (MAP 45) FROM HORTON IN RIBBLESDALE (MAP 48)

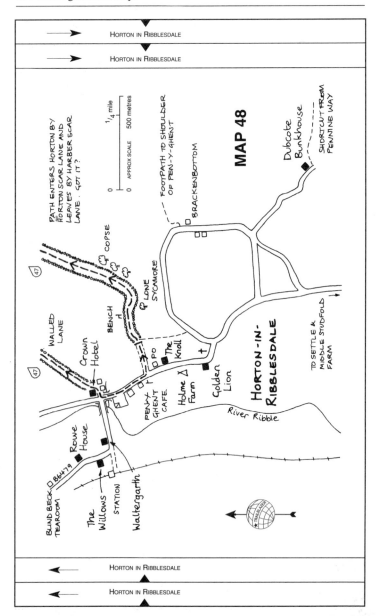

MAP 48

PATH ENTERS HORTON BY HORTON SCAR LANE AND LEAVES BY HARBER SCAR LANE. GOT IT?

¼ mile

APPROX SCALE

0   500 metres

FOOTPATH TO SHOULDER OF PEN-Y-GHENT

BRACKENBOTTOM

Dubcote Bunkhouse

SHORTCUT FROM PENNINE WAY

COPSE

LONE SYCAMORE

BENCH

WALLED LANE

Crown Hotel

PO

The Knoll

PEN-Y-GHENT CAFE

Holme Farm

Golden Lion

HORTON-IN-RIBBLESDALE

TO SETTLE & MIDDLE STUDFOLD FARM

River Ribble

Rowe House

BLIND BECK TEAROOM

B6479

The Willows

STATION

Waltergarth

TRAIL BLAZER

HORTON-IN-RIBBLESDALE TO HAWES   MAPS 48-55

This **14-mile (23km, 5¼-6¾hrs)** section is a classic fell-walk that takes some beating. It follows stony-walled tracks that have been used for centuries as the thoroughfares over the wild limestone moors where the wind is never still and where the lonely call of the curlew and golden plover will be the only sound you will hear.

Climbing out of Horton by way of Harber Scar Lane from the doorstep of the Crown Hotel, the lane tops out on **Jackdaw Hill** (400m/1312ft) then traces a line along a prominent green road past pot holes and limestone outcrops to reach the delightful **Ling Gill** ravine where the beck has carved a deep gash in the earth and created a unique natural environment for trees, wildflowers and wildlife. The trail crosses Ling Gill Bridge and a more perfect picnic spot would be hard to find.

More uphill work follows, the path easily followed to the high crossroads known as **Cam End** where a sturdy signpost tells you that you are halfway between Horton and Hawes. The view of the Three Peaks country with Ribblehead Viaduct clearly visible in the wide valley between Ingleborough and Whernside is an unforgettable sight. You turn your back on it, however, and follow the broad, high-level track of Cam High Road along the contours of the hillside above dense forestry to reach **Kidhow Gate**. Here farmers have been gathering their sheep for driving to market for as long as flocks have been grazed on the springy turf of these wide open moors.

Another green road, West Cam Road, leads along the shoulder of **Dodd Fell** high above the secretive valley of Sleightholme, a long trudge that seems reluctant to end. **Hawes** at last comes into view, seen first in the distance like a mirage, gradually becoming solid, the stone houses clustering together as if sheltering against the elements. Hawes is a welcoming village and holds all the services a walker will need for rest and recuperation.

❏ **Packhorse roads**
The trackways that criss-cross the mid-Pennines are the remains of a once-thriving traffic in goods transported on the backs of packhorses.

These hardy animals were tough, stocky breeds known variously as jaggers after the German Jaeger ponies from which their stock came, or galloways after the Scottish breed particularly suited to carrying loads over rough country.

Wool, coal, hides, iron, lead, stone, charcoal and peat were carried down to the towns, the tracks used taking the shortest way across unenclosed country. Over the years the way would become heavily worn and sunken and we find names such as Hollow Way (Holloway) on maps where the traffic has cut a deep groove. Stones would be used to fill up holes and reinforce the road.

Most of the upland roads were abandoned when turnpikes were adopted for wheeled traffic (1770-1830) and it was only farmers who continued to use the old tracks to get up onto the high fells. Now walkers use them more than farmers. With the advent of quad-bikes, powerful four-wheelers with springs and tyres that will allow them to go anywhere, there is no need to follow the tracks; farmers simply drive straight across a field to the nearest gate.

HAWES

There's nothing pretentious about Hawes. It's a down-to-earth Yorkshire town with a vibrant centre full of pubs and cafés. If you're in need of a break this could be the place to relax for a day or so. There's plenty to see: a good local museum, a traditional ropemaker – and this is the home of the world-famous Wensleydale cheese.

Services

There are **buses** to Garsdale station and an hourly service to Leyburn and Northallerton where you can connect with the east-coast rail network (see public transport map, pp36-9). For **taxis** try either Cliff Ellis (☎ 01969-667598) or Ray Harrington (☎ 01969-650441 during the day and ☎ 01969-650682 after 6pm), who operates a minibus. The imaginative and informative **Dales Countryside Museum** houses both the **National Park Centre** and the **Tourist Information Centre** (☎ 01969-667450, ✉ hawes@ytbtic.co.uk) and is open daily 10am-5pm (last entry to the museum is at 4pm). There's a £3 charge for the museum. Nearby is another place to visit, the **Hawes Ropemaker**, open daily.

The **Wensleydale Cheese Factory Visitors' Centre** (Mon-Sat 9.30am-5pm, Sun 10am-4.30pm) is well worth visiting and they sell a wide range of their cheeses including interesting varieties such as garlic, cranberry and ginger. The best time to see the cheesemaking process is 10am-2pm.

There's a **Spar supermarket** (Mon-Fri 8am-7pm, Sat 8am-7.30pm, Sun 10am-5pm). If you're after something for a picnic try **Elijah Allen & Sons**, a wonderful old

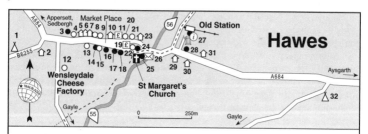

Where to stay
1 Honeycott Caravan Park
2 Hawes Youth Hostel
5 Cockett's Hotel
6 The Board Hotel
7 The Crown Hotel
10 The Bull's Head Hotel
23 Laburnum House
29 Spring Bank House
31 Ebor House
30 Fair View House
32 Bainbridge Ings Camping

Where to eat
4 Paul's Pizzas
8 Prachin
9 Fountain Hotel
12 Wensleydale Cheese Factory
    Restaurant
13 The Chippie

Where to eat (cont'd)
15 Wensleydale Pantry
20 Bay Tree Café & Bistro
21 Laura's Cottage Tea Shop
22 The White Hart

Other
3 Littlefair Ironmongery
11 Barclays Bank
14 Spar Supermarket
16 Stewart R Cunningham
17 Elijah Allen & Sons
18 Chemist and Wine Merchant
19 HSBC Bank
24 Launderette
25 Three Peaks (Gear Shop)
26 Post Office
27 Dales Countryside Museum,
    National Park Centre & Tourist Info
28 Hawes Ropemaker

grocery store that's been run by the same family since 1870.

For **outdoor gear** there's Three Peaks, which has a huge selection of boots and some other stuff, or the well-stocked Stewart R Cunningham (daily 9.30am-5pm). The **ironmonger** Littlefair has some camping fuels.

There's a **launderette** (Mon-Sat 9.30am-4pm closed Wed) and a **post office** (early closing Wed). Barclays and HSBC **banks** both have cash machines. There's also a **chemist**, which doubles as the **wine merchant** so you can buy both the cause and the cure for your hangover in one shop!

Where to stay

You can **camp** either side of the village. If you're feeling energetic head for *Bainbridge Ings Caravan and Camping Site* (☎ 01969-667354, 🖳 www.bainbridge-ings .co.uk, April-October), three-quarters of a mile east of the Market Place, where you can pitch your tent in beautiful countryside for £3.50 per person. They sell milk and eggs. A bit nearer but on the B6255 to the west is the seasonal *Honeycott Caravan Park* (☎ 01969-667310, Mar-Oct), which also charges £3.50 per person.

The modern and rather unattractive *Hawes Youth Hostel* (☎ 01969-667368, bookings ☎ 0870-770 5854, 🖳 hawes@yha .org.uk, open Apr-Aug, plus daily except Sun-Mon mid-Feb to Mar, Fri-Sat only Nov to mid-Dec) has beds for £10.60 (under 18s £7.20) and serves evening meals at 7pm.

To the east on the A684 to *Ebor House* (☎ 01969-667337, 🖳 gwen@eborhouse .freeserve.co.uk, 1S/1T/2D) which costs from £21. They offer laundry services, boot and clothes drying and packed lunches. *Laburnum House Tearoom* (☎ 01969-667717, 🖳 www.stayatlaburnumhouse.co .uk, The Holme, 1T/2D/1F) has all en suite rooms costing £23 and is just off Market Place but set back from the road and with good views. *Spring Bank House* (☎ 01969-667376, Townfoot, 2D/1T) is also set back from the road and has en suite rooms for £23 and they can do a packed lunch on request. You could also try *Fair View House* (☎ 01969-667348, 🖳 info@

fairview-hawes.co.uk, 2S/1T/2D/1F most en suite) which charges £27.50.

The **hotels** are largely similar in price and style. Probably the best is *Cockett's Hotel* (☎ 01969-667312, 🖳 www.cock etts.co.uk, 2T/6D all en suite) charges £32 per person for B&B. They can do a packed lunch, too. *The Crown Hotel* (☎ 01969-667212, 🖳 jdthprds@aol.com, 1D/1T/2F some en suite) in the Market Place does B&B from £22.50 per person. There is also *The Board Hotel* (☎ 01969-667223, 🖳 www.theboardhotel.com, 2T/3D) at £28 en suite, and *The Bull's Head Hotel* (☎ 01969-667437, 🖳 www.bullsheadhotel.com, 3D/2T/1F mostly en suite) from £25, or £20 for a basement room.

Where to eat

The *Wensleydale Cheese Visitors' Centre* has a restaurant and café and does good food for around £6. For a starter you can taste their free samples. It's open 9.30am-5pm daily (to 4.30pm on Sunday).

Bay Tree Café & Bistro offers quiches and hot or cold filled baguettes with tasty fillings (eg Yorkshire blue cheese with grapes and mayo, £4.55). *The White Hart* (☎ 01969-667259) is a welcoming locals' pub, which stays open all day and from 12 noon to 2pm and 7-8.30pm will produce a square meal for around £7. Most of the hotels do pub grub for around the same price. *Cockett's Hotel* is more upmarket and offers two courses for £14.95, three for £16.95.

The *Wensleydale Pantry* (☎ 01969-667202) is open daily from 8.30am to 8pm (to 9pm in the summer) and has an extensive menu for around £6. There's a good Indian and Bangladeshi restaurant, *Prachin* (☎ 01969-6673142, daily 5-11.30pm) opposite.

Laura's Cottage Tea Shop (daily 10.30am-5pm) serves local favourites such as roast beef, Yorkshire pudding and veg (£5.50) and giant Yorkshire puddings with chips and gravy (£3.50) and well as cream teas and cakes. Close by is *Laburnum House Tearoom* which also has a 'soup and a sandwich' type menu, in a nice setting.

For a takeaway there's *Paul's Pizzas*, and *The Chippie* (cod, chips and mushy peas for £3.40),

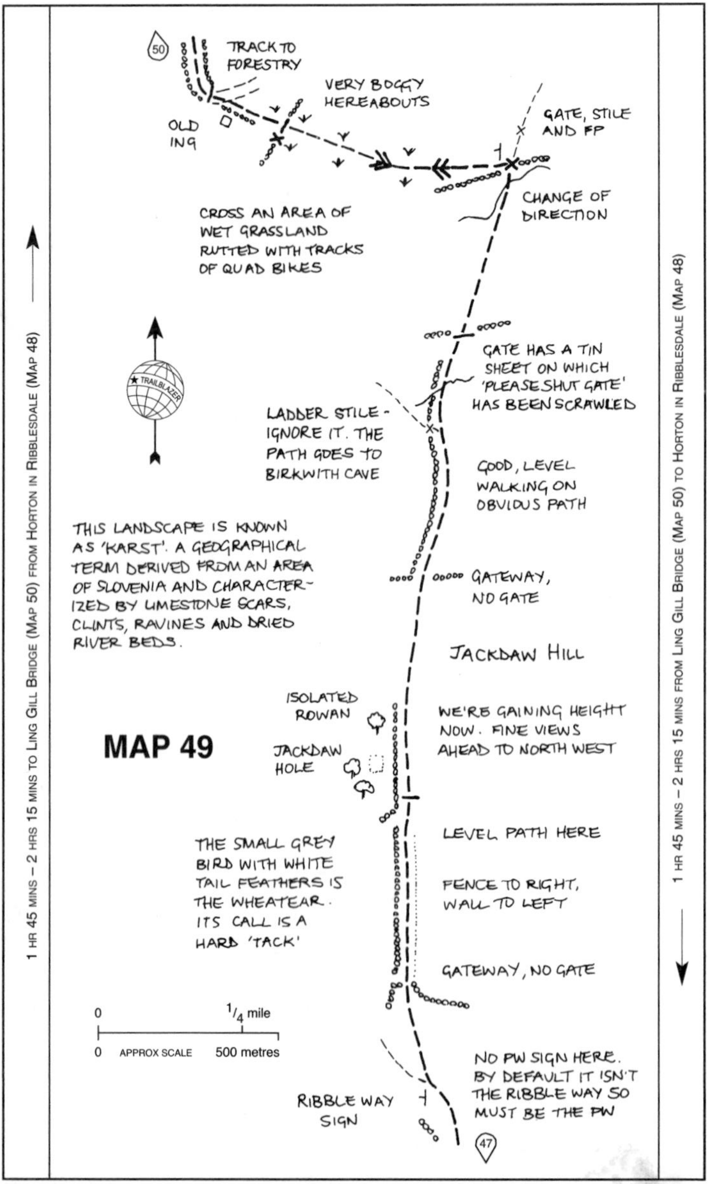

50

TRACK TO FORESTRY

VERY BOGGY HEREABOUTS

GATE, STILE AND FP

OLD ING

CHANGE OF DIRECTION

CROSS AN AREA OF WET GRASSLAND RUTTED WITH TRACKS OF QUAD BIKES

★ TRAILBLAZER

GATE HAS A TIN SHEET ON WHICH 'PLEASE SHUT GATE' HAS BEEN SCRAWLED

LADDER STILE - IGNORE IT. THE PATH GOES TO BIRKWITH CAVE

GOOD, LEVEL WALKING ON OBVIOUS PATH

THIS LANDSCAPE IS KNOWN AS 'KARST'. A GEOGRAPHICAL TERM DERIVED FROM AN AREA OF SLOVENIA AND CHARACTER- IZED BY LIMESTONE SCARS, CLINTS, RAVINES AND DRIED RIVER BEDS.

GATEWAY, NO GATE

JACKDAW HILL

ISOLATED ROWAN

JACKDAW HOLE

WE'RE GAINING HEIGHT NOW. FINE VIEWS AHEAD TO NORTH WEST

MAP 49

THE SMALL GREY BIRD WITH WHITE TAIL FEATHERS IS THE WHEATEAR. ITS CALL IS A HARD 'TACK'

LEVEL PATH HERE

FENCE TO RIGHT, WALL TO LEFT

GATEWAY, NO GATE

0   1/4 mile

0   APPROX SCALE   500 metres

NO PW SIGN HERE. BY DEFAULT IT ISN'T THE RIBBLE WAY SO MUST BE THE PW

RIBBLE WAY SIGN

47

1 HR 45 MINS – 2 HRS 15 MINS TO LING GILL BRIDGE (MAP 50) FROM HORTON IN RIBBLESDALE (MAP 48)

1 HR 45 MINS – 2 HRS 15 MINS FROM LING GILL BRIDGE (MAP 50) TO HORTON IN RIBBLESDALE (MAP 48)

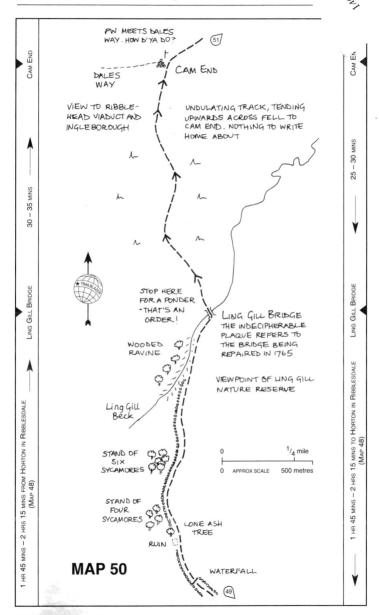

MAP 50

PW MEETS DALES WAY. HOW D'YA DO?

51

CAM END

DALES WAY

VIEW TO RIBBLE-HEAD VIADUCT AND INGLEBOROUGH

UNDULATING TRACK, TENDING UPWARDS ACROSS FELL TO CAM END. NOTHING TO WRITE HOME ABOUT

★ TRAILBLAZER

STOP HERE FOR A PONDER - THAT'S AN ORDER!

LING GILL BRIDGE
THE INDECIPHERABLE PLAQUE REFERS TO THE BRIDGE BEING REPAIRED IN 1765

WOODED RAVINE

VIEWPOINT OF LING GILL NATURE RESERVE

Ling Gill Beck

0   1/4 mile

0   APPROX SCALE   500 metres

STAND OF SIX SYCAMORES

STAND OF FOUR SYCAMORES

LONE ASH TREE

RUIN

WATERFALL

49

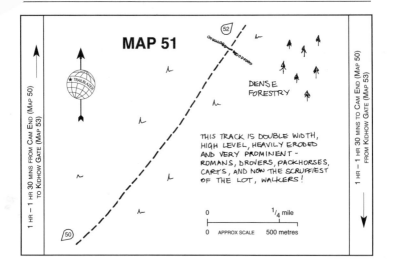

MAP 51

★ TRAILBLAZER

52

50

DENSE FORESTRY

THIS TRACK IS DOUBLE WIDTH, HIGH LEVEL, HEAVILY ERODED AND VERY PROMINENT – ROMANS, DROVERS, PACKHORSES, CARTS, AND NOW THE SCRUFFIEST OF THE LOT, WALKERS!

0   ¼ mile

0   APPROX SCALE   500 metres

1 HR – 1 HR 30 MINS FROM CAM END (MAP 50)
TO KIDHOW GATE (MAP 53)

1 HR – 1 HR 30 MINS TO CAM END (MAP 50)
FROM KIDHOW GATE (MAP 53)

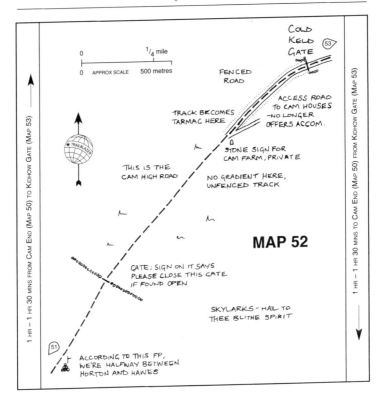

COLD KELD GATE 53

FENCED ROAD

ACCESS ROAD TO CAM HOUSES - NO LONGER OFFERS ACCOM.

TRACK BECOMES TARMAC HERE

STONE SIGN FOR CAM FARM, PRIVATE

THIS IS THE CAM HIGH ROAD

NO GRADIENT HERE, UNFENCED TRACK

MAP 52

GATE; SIGN ON IT SAYS PLEASE CLOSE THIS GATE IF FOUND OPEN

SKYLARKS - HAIL TO THEE BLITHE SPIRIT

51 ACCORDING TO THIS FP, WE'RE HALFWAY BETWEEN HORTON AND HAWES

0 ¼ mile

0 APPROX SCALE 500 metres

★ TRAILBLAZER

1 HR – 1 HR 30 MINS FROM CAM END (MAP 50) TO KIDHOW GATE (MAP 53)

1 HR – 1 HR 30 MINS TO CAM END (MAP 50) FROM KIDHOW GATE (MAP 53)

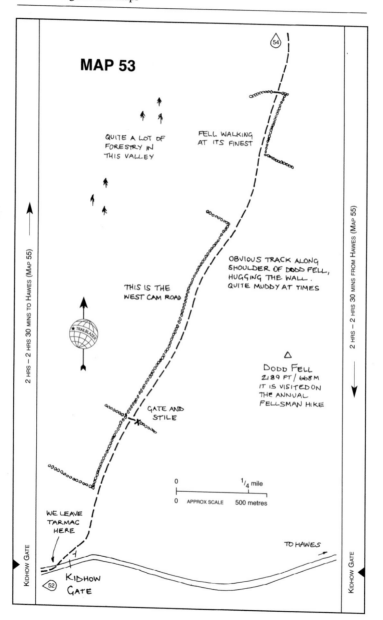

MAP 53

QUITE A LOT OF
FORESTRY IN
THIS VALLEY

FELL WALKING
AT ITS FINEST

THIS IS THE
WEST CAM ROAD

★ TRAILBLAZER

OBVIOUS TRACK ALONG
SHOULDER OF DODD FELL,
HUGGING THE WALL.
QUITE MUDDY AT TIMES

△
DODD FELL
2189 FT / 668M
IT IS VISITED ON
THE ANNUAL
FELLSMAN HIKE

GATE AND
STILE

0   ¼ mile
0   APPROX SCALE   500 metres

WE LEAVE
TARMAC
HERE

TO HAWES

KIDHOW
GATE

2 HRS – 2 HRS 30 MINS TO HAWES (MAP 55)

2 HRS – 2 HRS 30 MINS FROM HAWES (MAP 55)

KIDHOW GATE

KIDHOW GATE

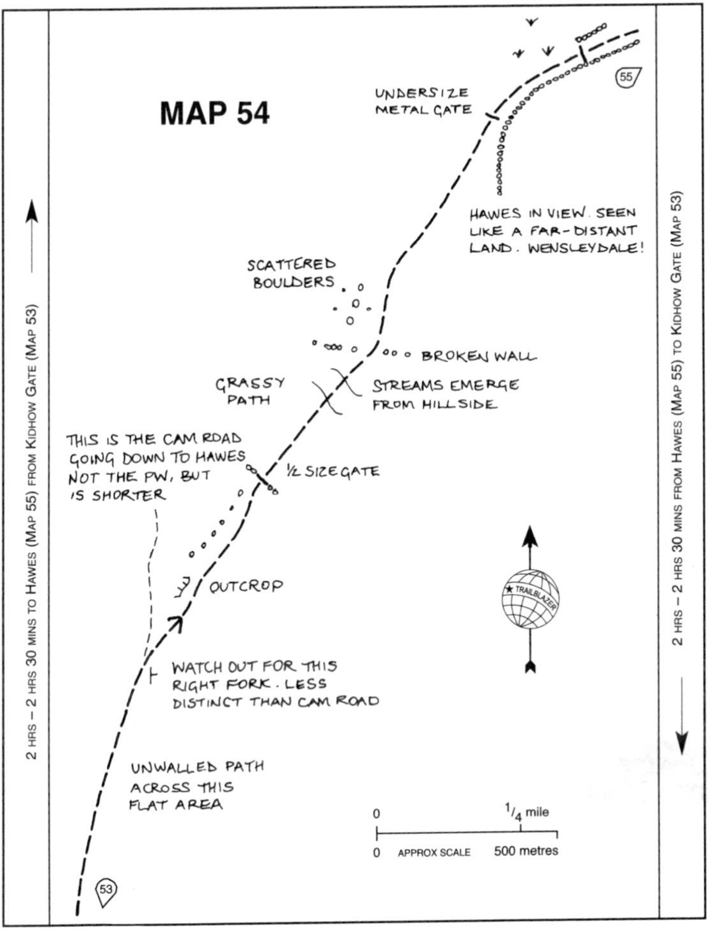

MAP 54

UNDERSIZE METAL GATE

55

HAWES IN VIEW. SEEN LIKE A FAR-DISTANT LAND. WENSLEYDALE!

SCATTERED BOULDERS

BROKEN WALL

GRASSY PATH

STREAMS EMERGE FROM HILLSIDE

THIS IS THE CAM ROAD GOING DOWN TO HAWES NOT THE PW, BUT IS SHORTER

½ SIZE GATE

OUTCROP

TRAILBLAZER

WATCH OUT FOR THIS RIGHT FORK. LESS DISTINCT THAN CAM ROAD

UNWALLED PATH ACROSS THIS FLAT AREA

0	¼ mile
0 APPROX SCALE	500 metres

53

2 HRS – 2 HRS 30 MINS TO HAWES (MAP 55) FROM KIDHOW GATE (MAP 53)

2 HRS – 2 HRS 30 MINS FROM HAWES (MAP 55) TO KIDHOW GATE (MAP 53)

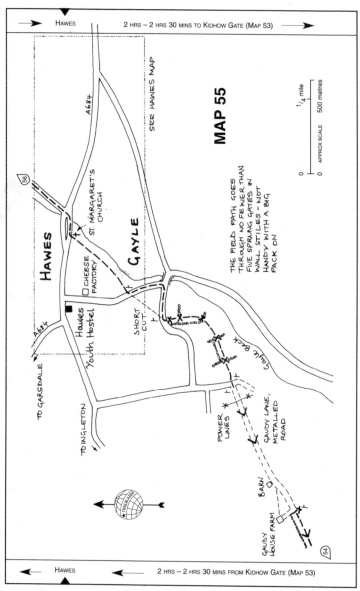

MAP 55

HAWES — 2 HRS – 2 HRS 30 MINS TO KIDHOW GATE (MAP 53) →

HAWES ← 2 HRS – 2 HRS 30 MINS FROM KIDHOW GATE (MAP 53)

SEE HAWES MAP

A684

56

HAWES

ST. MARGARET'S CHURCH

GAYLE

CHEESE FACTORY

Hawes Youth Hostel

A684

TO GARSDALE

TO INGLETON

SHORT CUT

THE FIELD PATH GOES THROUGH NO FEWER THAN FIVE SPRING GATES IN WALL STILES – NOT HANDY WITH A BIG PACK ON

GAYLE BECK

POWER LINES

GAUDY LANE, METALLED ROAD

BARN

GAUDY HOUSE FARM

54

TRAILBLAZER

0 — ¼ mile
0 — 500 metres
APPROX SCALE

Opposite Top: Lumb Head Beck, Ickornshaw (see p111). **Bottom**: Lothersdale (see p108).

HAWES TO KELD   MAPS 55-62

Many of the days on the Pennine Way have an upside and a downside. On today's **12½-mile (20km, 6-7¾hrs)** walk the plus side is the delightful early ramble through the meadows to **Hardraw** and the late limestone gallery along the Swale to reach the lonely outpost of the village of Keld.

The downside is **Great Shunner Fell**, a major hill massif involving five gruelling miles (8km) of climbing to top out on the 716-metre (2349ft) summit. On a clear day you have the view over the Buttertubs Pass to admire and the shapely summit of Lovely Seat to gaze upon but in mist or rain there is nothing to relieve the punishing toil up these slopes. Continue down the other side on slabs and tussocky grass and you reach **Thwaite** where there's a fine licensed café-cum-hotel, the Kearton Country Hotel (see below).

From Thwaite the walking soars in quality, first through the field paths and hay meadows of **Swaledale** then high above the valley of the infant River Swale on the exposed shoulder of **Kisdon Hill**. In no more than two hours the path drops down to cross the river but by keeping straight on along a dog-walkers' path you emerge at curious little **Keld**, a uniquely perfect limestone settlement where Pennine Way and the Coast to Coast Path meet, a conjunction that tests to the full the limited accommodation available.

HARDRAW   [Map 56]
Just north of Hawes is Hardraw, known for the **Green Dragon Inn** (☎ 01969-667392, 🖥 www.greendragoninn.fsnet.co.uk, 2S/2T/5D/1F en suite), where B&B is £25 per person, and it's £3 for campers at the back of the pub. Food is served at the pub between 10am and 9.30pm. Main dishes are around £6.50.

Access to the famous, though somewhat disappointing, **Hardraw Force waterfall** (supposedly the highest in England) is through the pub where a charge of £2 is levied. The falls vary in volume depending on the rainfall; in very dry weather there is hardly a trickle.

Camping can also be had at **Old Hall Cottage** (☎ 01969-667296) for £3 per person plus £1 per tent.

To the east of the village there are more accommodation possibilities: the very quiet **Shaw Ghyll Campsite** (☎ 01969-667359, 🖥 rogerstott@aol.com), which charges £10 per tent; and, for some luxury,

the **Simonstone Hall Hotel** (☎ 01969-667255, 🖥 www.simonstonehall.com, 20 rooms, en suite) with B&B from £60; bar meals are available for around £7.

THWAITE   [Map 61]
The village is notable for the excellent café and tea room at **Kearton Country Hotel** (☎ 01748-886277, 🖥 www.keartoncountry hotel.co.uk, 1S/1T/6D/5F) where you can have morning coffee, a pint with bar meals or choose something from the proper lunch menu. If you're in the mood for afternoon tea there's nowhere better and the evening menu is inventive and the food delicious. B&B costs £27.50 en suite, £33.50 with an evening meal. While walkers can find everything they could possibly want here, most will almost certainly push on to Keld even though there is nothing there to approach it in terms of quality or amenities.

There's an infrequent **bus** service to Richmond (see public transport map, pp36-9).

Opposite Top: Malham Cove (see p125). **Bottom left**: Watlowes, looking south (see p128).

MUKER [Map 61]

For campers, just over half a mile east through the meadows brings you to the campsite at *Usha Gap* (☎ 01748-886214, 🖳 www.ushagap.btinternet.co.uk, Map 61), a lovely riverside field where you can pitch for £4 including showers. Another half a mile and you reach Muker. This is a very pleasant little place and a favourite of James Herriot (the Yorkshire vet who wrote about his experiences in *All Creatures Great and Small*). It has a church, a small **shop** and a fine pub, the *Farmers Arms* (☎ 01748-886297) which serves food daily 12-2pm and 6-9pm.

There are several B&Bs in the village. *Muker Tea Shop* (☎ 01748-886409, 🖳 www.mukervillage.co.uk, 1T en suite + extra bed) charges £50 for two or £60 for three for B&B. *Bridge House* (☎ 01748-886461, 🖳 bridgehouse@mukervillage .co.uk, 3D/1T, some en suite) is by the river and they charge from £25. Near the church is *Hylands* (☎ 01748-886003, 2D en suite or private bathroom) with B&B for £29 per person, less if you stay longer than one night.

Muker has also been the home for 30 years of **Swaledale Woollens** (🖳 www .swaledalewoollens.co.uk), its products made from the wool of Swaledale sheep, a hardy breed whose tough wool is considered ideal for carpets. The shop boasts that it actually saved the village following the depression caused by the collapse of the mining industry. Following a meeting in the pub, a decision was made to set up a local cottage industry producing knitwear, and today nearly 40 home-workers are employed in knitting the jumpers, hats and many other items available in the store, which is near the pub.

KELD [Map 62]

If you want to take a day off and do not need to do it in a place with plenty of facilities Keld is as perfect as anywhere gets. It is a small and cut off farming village with delightful people. You can buy basic groceries here, and most B&Bs will do an evening meal for you, but note that there is no pub.

There's an infrequent **bus** service to Richmond via Thwaite (see public transport map, pp36-9).

You can **camp** at *Park Lodge*, (☎ 01748-886274, open Easter-Oct) where it costs £2.75 per person and there's a café and farm shop; well worth a visit for an idyllic rural experience. Half a mile west of Keld is *Park House Campsite* (☎ 01748-886549, 🖳 park.house@btinternet.co.uk). It's a lovely riverside site and they charge £3 per person. There's a food shop and indoor sitting area.

Keld Youth Hostel, (☎ 01748-886259, bookings ☎ 0870-770 5888, 🖳 keld@yha .org.uk, open Apr-Oct, except Mon Apr-June and Sun-Mon Sep-Oct) is adequate but school parties tend to swallow up all of the beds. A pet rabbit, the subject of a famous occasion when the area health inspector visited, also inhabits the place. The cost is £10.60 (under 18s £7.20) and evening meals are served at 7pm.

Greenlands (☎ 01748-886778, 🖳 www.yorkshirenet.co.uk/stayat/greenlands, 1T/1D en suite + 1S), three-quarters of a mile from the Pennine Way and a little south of Keld, has en suite rooms that are as good a bet as any. It costs £22 and they will do an evening meal for walkers by arrangement.

You will probably get the most complete service at Doreen Whitehead's *Butt House* (☎ 01748-886374, 🖳 butthouse@bt internet.com, 1S/1T/1D/1F) where en suite rooms cost £20. This is the only B&B in Keld itself. They are licensed, which may just give that evening meal (£10) a much-needed 'je ne sais quoi'. Doreen's name is mentioned wherever Pennine Way walkers gather. She runs a tight ship. Perhaps it was her forceful personality that led William Hague, former Conservative leader, to call for afternoon tea when he wanted to get back to the grassroots.

Smaller but no less comfortable an establishment is *Frith Lodge* (☎ 01748-886489, 1D/2T/1F, Map 63), which offers dinner (there's nowhere else to eat within three miles) plus B&B for £29. It's a mile or so out of the village, but right on the trail.

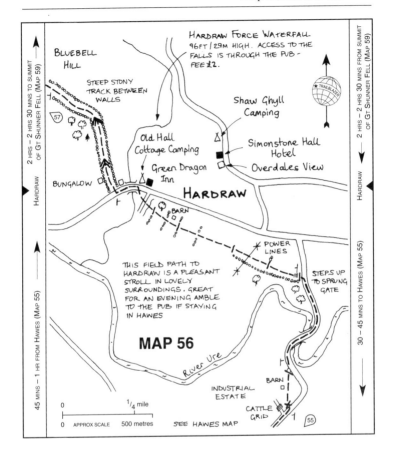

HARDRAW FORCE WATERFALL
96FT / 29M HIGH. ACCESS TO THE
FALLS IS THROUGH THE PUB -
FEE £2.

BLUEBELL
HILL

STEEP STONY
TRACK BETWEEN
WALLS

57

★ TRAILBLAZER

Shaw Ghyll
Camping

Old Hall
Cottage Camping

Green Dragon
Inn

Simonstone Hall
Hotel

Overdales View

BUNGALOW

HARDRAW

BARN

POWER
LINES

STEPS UP
TO SPRUNG
GATE

THIS FIELD PATH TO
HARDRAW IS A PLEASANT
STROLL IN LOVELY
SURROUNDINGS. GREAT
FOR AN EVENING AMBLE
TO THE PUB IF STAYING
IN HAWES

MAP 56

River Ure

INDUSTRIAL
ESTATE

BARN

CATTLE
GRID

55

SEE HAWES MAP

0   ¼ mile
0   APPROX SCALE   500 metres

2 HRS – 2 HRS 30 MINS TO SUMMIT OF GT SHUNNER FELL (MAP 59)

45 MINS – 1 HR FROM HAWES (MAP 55)

2 HRS – 2 HRS 30 MINS FROM SUMMIT OF GT SHUNNER FELL (MAP 59)

HARDRAW

30 – 45 MINS TO HAWES (MAP 55)

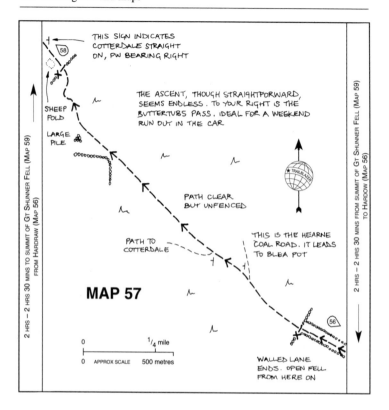

THIS SIGN INDICATES
COTTERDALE STRAIGHT
ON, PW BEARING RIGHT

THE ASCENT, THOUGH STRAIGHTFORWARD,
SEEMS ENDLESS. TO YOUR RIGHT IS THE
BUTTERTUBS PASS. IDEAL FOR A WEEKEND
RUN OUT IN THE CAR

SHEEP
FOLD

LARGE
PILE

PATH CLEAR
BUT UNFENCED

PATH TO
COTTERDALE

THIS IS THE HEARNE
COAL ROAD. IT LEADS
TO BLEA POT

MAP 57

★ TRAILBLAZER

2 HRS – 2 HRS 30 MINS TO SUMMIT OF GT SHUNNER FELL (MAP 59)
FROM HARDRAW (MAP 56)

2 HRS – 2 HRS 30 MINS FROM SUMMIT OF GT SHUNNER FELL (MAP 59)
TO HARDOW (MAP 56)

0   1/4 mile
0   APPROX SCALE   500 metres

WALLED LANE
ENDS. OPEN FELL
FROM HERE ON

❑ Black Grouse

Pennine Way walkers are unlikely to get as far as Bowes without seeing or at least hearing grouse. Their distinctive nagging croak which has been likened to the warning 'go-back, go-back, go-back' is a familiar sound on wild heather moors, as familiar as the lonely bubbling call of the curlew or the insistent pipe of the golden plover.

While the red grouse is the primary target of many a landowner's gun, the black grouse is a different matter altogether. Shot almost to extinction across most of Northern England, it is now only plentiful in the Scottish hills where the vast space and better cover have enabled it to survive in some numbers. In the Pennines only a few remnants remain and these are carefully protected by gamekeepers and conservationists alike. Most keepers now appreciate the bird for its own sake and, like their changing attitudes to birds of prey, are simply glad it has survived.

In Baldersdale black grouse have been seen in the vicinity of the youth hostel where their curious courtship ritual was described to me by the warden. The hen birds line up on the branch of a tree like spectators grabbing the best seats in the stands to watch the cock birds perform their 'lek', a display acted out on a piece of prepared ground on which they parade, each trying to outdo the others in their strutting and posturing. Their lyre-shaped tail feathers are fanned out in a magnificent demonstration intended to win the hens' affections.

There are reports that the black grouse is making a comeback. Pennine Way walkers would be the richer if this is so.

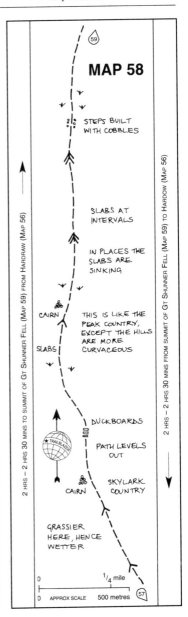

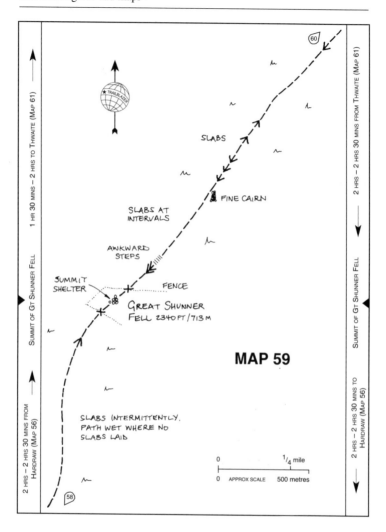

1 HR 30 MINS – 2 HRS TO THWAITE (MAP 61)

SUMMIT OF GT SHUNNER FELL

2 HRS – 2 HRS 30 MINS FROM HARDRAW (MAP 56)

2 HRS – 2 HRS 30 MINS FROM THWAITE (MAP 61)

SUMMIT OF GT SHUNNER FELL

2 HRS – 2 HRS 30 MINS TO HARDRAW (MAP 56)

★ TRAILBLAZER

SLABS

FINE CAIRN

SLABS AT INTERVALS

AWKWARD STEPS

SUMMIT SHELTER

FENCE

GREAT SHUNNER FELL 2340 FT / 713 M

MAP 59

SLABS INTERMITTENTLY. PATH WET WHERE NO SLABS LAID

0   1/4 mile

0   APPROX SCALE   500 metres

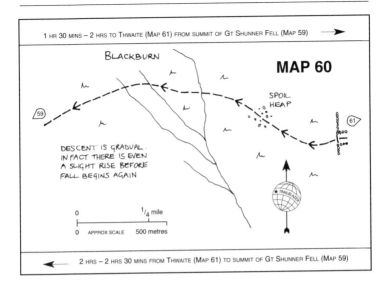

1 HR 30 MINS – 2 HRS TO THWAITE (MAP 61) FROM SUMMIT OF GT SHUNNER FELL (MAP 59)

BLACKBURN

MAP 60

SPOIL
HEAP

59

61

DESCENT IS GRADUAL.
IN FACT THERE IS EVEN
A SLIGHT RISE BEFORE
FALL BEGINS AGAIN

0   ¼ mile

0   APPROX SCALE   500 metres

★ TRAILBLAZER

2 HRS – 2 HRS 30 MINS FROM THWAITE (MAP 61) TO SUMMIT OF GT SHUNNER FELL (MAP 59)

❏ Field barns

As you pass through the Yorkshire Dales the prevalence of field barns will have been obvious. Swaledale is particularly noted for these isolated stone barns which are also known as laithes. It has been estimated that within a thousand metre radius of the village of Muker there are 60 barns of this type. They were part and parcel of the traditional farming methods of the area which saw grazing land enclosed between stone walls, the cattle kept in the barns between October and May, fed on hay stored in the upper roof space of the barn. Cows were milked where they stood and their manure was spread on the surrounding fields. Typically, a field barn would house four or five cows, hence a farmer with a large herd would need plenty of barns to keep them in.

Today, field barns are largely redundant due to farmers making hay on a semi industrial basis with automated machinery, the hay being baled and stored in huge modern barns close to the farm buildings for convenience. Field barns are used mainly for storage. In some cases farmers have converted them into tourist accommodation, thanks to the availability of grants encouraging them to do so.

Most of the stone walls which make the Yorkshire Dales so distinctive date from the era of the Enclosure Acts in the late 18th and early 19th centuries.

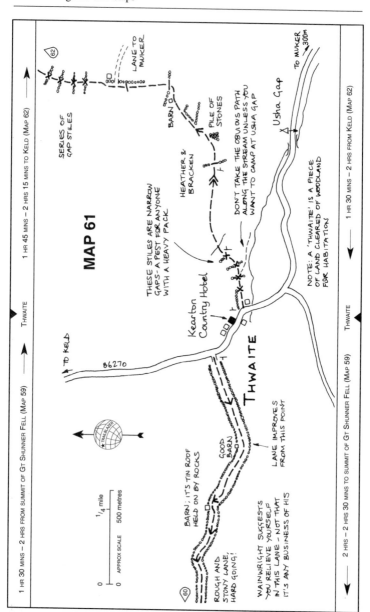

1 HR 30 MINS – 2 HRS FROM SUMMIT OF GT SHUNNER FELL (MAP 59) ▶ THWAITE ▲ 1 HR 45 MINS – 2 HRS 15 MINS TO KELD (MAP 62)

MAP 61

SERIES OF GAP STILES

THESE STILES ARE NARROW GAPS – A PEST FOR ANYONE WITH A HEAVY PACK

LANE TO MUKER

62

HEATHER & BRACKEN

BARN

PILE OF STONES

DON'T TAKE THE OBVIOUS PATH ALONG THE STREAM UNLESS YOU WANT TO CAMP AT USHA GAP

USHA GAP

TO MUKER 300m

TO KELD

B6270

Kearton Country Hotel

THWAITE

NOTE: A 'THWAITE' IS A PIECE OF LAND CLEARED OF WOODLAND FOR HABITATION

LANE IMPROVES FROM THIS POINT

GOOD BARN

BARN; ITS TIN ROOF HELD ON BY ROCKS

ROUGH AND STONY LANE, HARD GOING!

WAINWRIGHT SUGGESTS YOU RELIEVE YOURSELF IN THIS LANE – NOT THAT IT'S ANY BUSINESS OF HIS

60

TRAILBLAZER

0 ———— 1/4 mile
0 ———— 500 metres
APPROX SCALE

1 HR 30 MINS – 2 HRS FROM KELD (MAP 62) ◀ THWAITE ▶ 2 HRS – 2 HRS 30 MINS TO SUMMIT OF GT SHUNNER FELL (MAP 59)

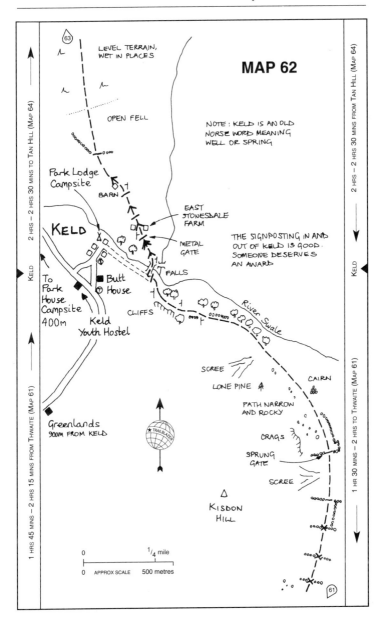

MAP 62

LEVEL TERRAIN, WET IN PLACES

OPEN FELL

NOTE: KELD IS AN OLD NORSE WORD MEANING WELL OR SPRING

Park Lodge Campsite

BARN

KELD

EAST STONESDALE FARM

METAL GATE

THE SIGNPOSTING IN AND OUT OF KELD IS GOOD. SOMEONE DESERVES AN AWARD

Butt House

FALLS

To Park House Campsite 400m

Keld Youth Hostel

CLIFFS

River Swale

SCREE

LONE PINE

CAIRN

Greenlands 900M FROM KELD

PATH NARROW AND ROCKY

CRAGS

SPRUNG GATE

SCREE

★ TRAILBLAZER

Kisdon Hill

0   ¼ mile

0   APPROX SCALE   500 metres

2 HRS – 2 HRS 30 MINS TO TAN HILL (MAP 64)

1 HRS 45 MINS – 2 HRS 15 MINS FROM THWAITE (MAP 61)

2 HRS – 2 HRS 30 MINS FROM TAN HILL (MAP 64)

KELD

1 HR 30 MINS – 2 HRS TO THWAITE (MAP 61)

KELD TO TAN HILL   MAPS 62-64

It is **4 miles (6km, 2-2¹/₂hrs)** across Stonesdale Moor to Tan Hill but for those who overnighted in Keld they'll be passing the door of the famous Inn (see below) between 10am and 11am and may not be ready for a break.

The moor has a well-defined track across it, marked by the passage of countless feet, but is very prone to bogginess and the chances are you'll get wet feet and will arrive at the Inn thoroughly hot and bothered. The next section along the Frumming Beck is no better and may even earn the epithet of the worst yet. It might be wise to pause at the highest pub in England before squelching onward.

TAN HILL   [Map 64]

Tan Hill Inn (☎ 01833-628246, 🖳 www .tanhillinn.co.uk, 5T/2D) charges a steep £32 per head for singles and £25 for en suite doubles. You can camp for £1 but there are no facilities except for a tap and an outside loo.

Tan Hill Inn stands completely on its own amid rolling moorland, and you are as likely to see signs of life from the deck of a boat in the middle of the Atlantic as you are from the doorstep of this pub. Inside is a different matter. There have been stories told of things getting quite animated late at night so turning in early might not be such a good idea.

Food is available daily between 12 noon and 2.30pm and in the evening between 7pm and 9pm. These times may vary a little, though. As the landlord said: 'If the menu's up you can have food. If it isn't, you can't'!

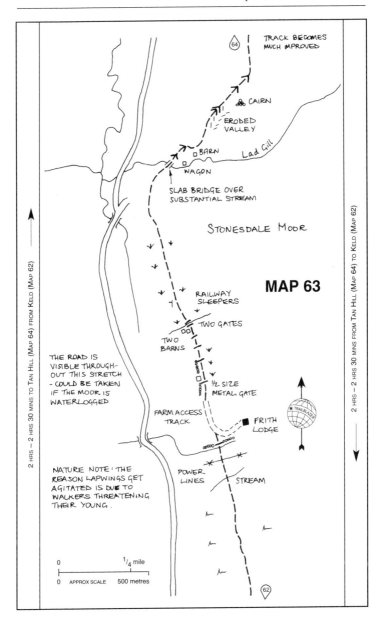

64

TRACK BECOMES
MUCH IMPROVED

CAIRN

ERODED
VALLEY

Lad Gill

BARN

WAGON

SLAB BRIDGE OVER
SUBSTANTIAL STREAM

STONESDALE MOOR

RAILWAY
SLEEPERS

MAP 63

TWO GATES

TWO
BARNS

½ SIZE
METAL GATE

FARM ACCESS
TRACK

FRITH
LODGE

★ TRAILBLAZER

THE ROAD IS
VISIBLE THROUGH-
OUT THIS STRETCH
- COULD BE TAKEN
IF THE MOOR IS
WATERLOGGED

NATURE NOTE! THE
REASON LAPWINGS GET
AGITATED IS DUE TO
WALKERS THREATENING
THEIR YOUNG.

POWER
LINES

STREAM

0   ¼ mile

0   APPROX SCALE   500 metres

62

2 HRS – 2 HRS 30 MINS TO TAN HILL (MAP 64) FROM KELD (MAP 62)

2 HRS – 2 HRS 30 MINS FROM TAN HILL (MAP 64) TO KELD (MAP 62)

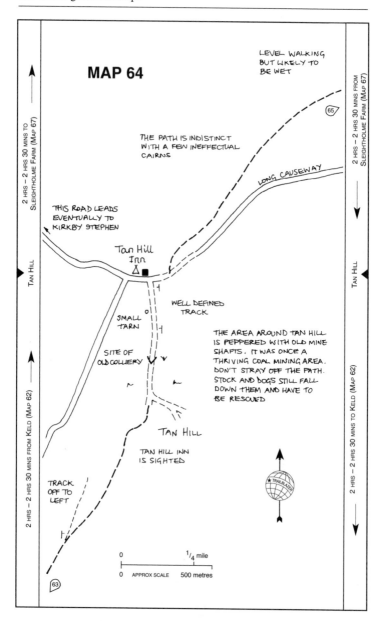

MAP 64

LEVEL WALKING BUT LIKELY TO BE WET

THE PATH IS INDISTINCT WITH A FEW INEFFECTUAL CAIRNS

LONG CAUSEWAY

2 HRS – 2 HRS 30 MINS TO SLEIGHTHOLME FARM (MAP 67)

2 HRS – 2 HRS 30 MINS FROM SLEIGHTHOLME FARM (MAP 67)

THIS ROAD LEADS EVENTUALLY TO KIRKBY STEPHEN

Tan Hill Inn

TAN HILL

TAN HILL

WELL DEFINED TRACK

SMALL TARN

SITE OF OLD COLLIERY

THE AREA AROUND TAN HILL IS PEPPERED WITH OLD MINE SHAFTS. IT WAS ONCE A THRIVING COAL MINING AREA. DON'T STRAY OFF THE PATH. STOCK AND DOGS STILL FALL DOWN THEM AND HAVE TO BE RESCUED

TAN HILL

TAN HILL INN IS SIGHTED

2 HRS – 2 HRS 30 MINS FROM KELD (MAP 62)

2 HRS – 2 HRS 30 MINS TO KELD (MAP 62)

TRACK OFF TO LEFT

TRAILBLAZER

0   1/4 mile

0   APPROX SCALE   500 metres

TAN HILL TO BALDERSDALE   MAPS 64-69

This **10-mile (16km, 4³/₄-6¹/₄hrs)** stretch tends to get lumped in to a longer day's walk by those for whom the Pennine Way is a succession of route marches, hence Keld to Middleton-in-Teesdale, a mere 21 miles (34km), would not be unusual. All I can say is, resist the temptation. Head for the hostel at Baldersdale or better still for the camping barn at Clove Lodge.

Some walkers divert off the trail and wander into Bowes, which used to be an alternative route but is no longer considered as such. There's nothing of note in **Bowes** apart from the castle ruins, the pub (the Ancient Unicorn, see below) and the finicky meandering route into and out of the place is enough to try the patience of a saint.

Leaving Tan Hill to rowdies and revellers, their singing ringing in your ears, the trail launches out across a marshy waste keeping along the north side of the Frumming Beck until a moorland road is reached. You can now walk on terra firma again via the near-deserted Sleightholme Farm to cross the River Greta at **God's Bridge**, a natural limestone shelf not unlike Kinder Downfall.

Shortly after you have to cross the A66 via a tunnel, as litter-strewn and smelly as any inner-city underpass. The roar of the traffic reminds you of the crossing of the M62 back in the far distant past, before you'd earned your Pennine Way spurs. It's worse here because you will have forgotten how noisy fast-moving traffic can be. It takes till **Ravock Castle** on top of Bowes Moor before you finally leave the sound of it behind. Ravock Castle is, unfortunately not much of a castle, merely a collapsed pile of stones.

The reservoirs at **Blackton** are not far ahead and the descent into **Baldersdale** marks another milestone reached, indeed it is the **halfway mark** on the trail.

BOWES   [Map 67a]

For those who wish to follow the so-called **Bowes Variant** or **Loop** it is detailed on Maps 67a-c. However, I don't recommend it. It is hard to follow, further to walk and there's no valid reason for doing it other than the fact that it was created by Alfred Wainwright in his *Pennine Way Companion*. There have, though, been some major changes to the landscape since his guide was published.

That said, the *Ancient Unicorn* (☎ 01833-628321, 🖥 www.ancient-unicorn .co.uk, 4T/4D/1F en suite) is a friendly pub with open fires and a good choice of bar meals. B&B costs £25 and there's a six-bed room for walkers at £15 each for B&B.

Campers can pitch at *Westend Farm* (☎ 01833-628239) for £2 each including the use of the showers and toilets. A stroll to the pub could include a look at the church-yard where Dickens found inspiration for the character of Smike in *Nicholas Nickleby*. Headstones tell the stark truth about infant mortality during the 1800s. The **castle** ruins are nearby.

Across the A66 is *Clint House Farm* (☎ 01833-628214, 1T/2D/2F), with B&B from £18 and camping for £2 per person. There are no facilities other than in house.

The **post office** (early closing Wed) is along the main street. The **village shop and newsagents** is open 7.30am-12.30pm, 2-5.30pm Mon-Fri except Wed afternoon when Bowes hibernates, but it opens Sat and Sun 8am-12pm.

There are a few **buses** to Kirkby Stephen where there's a train station, to Barnard Castle for connections on to the train station at Darlington, and to Middleton-in-Teesdale (see public transport map, pp36-9).

BALDERSDALE [Map 69]

Baldersdale Youth Hostel (☎ 01833-650629, bookings ☎ 0870-770 5684, ⌨ baldersdale@yha.org.uk, open Apr-Oct but book 48hrs in advance in Apr-June and Sep-Oct) is one of the more remote hostels on the trail as anyone who has tried to reach it by car will testify. You can **camp** here if you wish, using the showers inside and the evening meal served at 7pm is inventive and delicious. The area is likely to be beset by midges on a humid summer evening but the setting is superb. Adults are charged £10.60, under 18s £7.20.

Better though is the **camping barn** at *Clove Lodge* (☎ 01833-650030, ⌨ www.thepennineway.co.uk/clovelodge)

which sleeps at least eight, is one of the best on the trail and costs £6 which includes a hot shower, or £11 B&B. Dinner and breakfast are also available (£22) and can be brought to you in the barn where you can spread out your gear, dry your socks, fill the pot-bellied stove with wood and toast your toes to your heart's content. They'll rent you a sleeping bag too if you haven't got one. They also have a four-bed cottage (1D/1T), **B&B** there costs £22. Phil and Ann Heys are walkers themselves and know what walkers want. You will find it at Clove Lodge. For those who like browsing through visitors' books, theirs is full of gems.

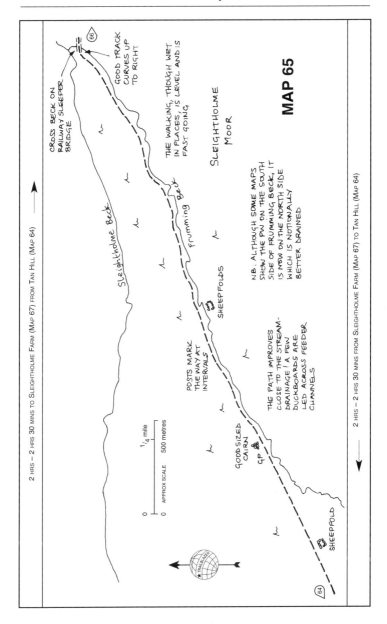

2 HRS – 2 HRS 30 MINS TO SLEIGHTHOLME FARM (MAP 67) FROM TAN HILL (MAP 64) →

← 2 HRS – 2 HRS 30 MINS FROM SLEIGHTHOLME FARM (MAP 67) TO TAN HILL (MAP 64)

MAP 65

SLEIGHTHOLME MOOR

CROSS BECK ON RAILWAY SLEEPER BRIDGE

GOOD TRACK CURVES UP TO RIGHT

THE WALKING, THOUGH WET IN PLACES, IS LEVEL AND IS FAST GOING.

Frumming Beck

Sleightholme Beck

N.B. ALTHOUGH SOME MAPS SHOW THE PW ON THE SOUTH SIDE OF FRUMMING BECK, IT IS NOW ON THE NORTH SIDE WHICH IS NOTIONALLY BETTER DRAINED

SHEEPFOLDS

POSTS MARK THE WAY AT INTERVALS

THE PATH IMPROVES CLOSE TO THE STREAM - DRAINAGE / A FEW DUCKBOARDS ARE LED ACROSS FEEDER CHANNELS

GOOD SIZED CAIRN

GP

SHEEPFOLD

1/4 mile

APPROX SCALE   500 metres

0

0

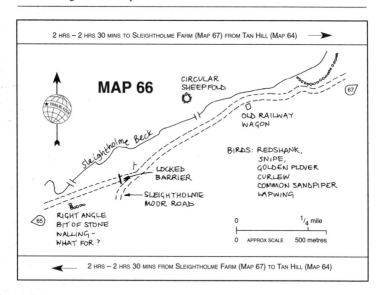

2 HRS – 2 HRS 30 MINS TO SLEIGHTHOLME FARM (MAP 67) FROM TAN HILL (MAP 64) ——→

MAP 66

★ TRAILBLAZER

CIRCULAR SHEEPFOLD

Sleightholme Beck

67

OLD RAILWAY WAGON

BIRDS: REDSHANK,
SNIPE,
GOLDEN PLOVER
CURLEW
COMMON SANDPIPER
LAPWING

LOCKED BARRIER

SLEIGHTHOLME MOOR ROAD

65

RIGHT ANGLE BIT OF STONE WALLING – WHAT FOR?

0   ¼ mile

0   APPROX SCALE   500 metres

←— 2 HRS – 2 HRS 30 MINS FROM SLEIGHTHOLME FARM (MAP 67) TO TAN HILL (MAP 64)

❑ Hannah Hauxwell   [See Map 69]

Right on the edge of Blackton Reservoir and beside the Pennine Way stands the farm of Low Birk Hat, home for many years to a remarkable lady. Hannah Hauxwell came to the notice of the public through a number of television programmes and books telling the story of the life of someone living at subsistence level in Baldersdale as recently as the 1970s. With a cow which had one calf a year, she allowed herself £250 a year for living expenses, without electricity or gas, surviving the harsh winters and keeping warm by the simple expedient of putting on another coat.

Miss Hauxwell became famous for her simplicity and courage and her natural understanding of the world and its follies. She travelled widely and the cameras recorded her impressions of cities around the world where her curiosity and common-sense enabled her to put her finger on the unusual and get pleasure from the com-monplace events of other people's lives.

Now retired and living in more comfort in Cotherstone, Hannah will be long remembered by those who followed her adventures. Her farm where at one time her father alone supported a family of seven, both sets of grandparents, himself, his wife and daughter by the sweat of his own brow, has been gentrified and a glimpse over the wall is like looking at a restored vintage car, cleaned up, pasteurized and merely an echo of the past and not the real thing.

Opposite Top: Pen-y-Ghent, near Horton-in-Ribblesdale (see p134). **Bottom**: Looking back to Horton from Harber Scar Lane.

Overleaf Top: Alston (see p195). **Bottom**: Langdon Beck Youth Hostel (see p179).

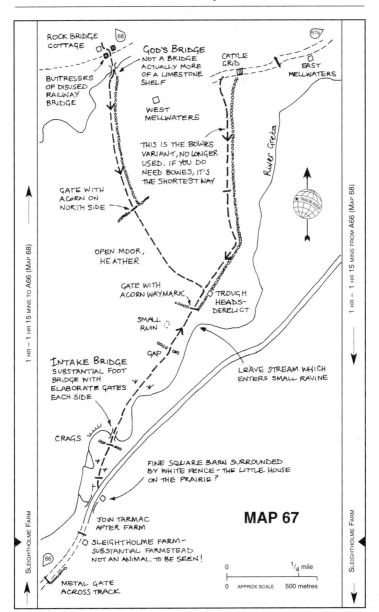

ROCK BRIDGE COTTAGE

68

GOD'S BRIDGE
NOT A BRIDGE
ACTUALLY MORE
OF A LIMESTONE
SHELF

CATTLE
GRID

67a

EAST
MELLWATERS

BUTTRESSES
OF DISUSED
RAILWAY
BRIDGE

WEST
MELLWATERS

River Greta

THIS IS THE BOWES
VARIANT, NO LONGER
USED. IF YOU DO
NEED BOWES, IT'S
THE SHORTEST WAY

GATE WITH
ACORN ON
NORTH SIDE

★ TRAILBLAZER

OPEN MOOR,
HEATHER

GATE WITH
ACORN WAYMARK

TROUGH
HEADS-
DERELICT

SMALL
RUIN

GAP

INTAKE BRIDGE
SUBSTANTIAL FOOT
BRIDGE WITH
ELABORATE GATES
EACH SIDE

LEAVE STREAM WHICH
ENTERS SMALL RAVINE

CRAGS

FINE SQUARE BARN SURROUNDED
BY WHITE FENCE - THE LITTLE HOUSE
ON THE PRAIRIE?

MAP 67

JOIN TARMAC
AFTER FARM

SLEIGHTHOLME FARM-
SUBSTANTIAL FARMSTEAD
NOT AN ANIMAL TO BE SEEN!

66

METAL GATE
ACROSS TRACK

0   1/4 mile

0   APPROX SCALE   500 metres

1 HR – 1 HR 15 MINS TO A66 (MAP 68)

1 HR – 1 HR 15 MINS FROM A66 (MAP 68)

SLEIGHTHOLME FARM

SLEIGHTHOLME FARM

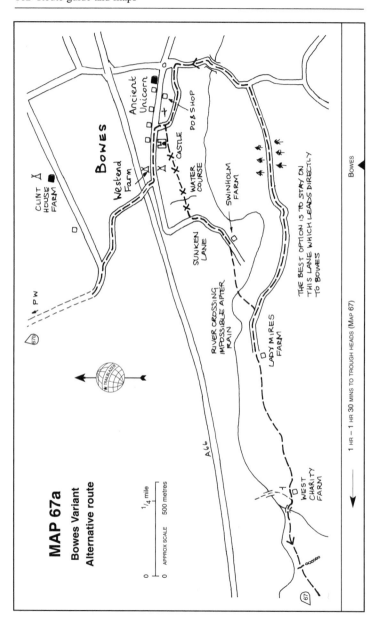

MAP 67a

Bowes Variant
Alternative route

1/4 mile

0   APPROX SCALE
0   500 metres

BOWES

CLINT
HOUSE
FARM

Westend
Farm

Ancient
Unicorn

PO & SHOP

CASTLE

WATER
COURSE

SWINHOLM
FARM

SUNKEN
LANE

PW

RIVER CROSSING
IMPOSSIBLE AFTER
RAIN

LADY MIRES
FARM

WEST
CHARITY
FARM

A66

THE BEST OPTION IS TO STAY ON
THIS LANE WHICH LEADS DIRECTLY
TO BOWES

BOWES

1 HR – 1 HR 30 MINS TO TROUGH HEADS (MAP 67)

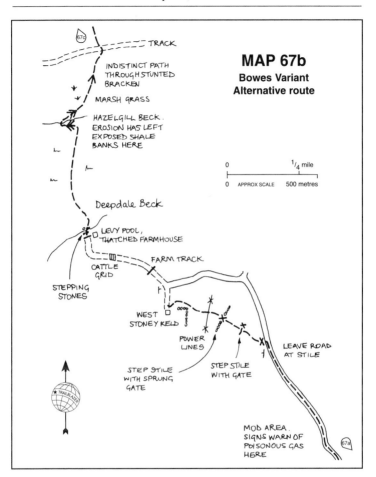

MAP 67b
Bowes Variant
Alternative route

67c

TRACK

INDISTINCT PATH
THROUGH STUNTED
BRACKEN

MARSH GRASS

HAZELGILL BECK.
EROSION HAS LEFT
EXPOSED SHALE
BANKS HERE

0   1/4 mile

0   APPROX SCALE   500 metres

Deepdale Beck

LEVY POOL,
THATCHED FARMHOUSE

CATTLE
GRID

FARM TRACK

STEPPING
STONES

WEST
STONEY KELD

POWER
LINES

LEAVE ROAD
AT STILE

STEP STILE
WITH SPRUNG
GATE

STEP STILE
WITH GATE

★ TRAILBLAZER

MOD AREA.
SIGNS WARN OF
POISONOUS GAS
HERE

67a

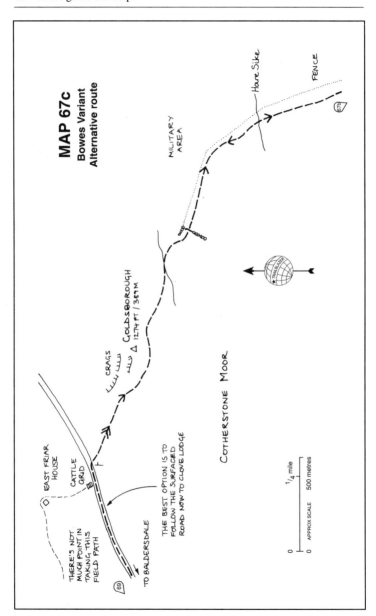

MAP 67c
Bowes Variant
Alternative route

Hare Sike

FENCE

67d

MILITARY AREA

TRAILBLAZER

COLDSBOROUGH
△ 1274 FT / 365M

CRAGS

EAST FRIAR HOUSE

CATTLE GRID

THERE'S NOT MUCH POINT IN TAKING THIS FIELD PATH

THE BEST OPTION IS TO FOLLOW THE SURFACED ROAD NOW TO CLOVE LODGE

COTHERSTONE MOOR

TO BALDERSDALE

69

¼ mile

0   500 metres
0   APPROX SCALE

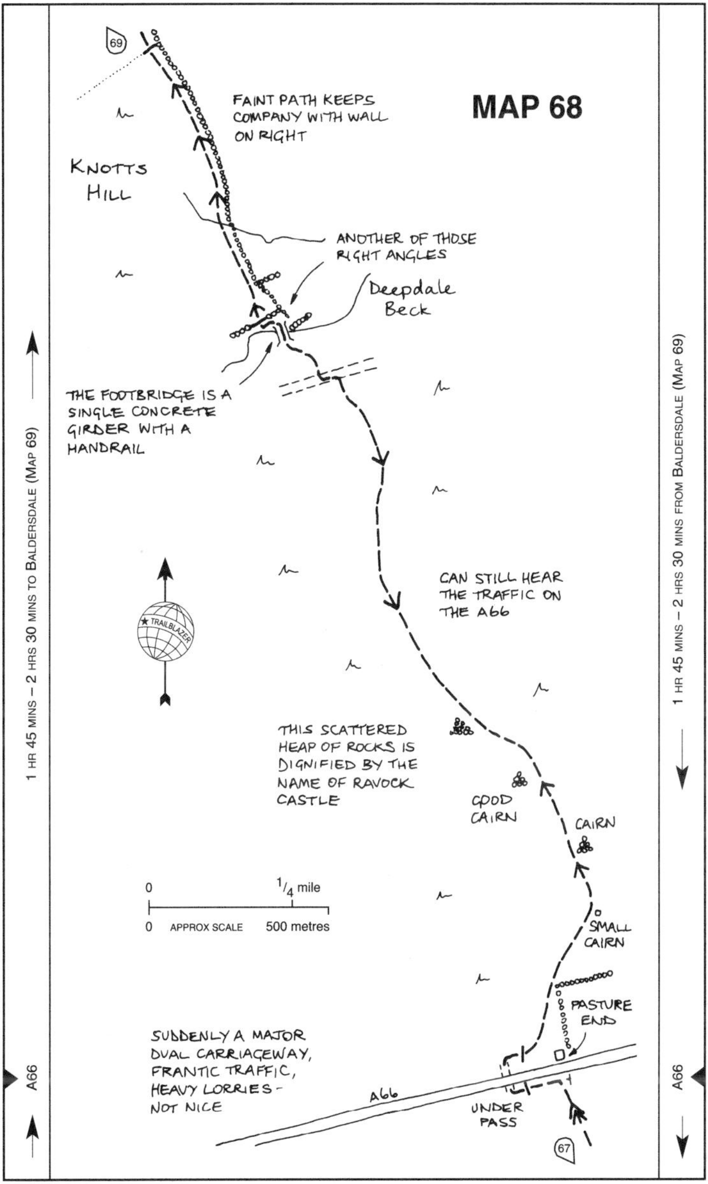

MAP 68

(69)

FAINT PATH KEEPS
COMPANY WITH WALL
ON RIGHT

KNOTTS
HILL

ANOTHER OF THOSE
RIGHT ANGLES

Deepdale
Beck

THE FOOTBRIDGE IS A
SINGLE CONCRETE
GIRDER WITH A
HANDRAIL

★ TRAILBLAZER

CAN STILL HEAR
THE TRAFFIC ON
THE A66

THIS SCATTERED
HEAP OF ROCKS IS
DIGNIFIED BY THE
NAME OF RAVOCK
CASTLE

GOOD
CAIRN

CAIRN

0   1/4 mile

0   APPROX SCALE   500 metres

SMALL
CAIRN

PASTURE
END

SUDDENLY A MAJOR
DUAL CARRIAGEWAY,
FRANTIC TRAFFIC,
HEAVY LORRIES -
NOT NICE

A66

UNDER
PASS

(67)

1 HR 45 MINS – 2 HRS 30 MINS TO BALDERSDALE (MAP 69)

1 HR 45 MINS – 2 HRS 30 MINS FROM BALDERSDALE (MAP 69)

A66

A66

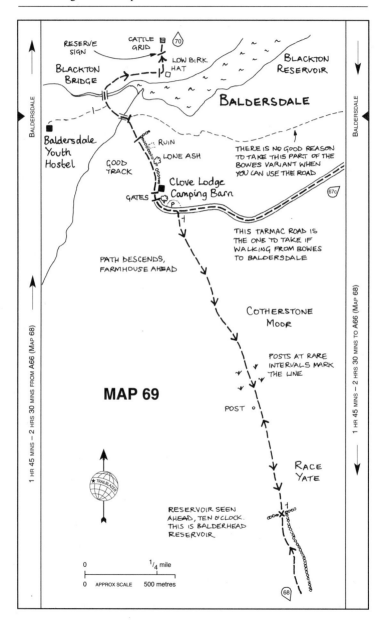

BALDERSDALE

BALDERSDALE

RESERVE SIGN

CATTLE GRID

70

LOW BIRK HAT

BLACKTON BRIDGE

BLACKTON RESERVOIR

BALDERSDALE

Baldersdale Youth Hostel

RUIN

LONE ASH

GOOD TRACK

Clove Lodge Camping Barn

GATES

THERE IS NO GOOD REASON TO TAKE THIS PART OF THE BOWES VARIANT WHEN YOU CAN USE THE ROAD

67c

THIS TARMAC ROAD IS THE ONE TO TAKE IF WALKING FROM BOWES TO BALDERSDALE

PATH DESCENDS, FARMHOUSE AHEAD

COTHERSTONE MOOR

POSTS AT RARE INTERVALS MARK THE LINE

POST

MAP 69

1 HR 45 MINS – 2 HRS 30 MINS FROM A66 (MAP 68)

1 HR 45 MINS – 2 HRS 30 MINS TO A66 (MAP 68)

★ TRAILBLAZER

RACE YATE

RESERVOIR SEEN AHEAD, TEN O'CLOCK. THIS IS BALDERHEAD RESERVOIR

0   1/4 mile

0   APPROX SCALE   500 metres

68

BALDERSDALE TO LANGDON BECK   MAPS 69-77

This **15-mile (24km, 6-8hrs)** section includes one minor gem, Middleton-in-Teesdale, and one major one, the riverside walk along the Tees including the spectacular effects of the river as it cascades over the dolerite rocks to create the impressive waterfalls of Low Force and the mighty High Force, one of the Seven Wonders of the Pennine Way.

You climb out of Baldersdale and down again to **Lunedale**, almost a copy of its neighbouring dale and home to yet another reservoir, Grassholme, and the usual dense plantation of conifers. More climbing follows to gain the high ground of **Harter Fell** and conquer another swathe of boggy moorland with which walkers who have got this far will be all too familiar. There will be more of the same in the days ahead. Wet weather can be the ruin of this kind of terrain since it holds water on or just below the surface to the detriment of the conditions underfoot.

Once the valley of the Tees is reached via the pleasant, purposeful town of **Middleton-in-Teesdale**, everything changes for the better. Ahead lie the sylvan banks of Teesdale, possibly the best walking along the entire Way. You take to the meadow-fringed footpath along the river where even those interested only in covering distance cannot fail to take notice of the surroundings. The best time is June or early July when the meadows are at their finest, a carpet of grasses and wild flowers that make the miles to Langdon Beck a genuine pleasure.

Beyond **High Force** the path becomes more eroded in places and at times there are some tricky scrambles where tumbled boulders require some care. The day ends at the scattered and lonely communities of **Forest-in-Teesdale** and **Langdon Beck**.

❏ **High Force**   **[See Map 75]**

High Force is so big it has to claim some distinction over others. The highest? The biggest? These seem to belong elsewhere so what they say is it's the highest unbroken fall of water in England. The drop is 21 metres (70ft). It's certainly impressive, especially after rain, which is always, when the water appears the colour of tea, tinged with the peat from the moors.

WA Poucher, the celebrated photographer and writer of a series of guides during the 1960s and '70s, said that it is a difficult subject to photograph well, facing north-east, hence having the wrong light conditions for effective photography. Its other problem, at least from the Pennine Way side of the river, is access for a good view. There are places where you can scramble through the undergrowth and cling on to the cliff edge but few where you can wield the camera effectively.

People have done some strange things here. Some have gone off the top, ending their days in the tumultuous water. Two canoeists were stopped at the last minute from attempting to canoe off the top and a visitor from abroad slipped on the flat shelf at the lip and though saving himself, catapulted the infant on his back over the edge.

There is an odd fascination about raging water which seems to compel people to get too close. For me there is something slightly discomforting about it, its power greater than mere mortals can cope with.

LUNEDALE [Map 71]

Among the scattered homesteads of Lunedale lie several places that may be of use to walkers. *Wemmergill Hall Farm* (☎ 01833-640379, 💻 www.wemmergill-farm .co.uk, 1D en suite/1F), 1¹/₂ miles to the west of the trail along the B6276, has outstanding views over Selset Reservoir and also charges £20 (£25 single); evening meal by arrangement £12.

Grassholme Farm (☎ 01833-640494), just by the reservoir of the same name, offers hot and cold snacks and teas. They are generally open Thur-Sun 10.30am-4.30pm but it is worth checking in advance especially if you are a group.

MIDDLETON-IN-TEESDALE

On the banks of the River Tees, this is a large attractive village that thrived during the 19th century when the now defunct lead-mining industry was in its heyday. It's mostly laid out along one street, with handsome architecture interspersed with a few quirky buildings. It has a friendly, open atmosphere and most people will go out of their way to help you.

You will find most things you want, and if your feet are getting tired the relaxing atmosphere may mean you find an excuse to stay for more than one night.

Services

The nearest **train** station is in Darlington, 25 miles (40km) away. To get there take a **bus** (see public transport map, pp36-9) to Barnard Castle and change there. Alternatively go by **taxi**: try Middleton-based Alston Rd Garage (☎ 01833-640213).

The **tourist information centre** (☎ 01833-641001, 💻 middletonplus@com puserve.com), 10 Market Place, is open daily from 10am to 1pm and 2 to 4.30pm.

For groceries try either the Co-op **supermarket** (daily 8am-10pm), which also has a range of foot-care products for those with sore feet, or R&L Armitage **off-licence and general store**.

There is also a **pharmacy**, a **post office** and Winter's **gear shop**, which stocks most camping fuels as well as boots and general walking kit. The Barclays **bank** here does not have a cash machine. Early closing for the town is on Wednesday.

Where to stay

The most convenient campsite is *Daleview Caravan Park and Camp Site* (☎ 01833-640233, 💻 daleview@caravanpark.onyxn er.co.uk, Mar-Oct) which you pass on your way in to town. They charge £4 per person and there's a very basic shop and a bar which also does food.

Bunkhouse accommodation is available at the friendly *Kingsway Adventure Centre* (☎ 01833-640881, 💻 www.kings waycentre.co.uk) for £10 bed only, or £20 full board. They also have 2S/2T for £13 B&B; camping £3. *Hudeway Outdoor Centre* (☎ 01833-640012) also has bunkhouse accommodation for £14.50 and £18 B&B. Both Hudeway and Kingsway tend to be block-booked by schools in June and July.

Grove Lodge (☎ 01833-640798, 2T/ 1F) is an old shooting lodge in a luxury location just outside the town. They are used to walkers and en suite B&B costs £26.50. If necessary, extra accommodation is available in a cottage curiously built under the front of the house. They have a washing machine, drying room and can provide full board or just a packed lunch.

Brunswick House (☎ 01833-640393, 💻 www.brunswickhouse.net, 2T/3D) is more central and their en suite rooms cost £25. They also do an evening meal (£17.50) and have a bar.

Next door is *Belvedere House* (☎ 01833-640884, 💻 www.thecoachhouse.net, 1T/ 2D) where an en suite room costs £19.

Nearby at 52-53 Market Place, *Norman Richardson House* (☎ 01833-640467, 💻 www.nrhouse.com) is a group accommodation centre currently with 4S/4T en suite from £18 per person; £30 with evening meal. It incorporates The King's Head pub.

16 Market Place (☎ 01833-640300, 2D) costs £44 per room (no single occupancy) en suite. The *Teesdale Hotel* (☎ 01833-640264, 2S/5D/3T) has pink décor and a drying room. An en suite room costs £32.50 per person or you may be able to get one of their cottages on a B&B basis.

You could also try *Ivy House* (☎ 01833-640603, 1F en suite/1D, £18) or *Snaisgill Farm* (☎ 01833-640343, 2D, from £18.50) both of which are over a mile north of the town. (off Map 72).

Where to eat
The Teesdale Hotel (see above) does pub grub for £5 upwards and has quite a wide vegetarian menu. Closest to the Way, *The Bridge Inn* is open for food 12-2.30pm and 6-9pm. Almost next door is *Sue's Café* where you can get an all-day breakfast for £4 or filling basics such as pie, chips, peas and gravy (£3.90).

For a pie or baked potato go to the *Country Style Bakery*. The *fish and chip shop* (☎ 01833-640404) has to be one of the cleanest in Britain.

HOLWICK   [Map 74]
Beyond Middleton there's the appealing little oasis of *Low Way Farm* (☎ 01833-640506) which offers basic **camping** for £2.50; ample **bunkhouse** accommodation in two barns for £6; and breakfast (£4.75) at the adjacent café, the *Farmhouse Kitchen*. There is a sign from the trail and the barns are only 200 yards off route.

Just over half a mile from the Way is *The Strathmore Arms* (☎ 01833-640362, ⌨ hojo@supanet.com, 2D/1T en suite) a pub with rooms from £23 B&B. Campers can use the nearby field for £2 with the use of the pub's toilet.

HIGH FORCE   [Map 75]
High Force Hotel (☎ 01833-622222, ⌨ www.highforcehotel.com, 2S/1T/3D, all en suite) is a popular and happening pub if you

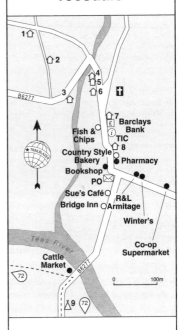

Middleton-in-Teesdale

Where to stay
1 Hudeway Outdoor Centre
2 Grove Lodge
3 Kingsway Adventure Centre
4 Brunswick House
5 Belvedere House
6 Norman Richardson House
7 Teesdale Hotel
8 16 Market Place
9 Daleview Caravan Park

catch it on a good day. On a wet Monday evening it didn't seem quite so appealing. B&B costs £30 a head.

FOREST-IN-TEESDALE AND
LANGDON BECK   [Map 77]

On reaching Cronkley Bridge the nearest place with accommodation is Forest-in-Teesdale, a scattered collection of houses along the main B6277 road which, to the casual visitor, seems a rather deserted spot. *The Dale* (☎ 01833-622303, 1D or T/1F) is one of those stalwarts among Pennine Way B&Bs. Mrs Bonner has catered for walkers for many years and knows how to please them with massive helpings of good food, comfortable beds and a coal fire to sit by. Mr Bonner used to be the security guard at the High Force waterfall and has some tales to tell. B&B costs £16 and an evening meal £9 but they will take you to the pub if you prefer. They will also do a packed lunch for £3.50; all in all outstanding value for money. You find them by first locating the school then turning right at the top of the lane.

Langdon Beck Youth Hostel (☎ 01833-622228, bookings ☎ 0870-770 5910, ☐ langdonbeck@yha.org.uk, open mid-Feb to Nov, but book 48hrs in advance mid-Feb to June and Sep-Nov) will be the chosen destination for many walkers, but note that it can get booked up with school parties in the summer months; walkers who booked weeks ahead will congratulate themselves on their forethought. Adults are charged £10.60, under 18s £7.20, and evening meals are available at 7pm.

There's an occasional **bus** from Langdon Beck to Middleton-in-Teesdale (see public transport map, pp36-9).

You can **camp** beside the river at *Sayer Hill Farm* (☎/▨ 01833-622203, 2S/1D/1F) for £2 but there is only a cold-water tap and a WC in an outhouse up at the farm. B&B costs £15 and is also fairly basic but is adequate for one night.

Half a mile north of the youth hostel is *Langdon Beck Hotel/Inn* (☎ 01833-622267, ▨ www.langdonbeckhotel.com, 1S/2D/3T). Some of the rooms are en suite, there's B&B from £19.50/25 std/en suite. The pub is open evenings only but not on Monday or Wednesday. There's food (eg steak and kidney pudding, £6.25) from 7pm, Thursday to Sunday.

❏ Hannah's Meadow   [See Map 70]

Part of the legacy of Hannah Hauxwell (see p160) has been the preservation of her farm land which has been given the status of a study area for meadow grasses and wild flowers.

Purchased by Durham Wildlife Trust in 1988, the site was later designated a Site of Special Scientific Interest qualifying by having 23 of the 47 species of rare and characteristic plants listed by English Nature. The meadows were never ploughed, being cut for hay in August and thereafter grazed by cows resulting in herb-rich meadows. Numerous kinds of birds are visitors to the meadows and no fewer than 16 kinds of dung-beetle have been identified.

One can only hope that they don't start selling Hannah Hauxwell memorabilia, creating out of an ordinary countrywoman an icon to be revered.

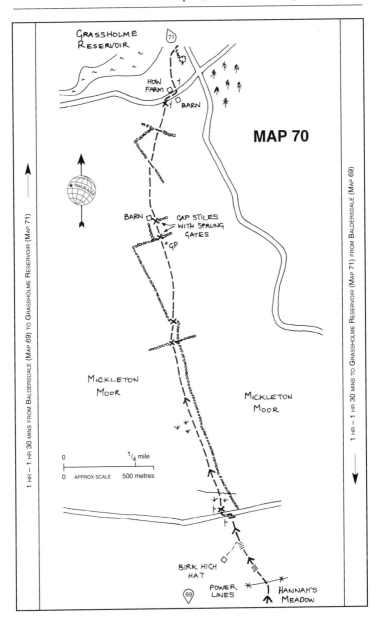

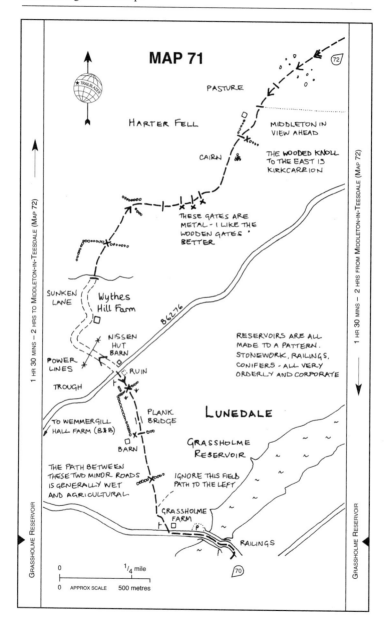

MAP 71

PASTURE

72

HARTER FELL

MIDDLETON IN
VIEW AHEAD

THE WOODED KNOLL
TO THE EAST IS
KIRKCARRION

CAIRN

THESE GATES ARE
METAL - I LIKE THE
WOODEN GATES
BETTER

SUNKEN
LANE

Wythes
Hill Farm

B 6276

NISSEN
HUT
BARN

POWER
LINES

RUIN

TROUGH

RESERVOIRS ARE ALL
MADE TO A PATTERN.
STONEWORK, RAILINGS,
CONIFERS - ALL VERY
ORDERLY AND CORPORATE

TO WEMMERGILL
HALL FARM (B&B)

PLANK
BRIDGE

LUNEDALE

BARN

GRASSHOLME
RESERVOIR

THE PATH BETWEEN
THESE TWO MINOR ROADS
IS GENERALLY WET
AND AGRICULTURAL

IGNORE THIS FIELD
PATH TO THE LEFT

GRASSHOLME
FARM

P

RAILINGS

70

0   1/4 mile

0   APPROX SCALE   500 metres

1 HR 30 MINS – 2 HRS TO MIDDLETON-IN-TEESDALE (MAP 72)

1 HR 30 MINS – 2 HRS FROM MIDDLETON-IN-TEESDALE (MAP 72)

GRASSHOLME RESERVOIR

GRASSHOLME RESERVOIR

MIDDLETON-IN-TEESDALE

TO SNAISGILL FARM & IVY HOUSE B&Bs

SUE'S CAFÉ

CATTLE MARKET

BRIDGE INN

River Tees

SEE MIDDLETON-IN-TEESDALE MAP   SEE P169

73

POWER LINES

B6277

Daleview Campsite

THE PW DOES NOT GO INTO MIDDLETON ITSELF BUT DEPARTS LEFT BEFORE THE BRIDGE

GPo

MAP 72

GREEN ROAD DESCENDS ON SPRINGY TURF TO GATE

71

0   1/4 mile

0   APPROX SCALE   500 metres

★ TRAILBLAZER

MIDDLETON-IN-TEESDALE

MIDDLETON-IN-TEESDALE

1 HR 30 MINS – 2 HRS FROM GRASSHOLME RESERVOIR (MAP 71)

1 HR 30 MINS – 2 HRS TO GRASSHOLME RESERVOIR (MAP 71)

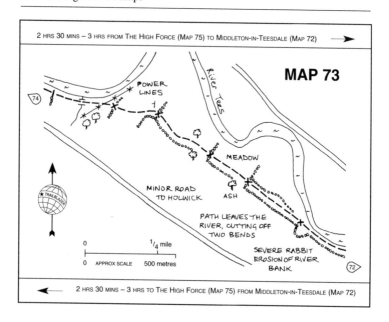

2 HRS 30 MINS – 3 HRS FROM THE HIGH FORCE (MAP 75) TO MIDDLETON-IN-TEESDALE (MAP 72) ⟶

MAP 73

POWER LINES

River Tees

74

MEADOW

MINOR ROAD TO HOLWICK

ASH

PATH LEAVES THE RIVER, CUTTING OFF TWO BENDS

★ TRAILBLAZER

0   ¼ mile

0   APPROX SCALE   500 metres

SEVERE RABBIT EROSION OF RIVER BANK

72

⟵ 2 HRS 30 MINS – 3 HRS TO THE HIGH FORCE (MAP 75) FROM MIDDLETON-IN-TEESDALE (MAP 72)

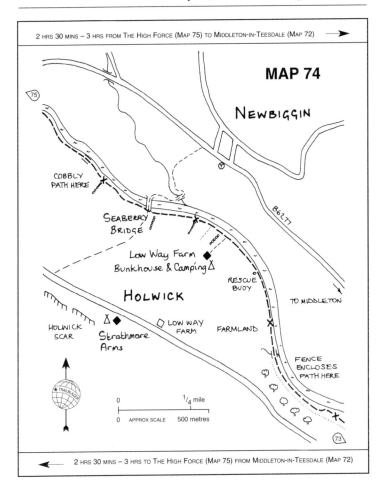

2 HRS 30 MINS – 3 HRS FROM THE HIGH FORCE (MAP 75) TO MIDDLETON-IN-TEESDALE (MAP 72) →

75

MAP 74

NEWBIGGIN

COBBLY PATH HERE

SEABERRY BRIDGE

Low Way Farm ◆
Bunkhouse & Camping △

HOLWICK

RESCUE BUOY

B6277

TO MIDDLETON

HOLWICK SCAR

△◆ Strathmore Arms

□ LOW WAY FARM

FARMLAND

FENCE ENCLOSES PATH HERE

★ TRAILBLAZER

0   ¼ mile
0   APPROX SCALE   500 metres

73

← 2 HRS 30 MINS – 3 HRS TO THE HIGH FORCE (MAP 75) FROM MIDDLETON-IN-TEESDALE (MAP 72)

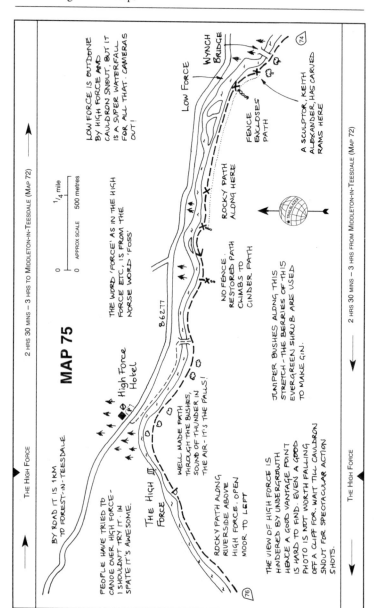

The High Force

2 HRS 30 MINS – 3 HRS TO MIDDLETON-IN-TEESDALE (MAP 72)

MAP 75

LOW FORCE IS OUTDONE BY HIGH FORCE AND CAULDRON SNOUT, BUT IT IS A SUPER WATERFALL FOR ALL THAT. CAMERAS OUT!

WYNCH BRIDGE

LOW FORCE

FENCE ENCLOSES PATH

A SCULPTOR, KEITH ALEXANDER, HAS CARVED RAMS HERE

ROCKY PATH ALONG HERE

NO FENCE RESTORED PATH CLIMBS TO CINDER PATH

THE WORD 'FORCE' AS IN THE HIGH FORCE ETC, IS FROM THE NORSE WORD 'FOSS'

0   1/4 mile
0 APPROX SCALE 500 metres

B6277

High Force Hotel

PEOPLE HAVE TRIED TO CANOE OVER HIGH FORCE - I SHOULDN'T TRY IT - IN SPATE IT'S AWESOME.

BY ROAD IT IS 1 KM TO FOREST-IN-TEESDALE.

The High Force

WELL MADE PATH THROUGH THE BUSHES, SOUND OF THUNDER IN THE AIR - IT'S THE FALLS!

JUNIPER BUSHES ALONG THIS STRETCH - THE BERRIES OF THIS EVERGREEN SHRUB ARE USED TO MAKE GIN.

ROCKY PATH ALONG RIVERSIDE ABOVE HIGH FORCE. OPEN MOOR TO LEFT

THE VIEW OF HIGH FORCE IS HINDERED BY UNDERGROWTH HENCE A GOOD VANTAGE POINT IS HARD TO FIND. EVEN A GOOD PHOTO IS NOT WORTH FALLING OFF A CLIFF FOR. WAIT TILL CAULDRON SNOUT FOR SPECTACULAR ACTION SHOTS.

The High Force

2 HRS 30 MINS – 3 HRS FROM MIDDLETON-IN-TEESDALE (MAP 72)

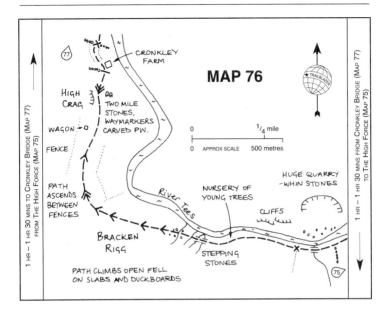

LANGDON BECK TO DUFTON   **MAPS 77-83**

At least half of this **12-mile (19km, 6-8hrs)** section is beside running water, first the fast-flowing River Tees, then Maize Beck which in wet weather can overflow, creating problems as you make towards the remarkable chasm of High Cup Nick. The path along the upper reaches of the Tees is notable for its wild scenery with splintered crags looming over you and bouldery obstructions to be clambered over. **Cauldron Snout** is an exhilarating sight, the ascent up the jumbled rocks beside it providing a thrilling experience, the roar of the torrent drowning any other sounds.

Beyond the dam wall of **Cow Green Reservoir** the track is prominent and the going straightforward until the isolated farmstead of **Birkdale** when you take to the open moor again.

After reaching **Maize Beck** (Map 80) the choice of route depends on the state of the water. If the stepping stones are flooded you have to stick to the east side of the beck and cross it on the footbridge over the gorge. If you can, it's better to cross the beck on the west side because the path is drier and more direct, leading straight to the rim of **High Cup** (see box p178). The sight of this colossal abyss is worth the rigours of this quite arduous day.

The descent by miners' tracks leads at last to the tidy village of **Dufton**, a quintessential English village with pub, local shop and village green, one of the more delightful destinations along the Pennine Way.

DUFTON [Map 83]

This quiet and attractive little village is an excellent place to stop. Almost all the places to stay offer drying facilities, which may be a reflection on the state in which walkers tend to arrive. The **village shop** has basic groceries, an off licence and a **post office** (open Mon, Tue, Thu).

The Stag Inn (☎ 017683-51608, 🖳 www.thestagdufton.co.uk, 2T/1D) has **B&B** in a nice adjacent cottage at £25 per person and is well known for its wonderful bar meals in the £6 range served from 12 noon to 2pm and 6.30 to 8.45pm.

Cheaper rooms are available a few doors along at *Sycamore House* (☎ 017683-51296, 🖳 www.sycamorehouse .org.uk, 2S/3D, some en suite) where en suite costs £21, Easter to September. The owners are keen walkers themselves and may entertain you with tales of their world-wide travels.

Coney Garth (☎/🖹 017683-52582, 🖳 coneygarth@onetel.net, 1T/1D or F) offers a warm welcome and costs £20 per person in the twin room and £25 for the double/family room and has drying facilities on the Aga. Both rooms are en suite. They will do 'anything requested', including making up a tasty packed lunch. If you prefer you can opt for self-catering.

Dufton Youth Hostel (☎ 01629-592708, bookings ☎ 0870-770 5800, 🖳 dufton@yha.org.uk, open Apr-Oct except Wed Apr-May and Tue-Wed Sep-Oct) is centrally located and provides an evening meal (7pm). Charges are £10.60 for adults and £7.20 for under 18s.

Dufton Hall Farm (☎ 017683-51573) has a basic **campsite** behind the public loos, with a shower back at the Hall costing £3.50 per person, open April to October.

Brow Farm (☎ 017683-52865, 🖳 www.browfarm.com, 1S/1T/1F en suite) permits camping (£2.50 per person, open from approx May to Oct) on one of their fields but there are no facilities. However, they offer comfortable B&B (all rooms en suite) for £25 Sep-June, £25.50 in July, £26 in Aug. Also at this end of the village is *Ghyll View* (☎ 017683-51855, 1S/3T), a friendly place open Mar-Oct only, with B&B from £20.

Currently the only **bus** is the Friday connection with Appleby (see pp36-9).

❑ High Cup

Northbound walkers come upon the massive glaciated valley of High Cup (also known as High Cup Nick) quite suddenly and are always surprised by this incredible sight. The entire mountain has fallen, as if all at once, into a bowl. The sides are layered with strata of hard rock, basalt or dolerite, interspersed with jumbled scree. Your first thought is likely to be whether this is indeed natural or has Man at his most destructive quarried out the whole lot and carted it away to make roads. Is this the work of Alfred McAlpine?

In fact, it is Nature that has fashioned this astonishing wonder. Strangely enough, none of the people who has seen fit to write about the Pennine Way has made much of it. Wainwright hardly mentions it, others gloss over it and even JHB Peel in his invaluable book, *Along the Pennine Way*, loses the plot when it comes to describing High Cup Nick.

Perhaps it doesn't need prose or poetry, speaking for itself so eloquently that even the most unimaginative will be moved by it.

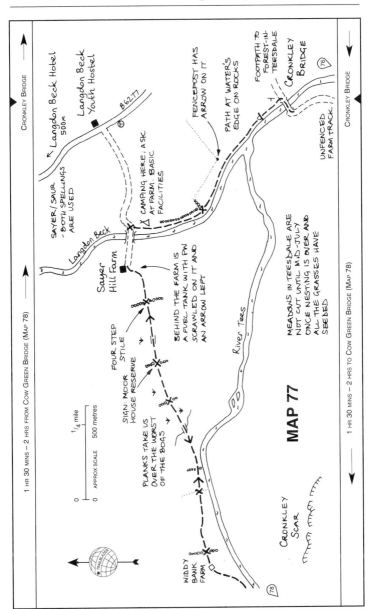

CRONKLEY BRIDGE

1 HR 30 MINS – 2 HRS FROM COW GREEN BRIDGE (MAP 78)

Langdon Beck Hotel

Langdon Beck Youth Hostel

500m

B6277

SAYER/SAUR – BOTH SPELLINGS ARE USED

Langdon Beck

Sauer Hill Farm

CAMPING HERE; ASK AT FARM. BASIC FACILITIES

FENCEPOST HAS ARROW ON IT

PATH AT WATER'S EDGE ON ROCKS

FOOTPATH TO FOREST-IN-TEESDALE

CRONKLEY BRIDGE

76

UNFENCED FARM TRACK

CRONKLEY BRIDGE

BEHIND THE FARM IS A FUEL TANK WITH PW SCRAWLED ON IT AND AN ARROW LEFT

FOUR STEP STILE

SIGN: MOOR HOUSE RESERVE

River Tees

MEADOWS IN TEESDALE ARE NOT CUT UNTIL MID-JULY ONCE NESTING IS OVER AND ALL THE GRASSES HAVE SEEDED

MAP 77

PLANKS TAKE US OVER THE WORST OF THE BOGS

¼ mile

0

APPROX SCALE   500 metres

0

TRAILBLAZER

CRONKLEY SCAR

WIDDY BANK FARM

78

1 HR 30 MINS – 2 HRS TO COW GREEN BRIDGE (MAP 78)

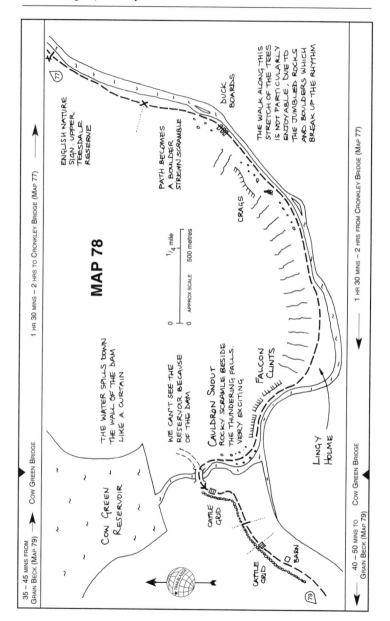

MAP 78

35 – 45 MINS FROM GRAIN BECK (Map 79) ⟶ COW GREEN BRIDGE

1 HR 30 MINS – 2 HRS TO CRONKLEY BRIDGE (MAP 77) ⟶

ENGLISH NATURE SIGN. UPPER TEESDALE RESERVE

DUCK BOARDS

PATH BECOMES A BOULDER STREWN SCRAMBLE

THE WALK ALONG THIS STRETCH OF THE TEES IS NOT PARTICULARLY ENJOYABLE, DUE TO THE JUMBLED ROCKS AND BOULDERS WHICH BREAK UP THE RHYTHM

CRAGS

THE WATER SPILLS DOWN THE WALL OF THE DAM LIKE A CURTAIN

WE CAN'T SEE THE RESERVOIR BECAUSE OF THE DAM

CAULDRON SNOUT ROCKY SCRAMBLE BESIDE THE THUNDERING FALLS. VERY EXCITING

FALCON CLINTS

LINGY HOLME

COW GREEN RESERVOIR

CATTLE GRID

CATTLE GRID

BARN

APPROX SCALE

0 — ¼ mile

0 — 500 metres

TRAIL BLAZER

1 HR 30 MINS – 2 HRS FROM CRONKLEY BRIDGE (MAP 77)

⟵ COW GREEN BRIDGE

40 – 50 MINS TO GRAIN BECK (MAP 79) ⟵

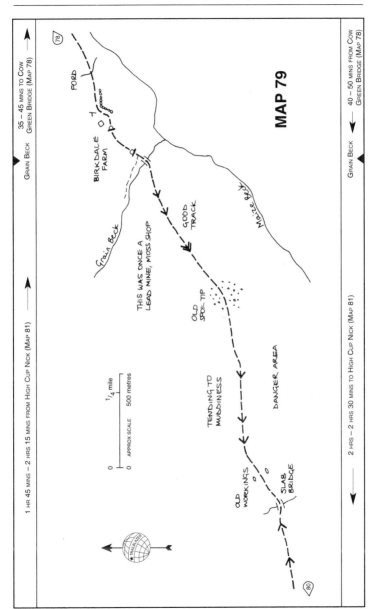

MAP 79

BIRKDALE FARM

FORD

78

Grain Beck

THIS WAS ONCE A LEAD MINE, MOSS SHOP

GOOD TRACK

Maize Beck

OLD SPOIL TIP

TENDING TO MUDDINESS

DANGER AREA

OLD WORKINGS

SLAB BRIDGE

80

1/4 mile

500 metres

0

0

APPROX SCALE

TRAILBLAZER

35 – 45 MINS TO COW GREEN BRIDGE (MAP 78)

GRAIN BECK

1 HR 45 MINS – 2 HRS 15 MINS FROM HIGH CUP NICK (MAP 81)

40 – 50 MINS FROM COW GREEN BRIDGE (MAP 78)

GRAIN BECK

2 HRS – 2 HRS 30 MINS TO HIGH CUP NICK (MAP 81)

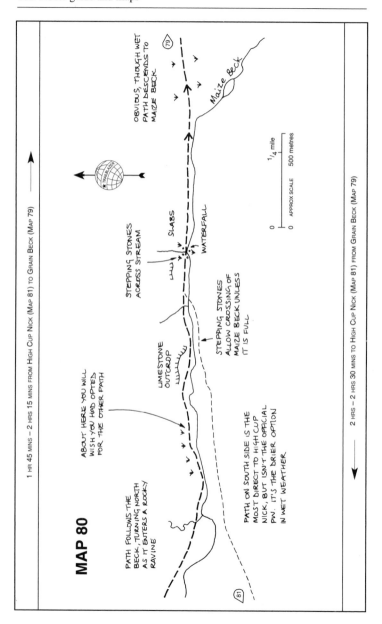

MAP 80

1 HR 45 MINS – 2 HRS 15 MINS FROM HIGH CUP NICK (MAP 81) TO GRAIN BECK (MAP 79)

2 HRS – 2 HRS 30 MINS TO HIGH CUP NICK (MAP 81) FROM GRAIN BECK (MAP 79)

OBVIOUS, THOUGH WET PATH DESCENDS TO MAIZE BECK

Maize Beck

79

TRAILBLAZER

¼ mile

0 APPROX SCALE 500 metres

STEPPING STONES ACROSS STREAM

SLABS

WATERFALL

STEPPING STONES ALLOW CROSSING OF MAIZE BECK UNLESS IT IS FULL

LIMESTONE OUTCROP

ABOUT HERE YOU WILL WISH YOU HAD OPTED FOR THE OTHER PATH

PATH FOLLOWS THE BECK, TURNING NORTH AS IT ENTERS A ROCKY RAVINE

PATH ON SOUTH SIDE IS THE MOST DIRECT TO HIGH CUP NICK, BUT ISN'T THE OFFICIAL PW. IT'S THE DRIER OPTION IN WET WEATHER.

81

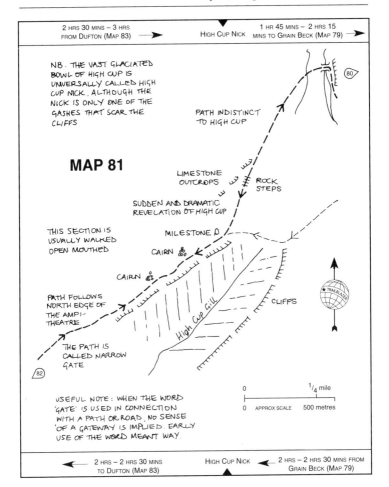

NB. THE VAST GLACIATED BOWL OF HIGH CUP IS UNIVERSALLY CALLED HIGH CUP NICK. ALTHOUGH THE NICK IS ONLY ONE OF THE GASHES THAT SCAR THE CLIFFS

PATH INDISTINCT TO HIGH CUP

MAP 81

LIMESTONE OUTCROPS

ROCK STEPS

SUDDEN AND DRAMATIC REVELATION OF HIGH CUP

THIS SECTION IS USUALLY WALKED OPEN MOUTHED

MILESTONE

CAIRN

CAIRN

PATH FOLLOWS NORTH EDGE OF THE AMPI-THEATRE

High Cup Gill

CLIFFS

THE PATH IS CALLED NARROW GATE

USEFUL NOTE: WHEN THE WORD 'GATE' IS USED IN CONNECTION WITH A PATH OR ROAD, NO SENSE OF A GATEWAY IS IMPLIED. EARLY USE OF THE WORD MEANT WAY.

0   1/4 mile

0   APPROX SCALE   500 metres

★ TRAILBLAZER

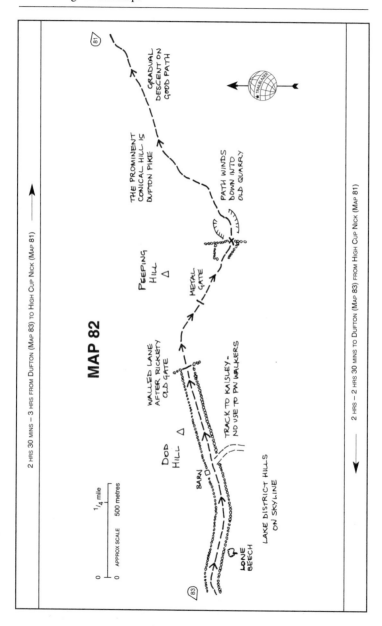

MAP 82

0 ──────── 1/4 mile
0 ──────── 500 metres
APPROX SCALE

Dod Hill △

BARN

LONE BEECH

LAKE DISTRICT HILLS ON SKYLINE

WALLED LANE AFTER RICKETY OLD GATE

TRACK TO KAISLEY – NO USE TO PW WALKERS

Peeping Hill △

METAL GATE

THE PROMINENT CONICAL HILL IS DUFTON PIKE

PATH WINDS DOWN INTO OLD QUARRY

GRADUAL DESCENT ON GOOD PATH

83

81

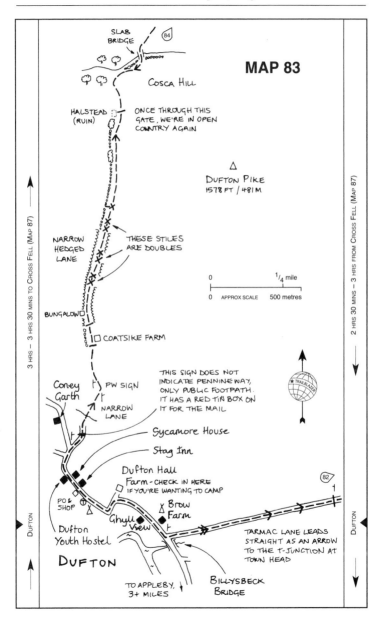

MAP 83

SLAB BRIDGE

84

Cosca Hill

HALSTEAD (RUIN)

ONCE THROUGH THIS GATE, WE'RE IN OPEN COUNTRY AGAIN

△ DUFTON PIKE 1578 FT / 481 M

NARROW HEDGED LANE

THESE STILES ARE DOUBLES

0 .... 1/4 mile
0   APPROX SCALE   500 metres

BUNGALOW

☐ COATSIKE FARM

Coney Garth

† PW SIGN

† NARROW LANE

THIS SIGN DOES NOT INDICATE PENNINE WAY, ONLY PUBLIC FOOTPATH. IT HAS A RED TIN BOX ON IT FOR THE MAIL

Sycamore House

Stag Inn

Dufton Hall Farm — CHECK IN HERE IF YOU'RE WANTING TO CAMP

82 1

PO & SHOP

✗ Brow Farm

Dufton Youth Hostel

Ghyll View

DUFTON

TARMAC LANE LEADS STRAIGHT AS AN ARROW TO THE T-JUNCTION AT TOWN HEAD

TO APPLEBY, 3+ MILES

BILLYSBECK BRIDGE

★ TRAILBLAZER

3 HRS – 3 HRS 30 MINS TO CROSS FELL (MAP 87)

2 HRS 30 MINS – 3 HRS FROM CROSS FELL (MAP 87)

DUFTON

DUFTON

DUFTON TO GARRIGILL   MAPS 83-91

There is one huge hill between Dufton and Garrigill and **16 miles (26km, 5-6hrs)** of hard walking, making this a tough section. Those who extend their route to walk on to Alston will certainly feel the effects at the end of the day. There are no places for refreshment on this tough walk so go well prepared.

The long ascent to the summit of **Cross Fell** begins gently through farm lanes and by-ways to skirt **Dufton Fell** before an extraordinary straight section that acts as a preliminary to the climb up **Knock Fell**.

The space-age buildings on **Little Dun Fell** act as a beacon ahead, the geodesic dome like a genetically modified golf ball set on a giant's tee for him to drive across the Vale of Eden. The chances are the weather will have begun to deteriorate, Cross Fell being a notorious catalyst for weather systems. Nobody should set out on this section without adequate protective clothing and supplies. To be caught out in a rain or even hail storm in July or August is not at all unlikely and many a walker has struggled in to **Greg's Hut** (see box opposite) in desperate straits, as the visitor's book testifies. The miners' path that winds and undulates down to **Garrigill** has a rough and stony surface that wears down the resolve but leads at last to the tiny haven where rest and hot showers can be found and a pint or two by the fire in the local pub. You will certainly have earned it.

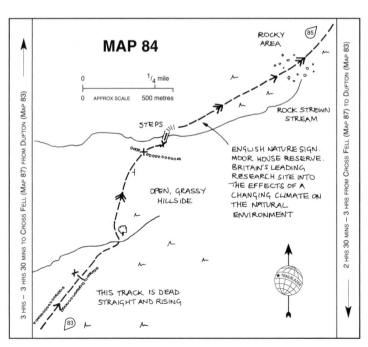

MAP 84

ROCKY AREA

ROCK STREWN STREAM

STEPS

ENGLISH NATURE SIGN. MOOR HOUSE RESERVE. BRITAIN'S LEADING RESEARCH SITE INTO THE EFFECTS OF A CHANGING CLIMATE ON THE NATURAL ENVIRONMENT

OPEN, GRASSY HILLSIDE

THIS TRACK IS DEAD STRAIGHT AND RISING

0   1/4 mile
0   APPROX SCALE   500 metres

3 HRS – 3 HRS 30 MINS TO CROSS FELL (MAP 87) FROM DUFTON (MAP 83)

2 HRS 30 MINS – 3 HRS FROM CROSS FELL (MAP 87) TO DUFTON (MAP 83)

GARRIGILL [Map 91]

Garrigill's **post office** (Mon-Sat 9am-5.30pm, to 12.30pm on Tue, Sun 8-11.30am) transacts the usual post office business but also sells a few essentials and is home to the *Garrigill Post Office Guesthouse* (☎/🖳 01434-381257, 🖳 www .garrigill-guesthouse.co.uk, 1S/1D/2T, £20). It is clean and comfortable but the rooms are a bit short on space. In order to do things properly Mrs Bramwell leaves notes everywhere informing guests of the house rules with injunctions against putting clothes on radiators, using the proper bath mats and leaving wet clothes (no wet boots) for drying at the bottom of the stairs up till 9pm. She may seem a little formidable but this is a good, well-run B&B.

The pub, *The George and Dragon* (☎ 01434-381293, 🖳 thegeorgeanddragon@bt openworld.com, 1D en suite + 2S/1T), has provided relief for many a walker in its time and does indeed do bar meals but don't be late. There's no flexibility in its opening hours: 12-1.30pm for food (not open for lunch on Tuesday) and it closes promptly at 2pm. In the evening food is served between 7pm and 8.30pm. On Saturday in summer, however, it's open all day. B&B is from £21 a head.

Ivy House (☎ 01434-382501, 🖳 www.garrigill.com, 1T/2D) was about to be put up for sale in mid-2004 but it has such a good reputation it's likely that it will remain a B&B. They charge £25 per person, but it's cheaper if there are three of you in one room. The current owner introduced a novel business idea in offering treks with llamas, only to find bureaucratic red tape from DEFRA stood in the way of a really resourceful idea. There are no plans, however, to let walkers hire one for the rest of the Pennine Way.

If you hope to **camp** at Garrigill, you can put your tent up behind the village hall. Check at the pub first and leave a donation to the funds before you leave.

A couple of miles towards Alston is *Alston Training and Adventure Centre* (☎ 01434-381886, 🖳 www.alstontrain ing.co.uk, see **Map 93**) which is not far off the Pennine Way and offers **camping** (£3.70 per person), **bunkhouse** accommodation (£10, £15.25 including breakfast), evening meals (£5.80) and packed lunches (£2.70). The owners are kind and flexible and will do everything they can to meet your needs.

❏ Greg's Hut [See Map 87]

Greg's Hut is a well-maintained bothy just over the summit of Cross Fell where walkers can take refuge from the wind and the rain. It's no hotel, having no comforts other than a roof that keeps out the rain, but holds a special place in the heart of wayfarers. It was originally used by lead miners who would stay here all week, walking home at the weekends.

Greg was John Gregson, a climber who lost his life in an epic climbing accident in the Alps in 1968 in spite of the heroic efforts of his companion who held him on the rope and tended his injuries all night until rescue came, alas, too late.

Thanks to the efforts of the Mountain Bothies Association, the hut has been repaired and maintained. There are two rooms, the inner one having a raised platform for sleeping on, with a stove, although fuel is scarce. Certainly you are unlikely to find any on the surrounding fell and I can only imagine that you'd have to bring your own wood with you if you hoped to light it.

This is a classic mountain bothy, unique along the Pennine Way, and it is hard to drag yourself out of it in horrible conditions. The visitors' book should be published as it stands, telling a multitude of stories, most of them epics of endurance.

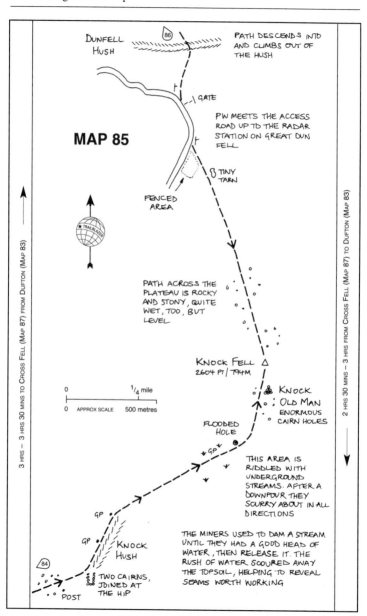

DUNFELL HUSH

86

PATH DESCENDS INTO AND CLIMBS OUT OF THE HUSH

GATE

MAP 85

PW MEETS THE ACCESS ROAD UP TO THE RADAR STATION ON GREAT DUN FELL

TINY TARN

FENCED AREA

★ TRAILBLAZER

PATH ACROSS THE PLATEAU IS ROCKY AND STONY, QUITE WET, TOO, BUT LEVEL

KNOCK FELL △
2604 PT / 794M

KNOCK OLD MAN
ENORMOUS CAIRN HOLES

0   ¼ mile
0   APPROX SCALE   500 metres

FLOODED HOLE

GP

THIS AREA IS RIDDLED WITH UNDERGROUND STREAMS. AFTER A DOWNPOUR THEY SCURRY ABOUT IN ALL DIRECTIONS

GP

GP   KNOCK HUSH

84

TWO CAIRNS, JOINED AT THE HIP

POST

THE MINERS USED TO DAM A STREAM UNTIL THEY HAD A GOOD HEAD OF WATER, THEN RELEASE IT. THE RUSH OF WATER SCOURED AWAY THE TOPSOIL, HELPING TO REVEAL SEAMS WORTH WORKING

3 HRS – 3 HRS 30 MINS TO CROSS FELL (MAP 87) FROM DUFTON (MAP 83)

2 HRS 30 MINS – 3 HRS FROM CROSS FELL (MAP 87) TO DUFTON (MAP 83)

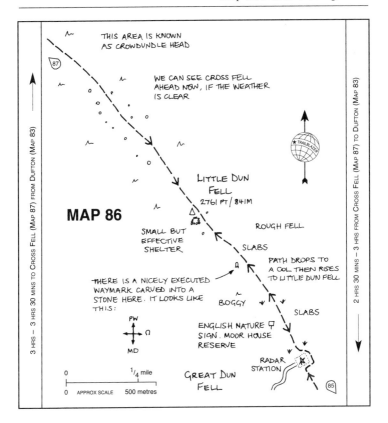

THIS AREA IS KNOWN AS CROWDUNDLE HEAD

WE CAN SEE CROSS FELL AHEAD NOW, IF THE WEATHER IS CLEAR

87

★ TRAILBLAZER

LITTLE DUN FELL
2761 PT / 841M

ROUGH FELL

MAP 86

SMALL BUT EFFECTIVE SHELTER

SLABS

PATH DROPS TO A COL THEN RISES TO LITTLE DUN FELL

THERE IS A NICELY EXECUTED WAYMARK CARVED INTO A STONE HERE. IT LOOKS LIKE THIS:

BOGGY

PW
Ω
MD

ENGLISH NATURE ☊ SIGN. MOOR HOUSE RESERVE

SLABS

RADAR STATION

0   ¼ mile
0   APPROX SCALE   500 metres

GREAT DUN FELL

85

3 HRS – 3 HRS 30 MINS TO CROSS FELL (MAP 87) FROM DUFTON (MAP 83)

2 HRS 30 MINS – 3 HRS FROM CROSS FELL (MAP 87) TO DUFTON (MAP 83)

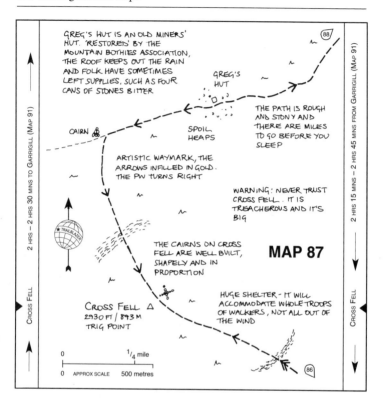

GREG'S HUT IS AN OLD MINERS' HUT. 'RESTORED' BY THE MOUNTAIN BOTHIES ASSOCIATION, THE ROOF KEEPS OUT THE RAIN AND FOLK HAVE SOMETIMES LEFT SUPPLIES, SUCH AS FOUR CANS OF STONES BITTER

GREG'S HUT

THE PATH IS ROUGH AND STONY AND THERE ARE MILES TO GO BEFORE YOU SLEEP

CAIRN

SPOIL HEAPS

ARTISTIC WAYMARK, THE ARROWS INFILLED IN GOLD. THE PW TURNS RIGHT

WARNING: NEVER TRUST CROSS FELL. IT IS TREACHEROUS AND IT'S BIG

THE CAIRNS ON CROSS FELL ARE WELL BUILT, SHAPELY AND IN PROPORTION

MAP 87

★ TRAILBLAZER

CROSS FELL △
2930 FT / 893 M
TRIG POINT

HUGE SHELTER - IT WILL ACCOMMODATE WHOLE TROOPS OF WALKERS, NOT ALL OUT OF THE WIND

0   ¹/₄ mile
0   APPROX SCALE   500 metres

88

86

2 HRS – 2 HRS 30 MINS TO GARRIGILL (MAP 91)

CROSS FELL

2 HRS 15 MINS – 2 HRS 45 MINS FROM GARRIGILL (MAP 91)

CROSS FELL

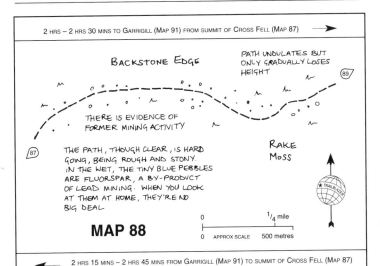

2 HRS – 2 HRS 30 MINS TO GARRIGILL (MAP 91) FROM SUMMIT OF CROSS FELL (MAP 87) ⟶

BACKSTONE EDGE

PATH UNDULATES BUT
ONLY GRADUALLY LOSES
HEIGHT

89

THERE IS EVIDENCE OF
FORMER MINING ACTIVITY

87

THE PATH, THOUGH CLEAR, IS HARD
GOING, BEING ROUGH AND STONY.
IN THE WET, THE TINY BLUE PEBBLES
ARE FLUORSPAR, A BY-PRODUCT
OF LEAD MINING. WHEN YOU LOOK
AT THEM AT HOME, THEY'RE NO
BIG DEAL

RAKE
MOSS

MAP 88

★ TRAILBLAZER

0 — 1/4 mile

0   APPROX SCALE   500 metres

⟵ 2 HRS 15 MINS – 2 HRS 45 MINS FROM GARRIGILL (MAP 91) TO SUMMIT OF CROSS FELL (MAP 87)

❑ Lead mining in the Pennines

The history of digging in the earth for lead in the Pennine hills goes back to the Romans and probably earlier, evidence having been uncovered that the Romans themselves exploited workings existing when they arrived.

The growth in the building of abbeys and castles increased the demand for lead for the roofs but it was not until the 19th century that mining assumed industrial proportions as the demand for lead increased with the Industrial Revolution.

The industry started to suffer when cheaper foreign sources threatened local production and by the early years of the 20th century the industry was in decline. Today there is no lead mining in Britain although some of the old pits have been re-opened to exploit other minerals found there such as barytes and fluorspar. The ore, galena, also has a use in producing X-ray equipment.

The ruins evident around Alston and in Swaledale around Keld are a reminder of the extensive industry involved in lead mining at one time. Old spoil tips, ruined mine buildings and the occasional remains of a chimney are all that is left of this activity, now long discarded as uneconomic. Traces of bell pits are often to be seen as hollows in the ground. They used to sink a shaft to a certain level then widen the bottom of the hole until it was unsafe to go further. Everything dug out went to the surface in a bucket, firstly by hand and then by a winch, sometimes drawn up on a wheel by a horse walking in a circle. It was a primitive industry in the early days, reliant on the muscle power of the miners themselves. With the advent of engineering, ways were found to mechanize production and so multiply the output, increasing profits for the owners.

Around Middleton-in-Teesdale mining rights were held by the London Lead Mining Company, a Quaker concern, active from the latter part of the 1700s until early in the 1900s when they pulled out in the face of cheap imported ore from Europe.

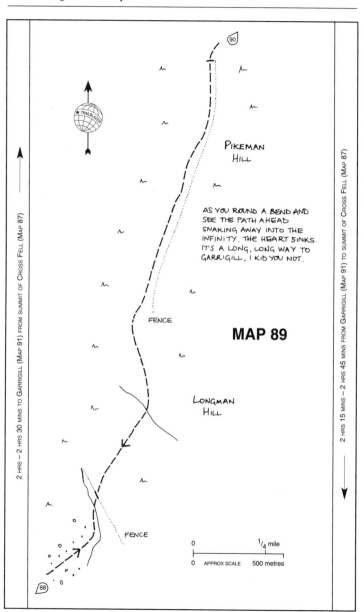

90

★ TRAILBLAZER

PIKEMAN
HILL

AS YOU ROUND A BEND AND
SEE THE PATH AHEAD
SNAKING AWAY INTO THE
INFINITY. THE HEART SINKS.
IT'S A LONG, LONG WAY TO
GARRIGILL, I KID YOU NOT.

FENCE

MAP 89

LONGMAN
HILL

FENCE

0   1/4 mile

0   APPROX SCALE   500 metres

88

2 HRS – 2 HRS 30 MINS TO GARRIGILL (MAP 91) FROM SUMMIT OF CROSS FELL (MAP 87)

2 HRS 15 MINS – 2 HRS 45 MINS FROM GARRIGILL (MAP 91) TO SUMMIT OF CROSS FELL (MAP 87)

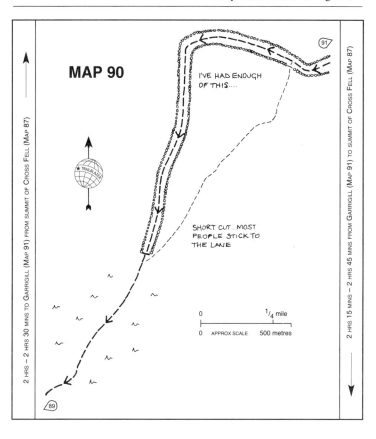

MAP 90

I'VE HAD ENOUGH OF THIS....

SHORT CUT. MOST PEOPLE STICK TO THE LANE

★ TRAILBLAZER

0   1/4 mile
0   APPROX SCALE   500 metres

2 HRS – 2 HRS 30 MINS TO GARRIGILL (MAP 91) FROM SUMMIT OF CROSS FELL (MAP 87)

2 HRS 15 MINS – 2 HRS 45 MINS FROM GARRIGILL (MAP 91) TO SUMMIT OF CROSS FELL (MAP 87)

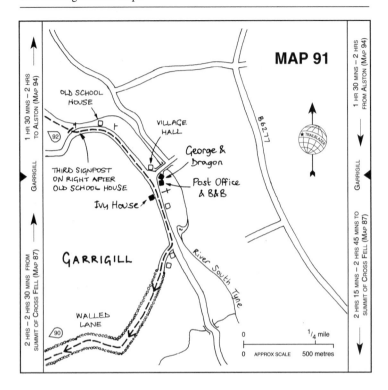

MAP 91

1 HR 30 MINS – 2 HRS TO ALSTON (MAP 94)

1 HR 30 MINS – 2 HRS FROM ALSTON (MAP 94)

GARRIGILL

GARRIGILL

2 HRS – 2 HRS 30 MINS FROM SUMMIT OF CROSS FELL (MAP 87)

2 HRS 15 MINS – 2 HRS 45 MINS TO SUMMIT OF CROSS FELL (MAP 87)

OLD SCHOOL HOUSE

VILLAGE HALL

George & Dragon

THIRD SIGNPOST ON RIGHT AFTER OLD SCHOOL HOUSE

Post Office & B&B

Ivy House

GARRIGILL

River South Tyne

WALLED LANE

B 62.77

TRAILBLAZER

0   1/4 mile

0   APPROX SCALE   500 metres

GARRIGILL TO ALSTON   MAPS 91-94

Whether this is the final effort of a hard day from Dufton or the start of the next day, it's a lovely **4-mile (6km, 1½-2hrs)** walk that follows the **South Tyne** river the whole way, at times along its very edge. You will negotiate field paths and climb numerous stiles but the goal is the delightful hilltop town of **Alston**.

ALSTON

You are now in Eden District, an area named after the River Eden that runs through it, although it is beautiful enough to get away with claims of an association with the Old Testament.

Alston is England's highest market town and is extremely pleasant with its steep cobbled roads and old buildings, many from the 17th and 18th centuries.

Services

If you want to break the walk here you can get a **bus** to Haltwhistle and catch a **train** on the Newcastle to Carlisle line. There are also buses to Carlisle, Penrith, Hexham and Nenthead (see public transport map, pp36-9). Alternatively a minibus **taxi** to Carlisle costs around £30 with Hendersons (☎ 01434-381204).

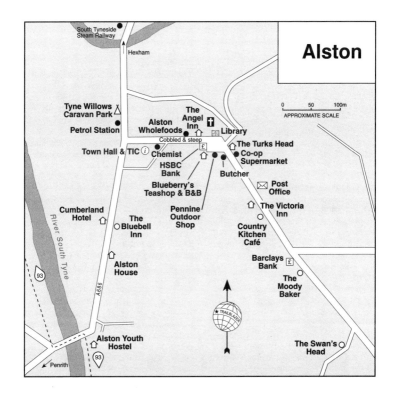

The **tourist information centre** (☎ 01434-382244, 🖳 alston.tic@eden.gov.uk), in the Town Hall on Front St, is open Apr-Oct Mon-Sat 10am-5pm, Sun 10am-4pm, Nov-Mar Tue and Sun 10am-3pm, other days 10am-5pm.

Alston Wholefoods sells fair-trade chocolate, interesting cheeses (eg Northumberland Nettle, Swaledale Ewe) and environmentally-friendly goods; the **Co-op** (Mon-Sat 8am-8pm, Sun 9am-5pm) has groceries; TG Blackstock, the **butcher,** has excellent cold ham for your sandwiches; and there's a **chemist** (early closing Tue and Sat) if your feet are in a bad way.

Both HSBC and Barclays **banks** have cash machines. The **post office** does foreign exchange and sells maps and cards.

Where to stay

If you want to **camp** and did not stop at the Alston Adventure Training Centre (see p187) make your way past lots of derelict cars behind the Texaco garage and seek out *Tyne Willows Caravan Park* (☎ 01434-382515). It costs £4 which includes showers.

Alston Youth Hostel (☎ 01629-529708, bookings ☎ 0870-770 5668, 🖳 alston@yha.org.uk, open Apr-Oct, except closed Wed-Thu Apr to mid-May and Sep-Oct) overlooks the South Tyne Valley and has beds for £10.60 (£7.20 under 18s) and serves evening meals at 7pm.

Blueberry's Tea Shop and B&B (☎ 01434-381928, 2T/1D) is pleasant and costs £38 for a twin/double room with shared bathroom (£25 for single occupancy) and £44 for a twin with a private bathroom (£29.50 for single occupancy). *The Victoria Inn* (☎ 01434-381194, 4S/2T/2F, some en suite) is an equally good bet and costs from £15.50.

The Angel Inn (☎ 01434-381363, 1S/1T/1D) also does B&B, none en suite, for £16.50, and is used to walkers. You should find a good fire burning if it's cold or wet. *Cumberland Hotel* (☎ 01434-381875, 🖳 www.milford.co.uk/hotels/alston-cumberland-hotel.html, 2D/2T/2F all en suite) is a good place offering B&B from £26.

Recently refurbished *Alston House* (☎ 01434-382200, 6 rooms/17 beds, all en suite) is walker friendly, with B&B for £28 per person or £24 in a triple and has a good bar-restaurant.

Just outside the town but near the Way (see Map 94) are two more B&Bs: *Grey Croft* (☎ 01434-381383, 2T), Middle Park, The Raise, is a tidy white bungalow where B&B is £26. Just 500m from the Way is *Bridge End Farm* (☎ 01434-381261, 1D/1F), with B&B for £25.

About a mile and a half south of Alston and three-quarters of a mile from the Way in the village of Leadgate, *Brownside House* (☎ 01434-382169, 1S/2T/1D) is a very pleasant place. The helpful owners charge £20 for B&B and £7.50 for an evening meal. To reach Leadgate see **Map 93**: cross the South Tyne River by the footbridge west of the Way and follow Black Burn until you reach the road bridge. Take the road over the bridge into Leadgate; turn right in the village and the B&B is signposted to the left after 200m.

Where to eat

The Victoria Inn (see above) does a daily roast lunch (including all the trimmings) for just £2.95. *The Turks Head* has a very friendly atmosphere, helped no doubt by the blazing fire, and does food from £5.

Blueberry's Tea Shop (see above) serves lunches (eg Boozy Pie, £5.45), jacket potatoes and an all-day breakfast (£4.15) 9am to 5pm. *The Angel Inn* (see above) has good pub food: sandwiches from £1.55, and local Cumberland sausage and fried egg for £4.95. *The Bluebell Inn* and *The Swan;s Head* also do pub food.

At *Country Kitchen Café* there's fish and chips and standard café fare. Nearby is *The Moody Baker*, a workers' co-operative shop offering excellent organic food to take away. Their stotties (flat bread rolls, white or brown) have a range of tasty fillings (eg stilton and walnut melt, £1.95).

The new bar-restaurant at Alston House (see above), *The House Bar*, is recommended and there's live music here sometimes. Interesting dishes include duck breast with Cointreau sauce (£11.50) and crêpes with chickpeas, vegetables, garlic and mozzarella cheese (£8).

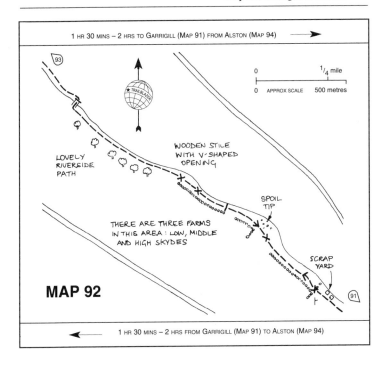

WOODEN STILE
WITH V-SHAPED
OPENING

LOVELY
RIVERSIDE
PATH

SPOIL
TIP

THERE ARE THREE FARMS
IN THIS AREA : LOW, MIDDLE
AND HIGH SKYDES

SCRAP
YARD

MAP 92

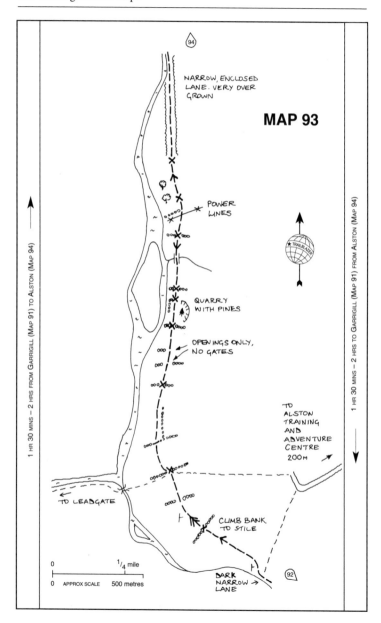

94

NARROW, ENCLOSED
LANE. VERY OVER
GROWN

MAP 93

POWER
LINES

★ TRAILBLAZER

QUARRY
WITH PINES

OPENINGS ONLY,
NO GATES

TO
ALSTON
TRAINING
AND
ADVENTURE
CENTRE
200M

TO LEADGATE

CLIMB BANK
TO STILE

0   ¼ mile

0   APPROX SCALE   500 metres

DARK
NARROW →
LANE

92

1 HR 30 MINS – 2 HRS FROM GARRIGILL (MAP 91) TO ALSTON (MAP 94)

1 HR 30 MINS – 2 HRS TO GARRIGILL (MAP 91) FROM ALSTON (MAP 94)

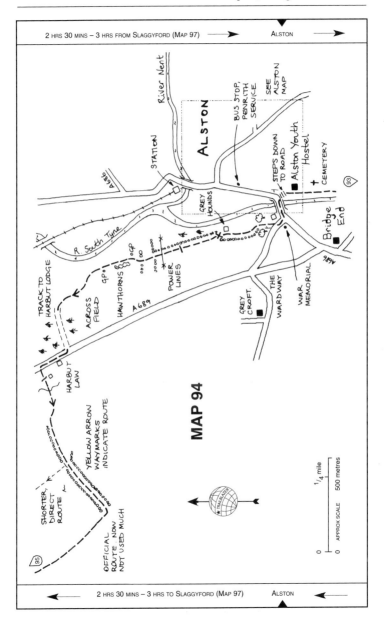

River Nent

ALSTON

BUS STOP, PENRITH SERVICE

SEE ALSTON MAP

STATION

A686

GREY HOUNDS

STEPS DOWN TO ROAD

Alston Youth Hostel

CEMETERY

93

Bridge End

R South Tyne

POWER LINES

HAWTHORNS

GP'S

TRACK TO HARBUT LODGE

ACROSS FIELD

A689

A689

THE WARDWAY

GREY CROFT

WAR MEMORIAL

HARBUT LAW

MAP 94

YELLOW ARROW WAYMARKS INDICATE ROUTE

SHORTER, DIRECT ROUTE

OFFICIAL ROUTE NOW NOT USED MUCH

95

TRAILBLAZER

¼ mile   500 metres

APPROX SCALE

0   0

ALSTON TO GREENHEAD

Is there anyone for whom **17 miles (27km, 7^{1}/$_{2}$-9^{1}/$_{2}$hrs)** is not a long way? If so, they will not be troubled by the walk from Alston to Greenhead though this involves no serious hills and no road walking to speak of. Added to which it does include an excellent pit-stop, the Kirkstyle Inn (see below) at Knarsdale, where you will be welcomed with open arms.

The first objective after leaving Alston is **Slaggyford**, a name that suggest a glum colliery town but which in reality is a sleepy village without the remotest hint of the kind of services walkers need; no café, pub or even a shop. It is residential and sedate. No doubt the homeowners who have taken refuge from the urban overcrowding would prefer not to be disturbed by the rucksack brigade. Walk on, pilgrim.

Once past Slaggyford and out of the parlour of the Kirkstyle Inn, the Way keeps pace with the course of the old railway, the track long since torn up. They have created the South Tynedale Trail out of it, a path that runs from Haltwhistle to Alston for use by strollers and cyclists, but the Way does not follow it. Perhaps it would have been an improvement if it had since Haltwhistle is a better destination than Greenhead.

The Pennine Way does at least follow the line of the Maiden Way, a Roman Road heading more or less due north over rough moor and marsh grass, usually damp underfoot. Some of the pasture through which we pass is in a dreadful condition, neglected and left to become overgrown with tussocky grass, in places waist deep, and nearly everywhere devoid of drainage. Those fields that have been reclaimed, the land drained and the grass and thistles cut, stand out in sharp contrast, the cattle benefiting accordingly.

After the A689 is crossed, the Way becomes more confused and unsure of itself, the sign-posting indifferent or just plain non-existent. Tiredness begins to wear you down and you may lose patience with the endless boggy pasture and sodden field paths. At length, after one last chunk of moorland, the crossing of which seems like an expedition over a country abandoned by man and beast, you come to a row of pylons and beyond to the frantic A69 dual carriageway. It has to be crossed, a panic-stricken scamper to reach the safety of the opposite embankment up which access can be gained to the old road, now overgrown, leading into the village of Greenhead.

SLAGGYFORD AND KNARSDALE
[Map 97]

After Alston you come to Slaggyford, where you can **camp** in the farmer's field across the road from the caravan site. Call at *Broadmea Farm* (☎ 01434-381375) before you put up your tent. There's no charge – and no facilities.

A little further on is the quiet *Kirkstyle Inn* (☎ 01434-381559) in Knarsdale, an absolute gem of a country pub which is

hard to beat between Edale and Kirk Yetholm. From the choice of beers to the tasty bar menu to the atmosphere this place has everything walkers go for.

Stone Croft (☎ 01434-382995, 2T) is conveniently close to Kirkstyle Inn and offers B&B for £20.

You can **camp** at *Stonehall Farm* (☎ 01434-381349) for £2.50 but it's quite basic with only a loo and a cold water tap.

GREENHEAD [Map 102]

This is a curious, spread-out settlement which has more to it than first meets the eye. It was the construction of the by-pass that sounded the death-knell for the village, killing off passing trade and turning it into a backwater with little incentive for local businesses to put any effort into attracting custom. The *Old Forge Tea Rooms* (☎ 01697-747174) is open Mon-Fri 10am-4pm, Sat 10am-3pm and Sun 11am-5pm. They serve a variety of snacks and of course teas. You may be able to get food at the **pub** but when I went by at the height of the season those dreaded words 'no food today' were chalked up outside.

There are hourly **buses** to Haltwhistle **railway** station, only 3 miles (5km) away and also services to Once Brewed, Hexham, Newcastle and Carlisle (see public transport map, pp36-9).

The *Roam-n-Rest Caravan Park* (☎ 01697-747213) is a tidy site which charges £4 per tent, the price reflecting the lack of drying facilities; it's open Mar-Oct.

Greenhead Youth Hostel (☎ 01629-592708, bookings ☎ 0870-770 5842, ▢ greenhead@yha.org.uk, Apr-Oct but book 48hrs in advance) in a converted Methodist chapel is the most likely choice for walkers. There's a pool table and a cavernous and gloomy common room. Beds cost £10.60 (£7.20 under 18s) and an evening meal is available at 7pm.

On the Way half a mile north of the village, *Holmhead Guest House* (☎ 01697-747402, ▢ www.bandbhadrians wall.com, 2T/2D en suite) is a delightful Northumbrian farm. The pleasant walk to it crosses a salmon river, follows a track along the bank (where you might see otters), through sheep fields and thence to the house. Pauline, who runs it, works as a local archaeological and historical guide and will be able to answer most of your questions as she serves up an evening meal (B&B guests only) or your selection from 'The Biggest Breakfast Menu in the World'. There is even a foot massager in the lounge, as well as a drying room and a payphone. If the prices are too steep (from £31 per person), they also have a basic **bunkhouse** (£9) and, if you ask nicely, may even let you **camp** (£3 including use of a chemical toilet, or £5 to use the bunkhouse facilities).

Alternatively there is *Braeside* (☎ 01697-747443) just above the caravan park, which has one versatile room that can be a twin, double or triple and costs £24 but with a £6 single person's supplement. An alternative would be *Four Wynds* (☎ 01697-747330, ▢ www.bed-breakfast-hadrianswall.com, 2T/1D), a more reasonably-priced B&B charging £20 and only £5 extra for solos. Neither of these two does an evening meal and it is worth repeating that you cannot rely on the pub. This presents a real problem at Greenhead and you may have to resort to a taxi into Haltwhistle to find a meal.

If you want a **hotel** your only choice is the pleasant-enough *Greenhead Hotel* (☎ 01697-747411, 1S/3D, doubles could be converted to twins) where B&B costs £25 per person. They claim to do food all day in the summer but in my experience this isn't always the case.

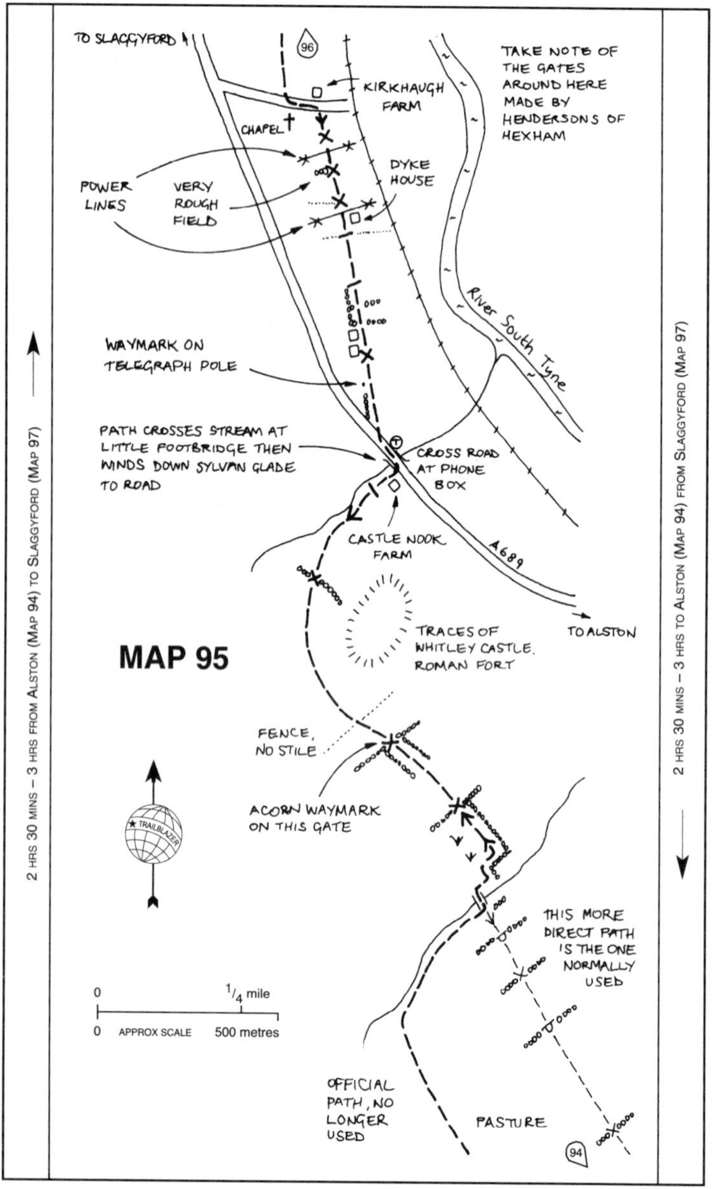

TO SLAGGYFORD

96

TAKE NOTE OF
THE GATES
AROUND HERE
MADE BY
HENDERSONS OF
HEXHAM

KIRKHAUGH
FARM

CHAPEL

DYKE
HOUSE

POWER
LINES

VERY
ROUGH
FIELD

River South Tyne

WAYMARK ON
TELEGRAPH POLE

PATH CROSSES STREAM AT
LITTLE FOOTBRIDGE THEN
WINDS DOWN SYLVAN GLADE
TO ROAD

CROSS ROAD
AT PHONE
BOX

CASTLE NOOK
FARM

A 689

TO ALSTON

MAP 95

TRACES OF
WHITLEY CASTLE.
ROMAN FORT

FENCE,
NO STILE

ACORN WAYMARK
ON THIS GATE

THIS MORE
DIRECT PATH
IS THE ONE
NORMALLY
USED

TRAILBLAZER

0   1/4 mile

0   APPROX SCALE   500 metres

OFFICIAL
PATH, NO
LONGER
USED

PASTURE

94

2 HRS 30 MINS – 3 HRS FROM ALSTON (MAP 94) TO SLAGGYFORD (MAP 97)

2 HRS 30 MINS – 3 HRS TO ALSTON (MAP 94) FROM SLAGGYFORD (MAP 97)

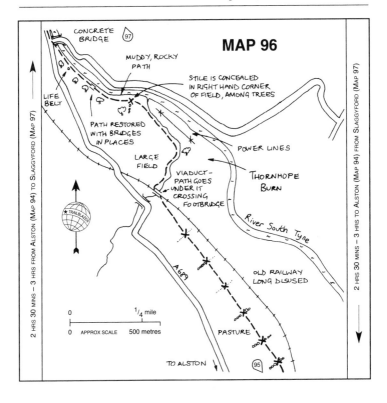

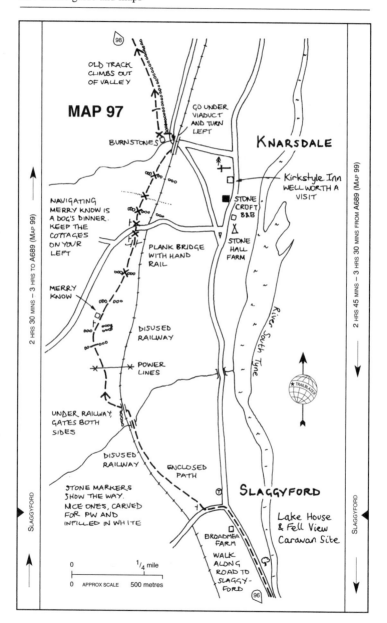

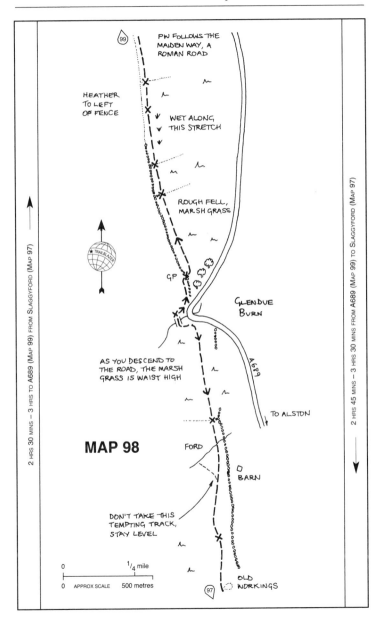

PW FOLLOWS THE MAIDEN WAY, A ROMAN ROAD

99

HEATHER TO LEFT OF FENCE

WET ALONG THIS STRETCH

ROUGH FELL, MARSH GRASS

★ TRAILBLAZER

GP

GLENDUE BURN

AS YOU DESCEND TO THE ROAD, THE MARSH GRASS IS WAIST HIGH

A689

TO ALSTON

MAP 98

FORD

BARN

DON'T TAKE THIS TEMPTING TRACK, STAY LEVEL

0   ¼ mile
0   APPROX SCALE   500 metres

OLD WORKINGS

97

2 HRS 30 MINS – 3 HRS TO A689 (MAP 99) FROM SLAGGYFORD (MAP 97)

2 HRS 45 MINS – 3 HRS 30 MINS FROM A689 (MAP 99) TO SLAGGYFORD (MAP 97)

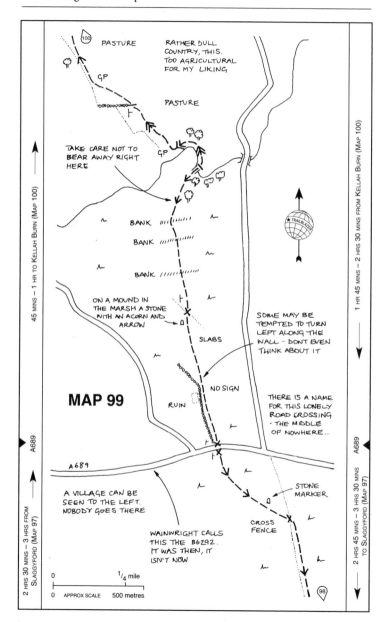

PASTURE

RATHER DULL
COUNTRY, THIS.
TOO AGRICULTURAL
FOR MY LIKING

GP

PASTURE

TAKE CARE NOT TO
BEAR AWAY RIGHT
HERE

GP

BANK

BANK

BANK

ON A MOUND IN
THE MARSH A STONE
WITH AN ACORN AND
ARROW

SLABS

SOME MAY BE
TEMPTED TO TURN
LEFT ALONG THE
WALL - DON'T EVEN
THINK ABOUT IT

NO SIGN

THERE IS A NAME
FOR THIS LONELY
ROAD CROSSING
- THE MIDDLE
OF NOWHERE...

MAP 99

RUIN

A689

A VILLAGE CAN BE
SEEN TO THE LEFT.
NOBODY GOES THERE

STONE
MARKER

CROSS
FENCE

WAINWRIGHT CALLS
THIS THE B6292.
IT WAS THEN, IT
ISN'T NOW

0   ¼ mile

0 APPROX SCALE   500 metres

45 MINS – 1 HR TO KELLAH BURN (MAP 100)

A689

2 HRS 30 MINS – 3 HRS FROM SLAGGYFORD (MAP 97)

1 HR 45 MINS – 2 HRS 30 MINS FROM KELLAH BURN (MAP 100)

A689

2 HRS 45 MINS – 3 HRS 30 MINS TO SLAGGYFORD (MAP 97)

★ TRAILBLAZER

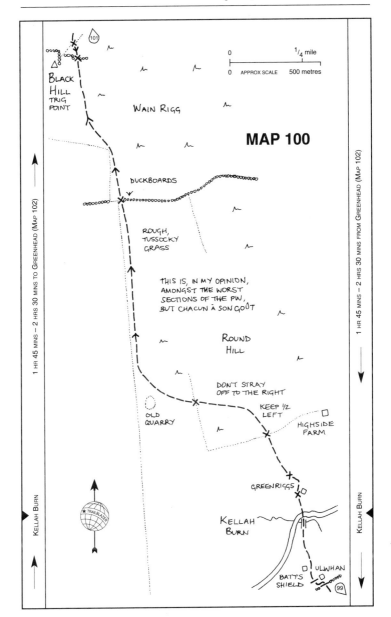

Map 100

(101)

BLACK
HILL
TRIG
POINT

WAIN RIGG

MAP 100

0   1/4 mile
0   APPROX SCALE   500 metres

DUCKBOARDS

ROUGH,
TUSSOCKY
GRASS

THIS IS, IN MY OPINION,
AMONGST THE WORST
SECTIONS OF THE PW,
BUT CHACUN À SON GOÛT

ROUND
HILL

DON'T STRAY
OFF TO THE RIGHT

KEEP 1/2
LEFT

OLD
QUARRY

HIGHSIDE
FARM

GREENRIGGS

KELLAH
BURN

★ TRAILBLAZER

ULWHAN

BATY'S
SHIELD

(99)

1 HR 45 MINS – 2 HRS 30 MINS TO GREENHEAD (MAP 102)

1 HR 45 MINS – 2 HRS 30 MINS FROM GREENHEAD (MAP 102)

KELLAH BURN

KELLAH BURN

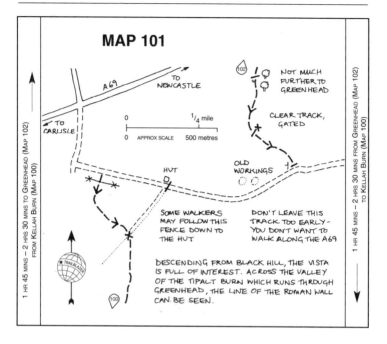

MAP 101

A69

TO
NEWCASTLE

TO
CARLISLE

102

NOT MUCH
FURTHER TO
GREENHEAD

CLEAR TRACK,
GATED

0   1/4 mile

0   APPROX SCALE   500 metres

HUT

OLD
WORKINGS

1 HR 45 MINS – 2 HRS 30 MINS TO GREENHEAD (MAP 102)
FROM KELLAH BURN (MAP 100)

1 HR 45 MINS – 2 HRS 30 MINS FROM GREENHEAD (MAP 102)
TO KELLAH BURN (MAP 100)

TRAILBLAZER

100

SOME WALKERS
MAY FOLLOW THIS
FENCE DOWN TO
THE HUT

DON'T LEAVE THIS
TRACK TOO EARLY –
YOU DON'T WANT TO
WALK ALONG THE A69

DESCENDING FROM BLACK HILL, THE VISTA
IS FULL OF INTEREST. ACROSS THE VALLEY
OF THE TIPALT BURN WHICH RUNS THROUGH
GREENHEAD, THE LINE OF THE ROMAN WALL
CAN BE SEEN.

GREENHEAD TO ONCE BREWED   MAPS 102-105

For those for whom a short day has been long overdue, this stretch will be very
welcome. Only **7 miles (11km, 2½-3hrs)**, the high-quality walking is along the
fascinating remains of **Hadrian's Wall**. The way-marking is generally good and
will get better now that the Wall has become a National Trail. This is a popular
and populous area and for the first time since leaving Malham you may feel that
too many other people are sharing your space. If so, raise your eyes to the horizon and the views ahead of the Wall following the Whin Sill, swooping and
soaring, lifting the spirits and dispelling negative thoughts brought on by the
proximity of 'crowds'.

Greenhead is left behind via the rather inflated ruin of **Thirlwall Castle**
(see box p210) which was built long after the Romans had departed, the stones
from their wall being used to good effect. Before long you join the Wall itself
at **Walltown Crags** and you follow the line of it for the remainder of this day's
walk. You may sometimes be tempted to jump up on it and stride along the very
top. Spoilsports say you shouldn't but it has survived two thousand years and is
unlikely to be seriously eroded by Vibram soles.

Refreshments are non-existent until you reach Once Brewed so you should
make sure you have plenty with you before setting out.

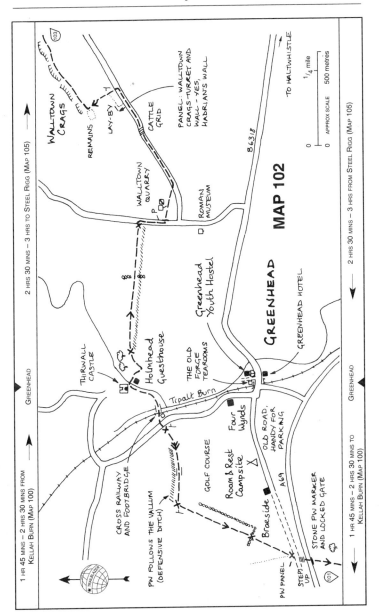

❑ Thirlwall Castle

Northumberland National Park Authority have done a great marketing job on what is in effect just an old ruin and all credit to them for bringing it to life. The truth is Thirlwall Castle is hardly the focus of massive historical interest and walkers may feel that they have taken in all they want from the interpretative panel on display. It was enough for me.

Built in the 14th century by a powerful local family for protection and defence against border raiders, Thirlwall must have represented an impregnable stronghold to men armed only with spear and sword but by the 17th century these lawless times had passed and the Thirlwall family moved to more comfortable quarters in Hexham.

As a reminder of a time when the Borders were the scene of raids and struggles, Thirlwall serves a purpose but we have more absorbing antiquities than this to investigate. Ahead lies The Wall!

ONCE BREWED   [Map 105]

This sporadically laid-out village is about half a mile from the Pennine Way on the B6318, the road everyone refers to as 'the military road'.

You may wonder about the origins of the settlement's odd name. Originally there was a drovers' inn, the Twice Brewed, a staging post for travellers between Carlisle and Newcastle. It's said that it had been called Twice Brewed because General Wade found the local ale so weak he said it needed to be brewed again. When the youth hostel was opened in the 1930s, its patron, Lady Trevelyan, remarked that she hoped the tea there would be brewed once, not twice like General Wade's ale. It's now a popular stop for many a Pennine Way walker.

There's nothing here of much note except a **tourist information centre** (☎ 01434-344396, open 9.30am-5pm Apr to Oct, to 6pm in the summer months, weekends only from Oct to Apr) with its own café, and that's about it.

For those who have set this day aside as a rest-day, there's nothing to do, unless you plan to catch the bus along the wall and visit one of the museums or preserved forts such as Housesteads.

Buses stop at the TIC throughout the season as a stop on the Hadrian's Wall Service (AD122; see public transport map, pp36-9), an excellent if under-used service which makes visiting the Wall very con-venient as it links all the main Roman sites.

Many of these buses also stop at the **railway station** at Haltwhistle on the Carlisle–Newcastle line with frequent trains throughout the day.

If you need a **taxi**, you can call one from Haltwhistle where Sprouls Taxis (☎ 01434-321064) run an efficient business. If you can't raise them, try Turnbulls (☎ 01434-320105).

The obvious choice for campers is **Winshields Farm** (☎ 01434-344243) right beside the main road, where the charge is £4 per person, the site flat and spacious and the facilities simple yet adequate. You can easily walk to the pub for a meal but there is no shop.

Once Brewed Youth Hostel (☎ 01434-344360, bookings ☎ 0870-770 5980, 🖥 once brewed@yha.org.uk, open early Feb to late Nov but closed Sun-Mon in Feb, Mar, Nov) has 90 beds, mostly in four-bedded rooms and is open from 1pm, which is unusual as most hostels leave you hanging about until 5pm. You can book an evening meal and beds cost £11.80 (£8.50 under 18s).

Other accommodation in the area includes the superior **Vallum Lodge** (☎ 01434-344248, 4T/3D) charging £23 for B&B (£28 in an en-suite double/twin; £33 for singles). There's also the **Crows Nest** (☎ 01434-344348, 1D/1T/1F) along the main road to the east, where you'll pay £22.50 per person.

Between the youth hostel and Vallum Lodge is *The Twice Brewed Inn* (☎ 01434-344534, 🖳 www.twicebrewedinn.co.uk, 3S/5T/4D) with B&B from £19.50 and with some en-suite rooms. The pub here most conveniently serves food all day (from 11am to 8.30pm): light meals such as baguettes (£3.25) or a ploughman's (£5.75) or main dishes at around £6-7. There are some good vegetarian options such as pan-fried Mediterranean vegetables with halloumi cheese (£5.25). The publican used to run the youth hostel.

Better value can be found at *Saughy Rigg Farm* (☎ 01434-344120, 🖳 www.saughyrigg.co.uk, 1S/4T/2F en suite) which has comfortable accommodation from £15-20 per person, evening meal £12.50. The Farm is about half a mile north of Hadrian's Wall.

❏ Hadrian's Wall

The Roman Emperor Hadrian first conceived the project after visiting Britain in AD 122 and finding out for himself the extent of the difficulty faced by the occupying army in northern Britain. It was impossible to hold any kind of control over the area now known as Scotland. It was too vast and was populated by lawless tribes who could not be conquered. Instead it was decided to build a defensive wall which none would be allowed to cross. The line of the wall, drawn from the Solway to the Tyne, followed the fault-line of the Whin Sill, a geological shelf of hard rock, basalt, which acted as a natural east–west barrier.

The Wall is approximately 80 Roman miles and 73 modern miles (117km) long and had turrets or milecastles every (Roman) mile and larger forts at intervals along its length. The forts would have had a garrison of 500 cavalry or 1000 foot soldiers. The milecastles were manned by 50 men each. The Wall was made of stone and turf and would have been five metres high and with a defensive ditch, the vallum, set between two mounds of earth, running the length of it on the southern side. Behind that ran a road to supply and provision the troops manning the wall.

The construction of the Wall was supervised by the Imperial Legate Aulus Platorius Nepos and the building took ten years. It remained in use for 200 years but as the Romans withdrew it fell into disuse and gradually the stones were plundered to build farmsteads and roads. Thirlwall Castle has stones from the Roman Wall in its walls.

Today English Heritage, the National Trust and the National Park authorities preserve and protect what remains of the wall, keeping it tidy and providing the information that we need to help us imagine what it was all for. It's well worth visiting **Housesteads Fort** (☎ 01434-344363, open daily, 10am-6pm 1 Apr-30 Sep and 10am-4pm 1 Oct-31 Mar, adult £3.50, child £1.60), less than a mile from the Way and one of the best examples of Roman remains in the whole of Britain. The communal latrines are particularly well preserved.

The information we have about the history of the Wall is fragmentary and circumstantial, historians having disputed for centuries over the finer details. What is certain is that the Wall is an extraordinary example of military might whilst demonstrating perhaps the futility of human endeavour. How can you hold back the tide of human expansion by anything so transient as a wall? Impressive, inspiring, unique, yes, but ultimately a failure. When we turn our back on it and head north into Wark Forest, the sight of the Whin Sill is like a breaking wave. The Wall blends into the landscape. The northern tribes had only to wait.

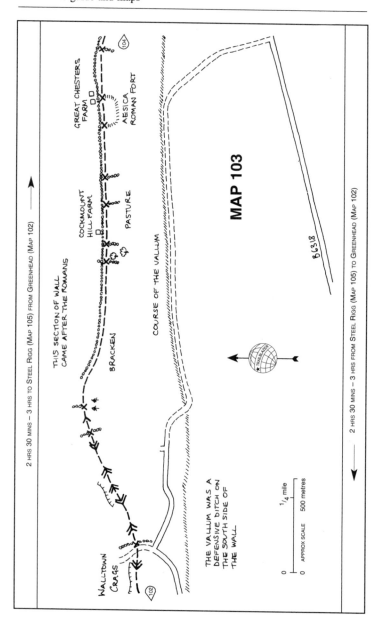

2 HRS 30 MINS – 3 HRS TO STEEL RIGG (MAP 105) FROM GREENHEAD (MAP 102)

THIS SECTION OF WALL
CAME AFTER THE ROMANS

GREAT CHESTERS
FARM

AESICA
ROMAN FORT

104

COCKMOUNT
HILL FARM

PASTURE

BRACKEN

COURSE OF THE VALLUM

MAP 103

B6318

WALLTOWN
CRAGS

102

THE VALLUM WAS A
DEFENSIVE DITCH ON
THE SOUTH SIDE OF
THE WALL

¼ mile

0   APPROX SCALE
0   500 metres

2 HRS 30 MINS – 3 HRS FROM STEEL RIGG (MAP 105) TO GREENHEAD (MAP 102)

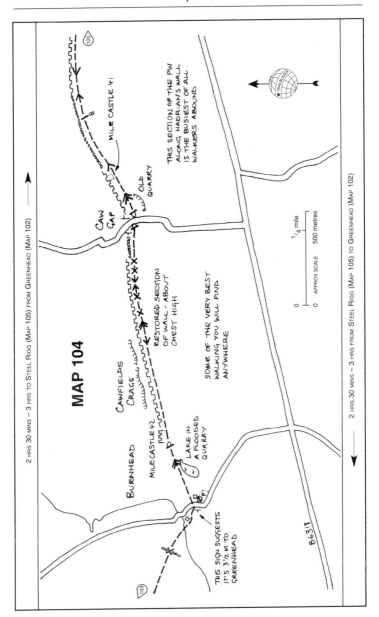

MAP 104

2 HRS 30 MINS – 3 HRS TO STEEL RIGG (MAP 105) FROM GREENHEAD (MAP 102)

2 HRS 30 MINS – 3 HRS FROM STEEL RIGG (MAP 105) TO GREENHEAD (MAP 102)

105

MILE CASTLE 41

OLD QUARRY

CAW GAP

THIS SECTION OF THE PW ALONG HADRIAN'S WALL IS THE BUSIEST OF ALL. WALKERS ABOUND.

RESTORED SECTION OF WALL – ABOUT CHEST HIGH

CAWFIELDS CRAGS

SOME OF THE VERY BEST WALKING YOU WILL FIND ANYWHERE

BURNHEAD

MILECASTLE 42

LAKE IN A FLOODED QUARRY

THIS SIGN SUGGESTS IT'S 3½ M TO GREENHEAD

103

B6318

TRAILBLAZER

0   ¼ mile
APPROX SCALE
0   500 metres

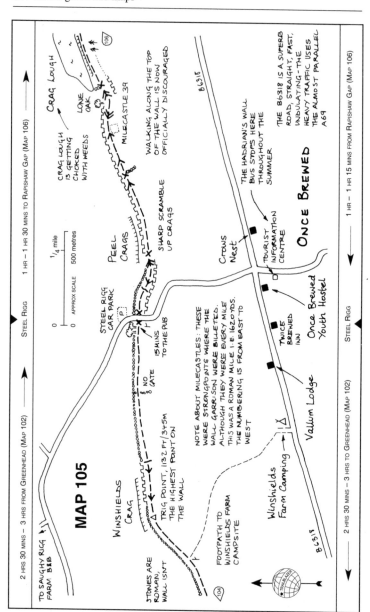

MAP 105

TO SAUGHY RIGG FARM B&B

WINSHIELDS CRAG

STONES ARE ROMAN, WALL ISN'T

TRIG POINT, 1132 FT/345M THE HIGHEST POINT ON THE WALL

FOOTPATH TO WINSHIELDS FARM CAMPSITE

NOTE ABOUT MILECASTLES: THESE WERE STRONGPOINTS WHERE THE WALL GARRISON WERE BILLETED. ALTHOUGH THEY WERE BILLETED EVERY MILE THIS WAS A ROMAN MILE I.E. 1620 YDS. THE NUMBERING IS FROM EAST TO WEST

Winshields Farm Camping

Vallum Lodge

Twice Brewed Inn

Once Brewed Youth Hostel

ONCE BREWED

TOURIST INFORMATION CENTRE

THE HADRIAN'S WALL BUS STOPS HERE THROUGHOUT SUMMER

THE B6318 IS A SUPERB ROAD, STRAIGHT, FAST, UNDULATING – THE HEAVY TRAFFIC USES THE ALMOST PARALLEL A69

B6318

Crows Nest

STEEL RIGG CAR PARK

NO GATE

15 MINS TO THE PUB

SHARP SCRAMBLE UP CRAGS

PEEL CRAGS

CRAG LOUGH IS GETTING CHOKED WITH WEEDS

MILECASTLE 39

LONE OAK

CRAG LOUGH

WALKING ALONG THE TOP OF THE WALL IS NOW OFFICIALLY DISCOURAGED

0   1/4 mile
0   500 metres
APPROX SCALE

ONCE BREWED TO BELLINGHAM   MAPS 105-112

This section is **14½ miles (23km, 6½-8¼hrs)** in length and feels every yard of it. The first hour is about the finest start to a day's march as you are likely to find, high along the line of the Wall, above the reedy **Crag Lough**, home to migrating wildfowl. After you have warmed up you reach a signpost which points away north towards the dark forests ahead, signalling your farewell to the Wall. The route isn't clear for the next few miles and it is not difficult to stray off the line and wander about in boggy ground like a lost sheep. The way through **Wark Forest** is mostly on forestry tracks, not an uplifting experience since large swathes of planted acres have been progressively cleared, leaving a lunar landscape of twisted stumps with ranks of plastic tree guards as evidence of extensive reforestation.

Emerging from the trees, the Way crosses an area of mixed pasture and farmland that lacks appeal until ahead a line of crags surmounted by a radio mast indicates that this is **Shitlington**. It's a tidy place so heavy-handed jokes are not appropriate. Beyond Shitlington lies **Bellingham**.

This has not been the most distinguished day you will experience on the trail and the last half-hour is the least distinguished of all, along the main road into town. Still, there is a sense that journey's end is not so far away now. In two days you could be sitting in the bar at the Border Hotel, patting yourself on the back.

Bellingham awaits. Nobody gives up here.

STONEHAUGH   [Map 109]
There are hardly any opportunities for refreshments on the route today except at the forestry outpost of Stonehaugh where if you feel that you simply cannot walk any further you could go to the Forestry Commission's *Stonehaugh Camp Site* (☎ 01434-230798). The site, which charges £3 per tent plus £3 per person, is open Easter-Oct and is well-run with showers and a Social Club (open Thur-Sun). It's a mile off the route and there are no shops for five miles but they can provide provisions if you call ahead.

HETHERINGTON   [Map 110]
Hetherington Farm (☎/🖹 01434-230260, 🖳 www.hetheringtonselfcater.co.uk, 2D /1F), just a few hundred metres from the Way, offers very comfortable B&B. They charge around £25 per person (£30 in the antique four-poster bed).

BELLINGHAM   [see Map p216]
This small old market town is set in glorious scenery. It's the last reasonably-sized place on the Pennine Way and has most things you will need.

Services
The **tourist information centre** (☎ 01434-220616, Easter-Oct Mon-Sat 9.30am-1pm, 2-5.30pm but to 5pm from Easter to mid-May, Sun 1-5pm, Nov to Easter Mon-Fri 2-5pm) has very helpful staff. There is a **chemist**, grocery shop and two butchers' as well as a small Co-op **supermarket** (Mon-Sat 8am-10pm, Sun 10am-10pm). You can buy a basic **camping kit**, including Coleman fuel and gas canisters, from Bellingham Country Stores (Mon-Wed and Fri 9am-12.30pm, 1.30-5pm, Thu and Sat 9am-12.30pm, 1.30-4pm). Rod's Snack Bar also sells Camping Gaz and Calor Gas. Barclays **bank** has a cash machine but Lloyds does not. The **post office** is opposite Rod's Snack Bar. Both Snaith Travel (☎ 01830-520609) and Bellingham and Hunshaugh (☎ 01434-220570) operate **taxis** or there's a regular **bus** service to Hexham (see public transport map, pp36-9). The nearest **hospital** is Hexham General Hospital (☎ 01434-655655).

Places to stay
On your way into town you pass the well set up *Brown Rigg Caravan and Camping*

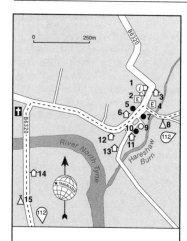

Bellingham

Where to stay
3 Lynn View
6 Cheviot Hotel
8 Demesne Farm Camping
11 The Rose & Crown
13 Lyndale GH
14 Crofter's End
15 Brown Rigg Camping Park

Other
1 TIC, Library &
  Fountain Cottage Tea Rooms
2 Barclays Bank
4 Lloyds Bank
5 Chemist
7 Bellingham Country Stores
9 Rod's Snack Bar
10 Co-op Supermarket
12 The Black Bull

Park (☎ 01434-220175, 🖳 www.northum berlandcaravanparks.com, Easter to Oct) which charges £4 per person July to August, otherwise £3.50. There's a washing machine big enough to take a sleeping bag (£1.50) and somewhere warm to hang your wet boots.

If you would rather be in the centre of town and on a working farm go to *Demesne*

Farm Camp Site (☎ 01434-220258/ 220107, 🖳 telfer@demesne.plus.com), which costs £4 per person per night.

Bellingham Youth Hostel (see Map 112; ☎ 01434-220313, bookings ☎ 0870-770 5694, 🖳 www.yha.org.uk, open Apr-Sep, closed Sun, Mon in Apr, May, Jun, Sep) is a simple traditional hostel, with self-catering facilities only, located in a cedarwood cabin high above the town. Beds cost £9.30 (£6.70 for under 18s).

Lynn View (☎ 01434-220344, 1S/1T/2D) promise to 'spoil walkers rotten' and have accommodation for £20, but are closed from November to around Easter. They will send you off with a packed lunch for £3.50. *Crofter's End* (☎ 01434-220034, 1S/1T) is a friendly place on your way into town where the rooms with shared bathroom cost £19, open Easter-Oct. *Lyndale Guest House* (☎ 01434-220361, 🖳 www.lyn daleguesthouse.co.uk, 1S/1T/2D) is a bright and friendly place where they charge £25 for B&B. They've even got a Jacuzzi, perfect after a long day on the Way.

Of the pubs *The Cheviot Hotel* (☎ 01434-220696, 🖳 www.thecheviothotel.co .uk, 1S/3T/1D en suite) is the most upmarket and costs £28 for B&B. *The Rose and Crown* (☎ 01434-220202, 3T) charges £17.50 but is often block-booked by soldiers for several months in the summer.

Places to eat
Rod's Snack Bar (☎ 01434-220288, Mon-Fri 9am-4pm, Sat 9am-1pm), on Lockup Lane close to the Co-op, is much better than it sounds, serving filled paninis or poonahs (Indian flat bread) for £2.95, takeaway salads (cheese flan, ham, tuna or prawn (£1.70-2.10) and a range of filter coffees (80p) as well as hearty portions of standard café food. The *Fountain Cottage Tea Rooms* (Tue-Sun 10am-5pm summer, 10am-4pm winter, and bank holidays) by the TIC, does home-cooked light lunches and teas.

The Cheviot Hotel (see above) is the best of the pubs, with favourites such as steak and ale pie (£6.25) or fish and chips (takeaway for £3.10). *The Black Bull* (open evenings only) and the *Rose and Crown* (see above) also do cheap pub grub.

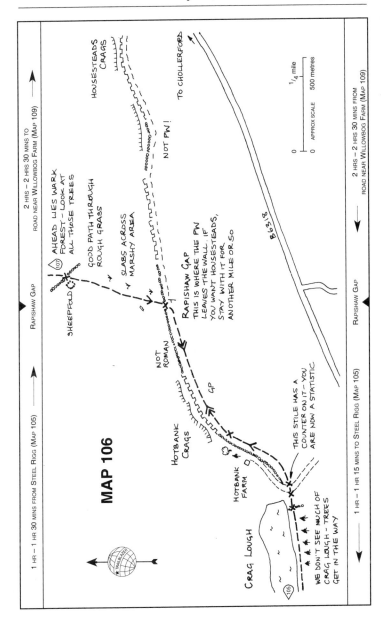

MAP 106

CRAG LOUGH

HOTBANK CRAGS

HOTBANK FARM

HOUSESTEADS CRAGS

SHEEPFOLD

NOT ROMAN

GP

RAPISHAW GAP
THIS IS WHERE THE PW LEAVES THE WALL. IF YOU WANT HOUSESTEADS, STAY WITH IT FOR ANOTHER MILE OR SO.

AHEAD LIES WARK FOREST - LOOK AT ALL THESE TREES

GOOD PATH THROUGH ROUGH GRASS

SLABS ACROSS MARSHY AREA

NOT PW!

THIS STILE HAS A COUNTER ON IT - YOU ARE NOW A STATISTIC

WE DON'T SEE MUCH OF CRAG LOUGH - TREES GET IN THE WAY

TO CHOLLERFORD

B6318

TRAIL BLAZER

0   ¼ mile
APPROX SCALE
0   500 metres

1 HR – 1 HR 30 MINS FROM STEEL RIGG (MAP 105)

2 HRS – 2 HRS 30 MINS TO ROAD NEAR WILLOWBOG FARM (MAP 109)

RAPISHAW GAP

2 HRS – 2 HRS 30 MINS FROM ROAD NEAR WILLOWBOG FARM (MAP 109)

RAPISHAW GAP

1 HR – 1 HR 15 MINS TO STEEL RIGG (MAP 105)

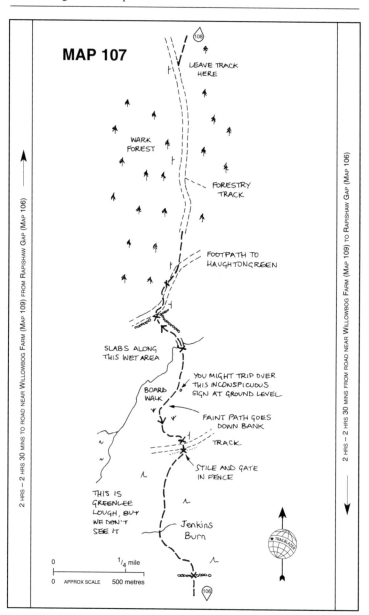

MAP 107

108

LEAVE TRACK
HERE

WARK
FOREST

FORESTRY
TRACK

FOOTPATH TO
HAUGHTONGREEN

SLABS ALONG
THIS WET AREA

YOU MIGHT TRIP OVER
THIS INCONSPICUOUS
SIGN AT GROUND LEVEL

BOARD
WALK

FAINT PATH GOES
DOWN BANK

TRACK

STILE AND GATE
IN FENCE

THIS IS
GREENLEE
LOUGH, BUT
WE DON'T
SEE IT

Jenkins
Burn

106

0   ¼ mile

0   APPROX SCALE   500 metres

TRAILBLAZER

2 HRS – 2 HRS 30 MINS TO ROAD NEAR WILLOWBOG FARM (MAP 109) FROM RAPISHAW GAP (MAP 106)

2 HRS – 2 HRS 30 MINS FROM ROAD NEAR WILLOWBOG FARM (MAP 109) TO RAPISHAW GAP (MAP 106)

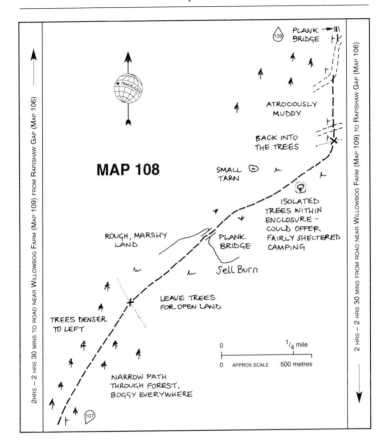

MAP 108

PLANK BRIDGE

ATROCIOUSLY MUDDY

BACK INTO THE TREES

SMALL TARN

ISOLATED TREES WITHIN ENCLOSURE – COULD OFFER FAIRLY SHELTERED CAMPING

ROUGH, MARSHY LAND

PLANK BRIDGE

Sell Burn

LEAVE TREES FOR OPEN LAND

TREES DENSER TO LEFT

NARROW PATH THROUGH FOREST, BOGGY EVERYWHERE

0   ¹/₄ mile
0   APPROX SCALE   500 metres

2HRS – 2 HRS 30 MINS TO ROAD NEAR WILLOWBOG FARM (MAP 109) FROM RAPISHAW GAP (MAP 106)

2 HRS – 2 HRS 30 MINS FROM ROAD NEAR WILLOWBOG FARM (MAP 109) TO RAPISHAW GAP (MAP 106)

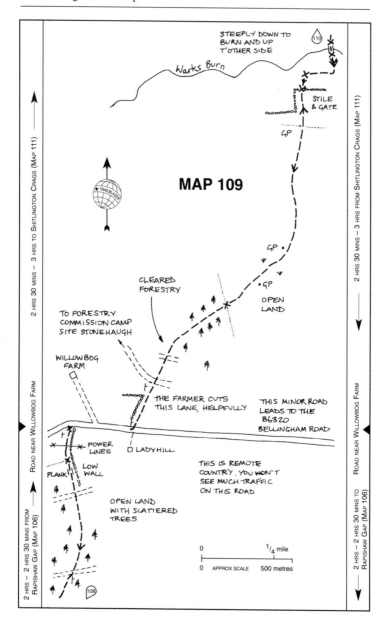

STEEPLY DOWN TO
BURN AND UP
T'OTHER SIDE

110

Warks Burn

STILE
& GATE

GP

MAP 109

★ TRAILBLAZER

GP

GP

OPEN
LAND

CLEARED
FORESTRY

TO FORESTRY
COMMISSION CAMP
SITE STONEHAUGH

WILLOWBOG
FARM

THE FARMER CUTS
THIS LANE, HELPFULLY

THIS MINOR ROAD
LEADS TO THE
B6320
BELLINGHAM ROAD

POWER
LINES

LADYHILL

PLANK

LOW
WALL

THIS IS REMOTE
COUNTRY. YOU WON'T
SEE MUCH TRAFFIC
ON THIS ROAD

OPEN LAND
WITH SCATTERED
TREES

108

0   1/4 mile

0   APPROX SCALE   500 metres

2 HRS 30 MINS – 3 HRS TO SHITLINGTON CRAGS (MAP 111)

ROAD NEAR WILLOWBOG FARM

2 HRS – 2 HRS 30 MINS FROM RAPISHAW GAP (MAP 106)

2 HRS 30 MINS – 3 HRS FROM SHITLINGTON CRAGS (MAP 111)

ROAD NEAR WILLOWBOG FARM

2 HRS – 2 HRS 30 MINS TO RAPISHAW GAP (MAP 106)

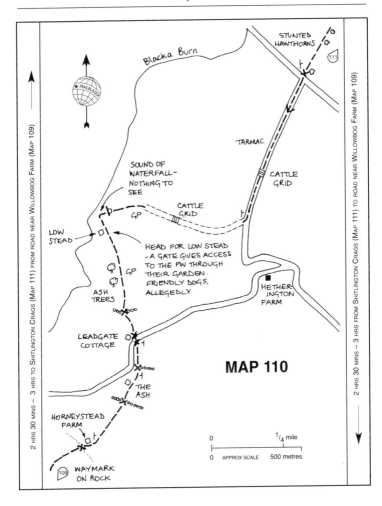

STUNTED
HAWTHORNS

111

Blacka Burn

★ TRAILBLAZER

TARMAC

CATTLE
GRID

SOUND OF
WATERFALL -
NOTHING TO
SEE

CATTLE
GRID

GP

LOW
STEAD

HEAD FOR LOW STEAD
- A GATE GIVES ACCESS
TO THE PW THROUGH
THEIR GARDEN.
FRIENDLY DOGS,
ALLEGEDLY

GP

HETHER-
INGTON
FARM

ASH
TREES

LEADGATE
COTTAGE

THE
ASH

MAP 110

HORNEYSTEAD
FARM

0   ¼ mile

0   APPROX SCALE   500 metres

109   WAYMARK
ON ROCK

2 HRS 30 MINS – 3 HRS TO SHITLINGTON CRAGS (MAP 111) FROM ROAD NEAR WILLOWBOG FARM (MAP 109)

2 HRS 30 MINS – 3 HRS FROM SHITLINGTON CRAGS (MAP 111) TO ROAD NEAR WILLOWBOG FARM (MAP 109)

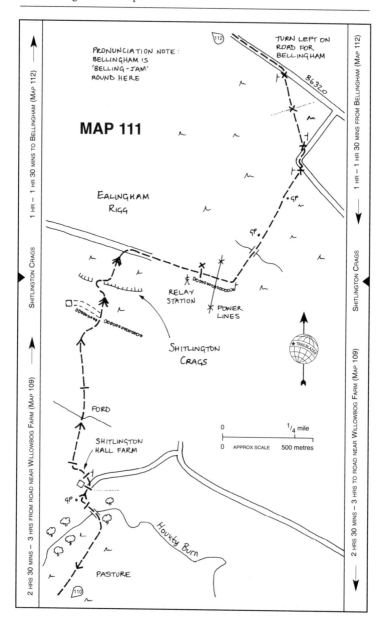

PRONUNCIATION NOTE:
BELLINGHAM IS
'BELLING-JAM'
ROUND HERE

TURN LEFT ON
ROAD FOR
BELLINGHAM

112

B 6320

MAP 111

EALINGHAM
RIGG

GP

GP

SHITLINGTON
CRAGS

RELAY
STATION

POWER
LINES

TRAILBLAZER

FORD

SHITLINGTON
HALL FARM

GP

Houxty Burn

PASTURE

110

0   1/4 mile

0   APPROX SCALE   500 metres

1 HR – 1 HR 30 MINS TO BELLINGHAM (MAP 112)

SHITLINGTON CRAGS

2 HRS 30 MINS – 3 HRS FROM ROAD NEAR WILLOWBOG FARM (MAP 109)

1 HR – 1 HR 30 MINS FROM BELLINGHAM (MAP 112)

SHITLINGTON CRAGS

2 HRS 30 MINS – 3 HRS TO ROAD NEAR WILLOWBOG FARM (MAP 109)

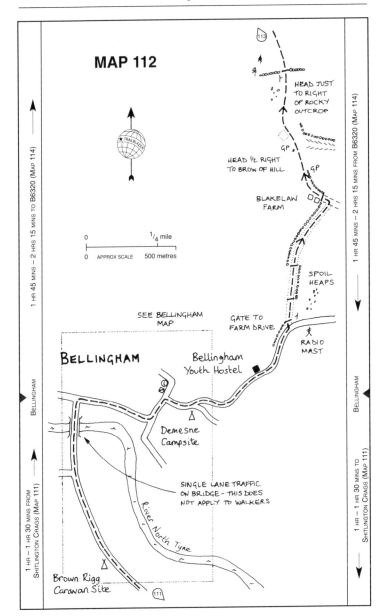

MAP 112

★ TRAILBLAZER

113

HEAD JUST
TO RIGHT
OF ROCKY
OUTCROP

GP

HEAD ½ RIGHT
TO BROW OF HILL

GP

BLAKELAW
FARM

0   ¼ mile

0   APPROX SCALE   500 metres

SPOIL
HEAPS

SEE BELLINGHAM
MAP

GATE TO
FARM DRIVE

RADIO
MAST

BELLINGHAM

Bellingham
Youth Hostel

Demesne
Campsite

SINGLE LANE TRAFFIC
ON BRIDGE - THIS DOES
NOT APPLY TO WALKERS

River North Tyne

Brown Rigg
Caravan Site

111

1 HR 45 MINS – 2 HRS 15 MINS TO B6320 (MAP 114)

BELLINGHAM

1 HR – 1 HR 30 MINS FROM SHITLINGTON CRAGS (MAP 111)

1 HR 45 MINS – 2 HRS 15 MINS FROM B6320 (MAP 114)

BELLINGHAM

1 HR – 1 HR 30 MINS TO SHITLINGTON CRAGS (MAP 111)

BELLINGHAM TO BYRNESS   MAPS 112-120

It's **15 miles (24km, 7¼-9hrs)** from Bellingham through a large chunk of Redesdale Forest to the isolated frontier settlement of Byrness, a place of minimal charm and slight interest other than its significance as an overnight stop on the Pennine Way.

The going underfoot is wet and boggy for much of the time, the waterlogged peat moors having absorbed so much rain that it can no longer drain away. You will need to be nimble-footed if you want to keep your feet dry. There is a fair amount of climbing over hills not exceeding 370 metres (1200ft) but none of them can claim much distinction. Padon Hill has a prominent cairn but the Way passes by on a path that avoids the summit.

Once you enter **Redesdale Forest** the walking is along well-made tracks used by forestry vehicles some of which drive at breakneck speeds regardless of passing walkers. A sign from the Forestry Commission welcomes Pennine Way walkers but that's where the welcome ends. The trees are being systematically cleared, a process that is heavily mechanized and brutal, leaving vast areas of blighted landscape that is no fun to walk through. The mature conifers, standing silent and untouched, have a quiet serenity that is totally destroyed once the uprooting starts.

The last mile from **Blakehope Burn** to **Byrness** is a pleasant walk through woodland and along the **River Rede**, a refreshing end to what has been a tiresome and soggy-bottomed day. This evening a drink is called for, but not a skinful. Tomorrow requires heroic effort.

BYRNESS   [Map 120]

This collection of buildings strung out along the busy A68 offers little to cheer the soul but enough to fortify you for the next day's long walk. That said, *The Byrness Hotel* (☎ 01830-520231, 🖥 www.thepennineway.co.uk/thebyrness, 1D en suite/1T/1F) provides a country-house-hotel atmosphere, a bed for £25 per person including breakfast and an evening meal from £6. They will also let people **camp** for £2.50. Campers can use the facilities in the hotel and are welcome for breakfast and supper. *Middle Byrness Cottage* (see Map 119; ☎ 01830-520294, 2T) does B&B for £20 per person.

Byrness Youth Hostel (☎ 01830-520425, bookings ☎ 0870-770 5740, 🖥 reservations@yha.org.uk, open Apr to early Oct) offers basic accommodation in two converted forestry cottages for £8.20 (£5.70 under 18s), or there's the friendly *Border Forest Caravan Park* (see Map 119; ☎ 01830-520259, 🖥 www.borderforestcaravanpark.co.uk) for **camping** (£4.20), **bunkhouse** (£10) and **B&B** (£23 per person, 2F en suite) in motel-type rooms; closed November to February. They are very keen to point out that the bunkhouse, with two four-bed rooms, is heated, has a basic kitchen and a boiler room for drying boots. You have to provide your own bedding. Showers are free and hot too!

First and Last Café in the garage sells good-value fast food for lorry drivers; a bit of stodge may be just what you need.

There's a daily **bus** service to Otterburn/Newcastle and to Edinburgh and an irregular one to Bellingham (see public transport map, pp36-9).

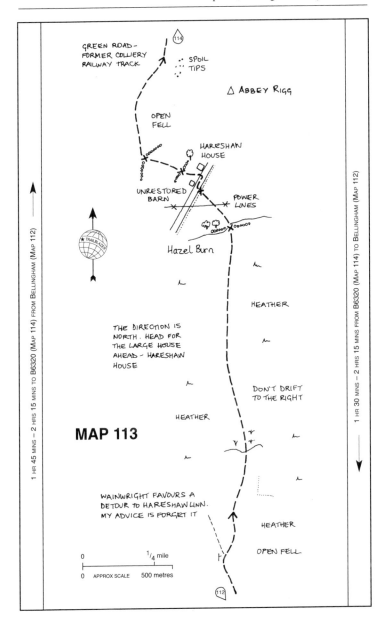

1 HR 45 MINS – 2 HRS 15 MINS TO B6320 (MAP 114) FROM BELLINGHAM (MAP 112)

1 HR 30 MINS – 2 HRS 15 MINS FROM B6320 (MAP 114) TO BELLINGHAM (MAP 112)

GREEN ROAD –
FORMER COLLIERY
RAILWAY TRACK

SPOIL
TIPS

△ ABBEY RIGG

OPEN
FELL

HARESHAW
HOUSE

UNRESTORED
BARN

POWER
LINES

★ TRAILBLAZER

Hazel Burn

HEATHER

THE DIRECTION IS
NORTH. HEAD FOR
THE LARGE HOUSE
AHEAD – HARESHAW
HOUSE

DON'T DRIFT
TO THE RIGHT

HEATHER

MAP 113

WAINWRIGHT FAVOURS A
DETOUR TO HARESHAW LINN.
MY ADVICE IS FORGET IT

HEATHER

OPEN FELL

0   ¹/₄ mile

0   APPROX SCALE   500 metres

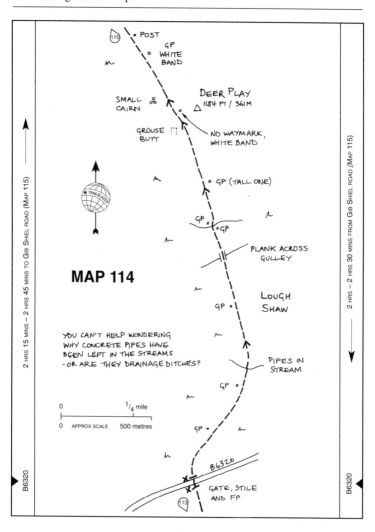

MAP 114

POST

GP
WHITE
BAND

DEER PLAY
△ 1184 FT / 361M

SMALL
CAIRN

NO WAYMARK,
WHITE BAND

GROUSE
BUTT

GP (TALL ONE)

GP
GP

PLANK ACROSS
GULLEY

LOUGH
SHAW

GP

YOU CAN'T HELP WONDERING
WHY CONCRETE PIPES HAVE
BEEN LEFT IN THE STREAMS
- OR ARE THEY DRAINAGE DITCHES?

PIPES IN
STREAM

GP

GP

B6320

GATE, STILE
AND FP

TRAILBLAZER

0   ¼ mile
0   APPROX SCALE   500 metres

2 HRS 15 MINS – 2 HRS 45 MINS TO GIB SHIEL ROAD (MAP 115)

2 HRS – 2 HRS 30 MINS FROM GIB SHIEL ROAD (MAP 115)

B6320

B6320

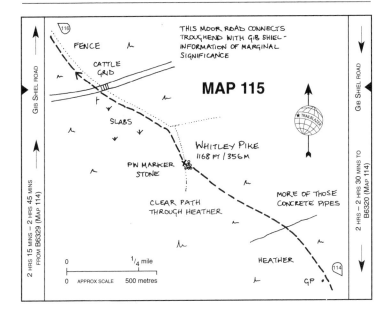

THIS MOOR ROAD CONNECTS
TROUGHEND WITH GIB SHIEL -
INFORMATION OF MARGINAL
SIGNIFICANCE

MAP 115

FENCE

CATTLE
GRID

SLABS

WHITLEY PIKE
1168 FT / 356 M

PW MARKER
STONE

CLEAR PATH
THROUGH HEATHER

MORE OF THOSE
CONCRETE PIPES

HEATHER

GP

★ TRAILBLAZER

GIB SHIEL ROAD

GIB SHIEL ROAD

2 HRS 15 MINS – 2 HRS 45 MINS
FROM B6329 (MAP 114)

2 HRS – 2 HRS 30 MINS TO
B6320 (MAP 114)

0   ¼ mile

0   APPROX SCALE   500 metres

116

114

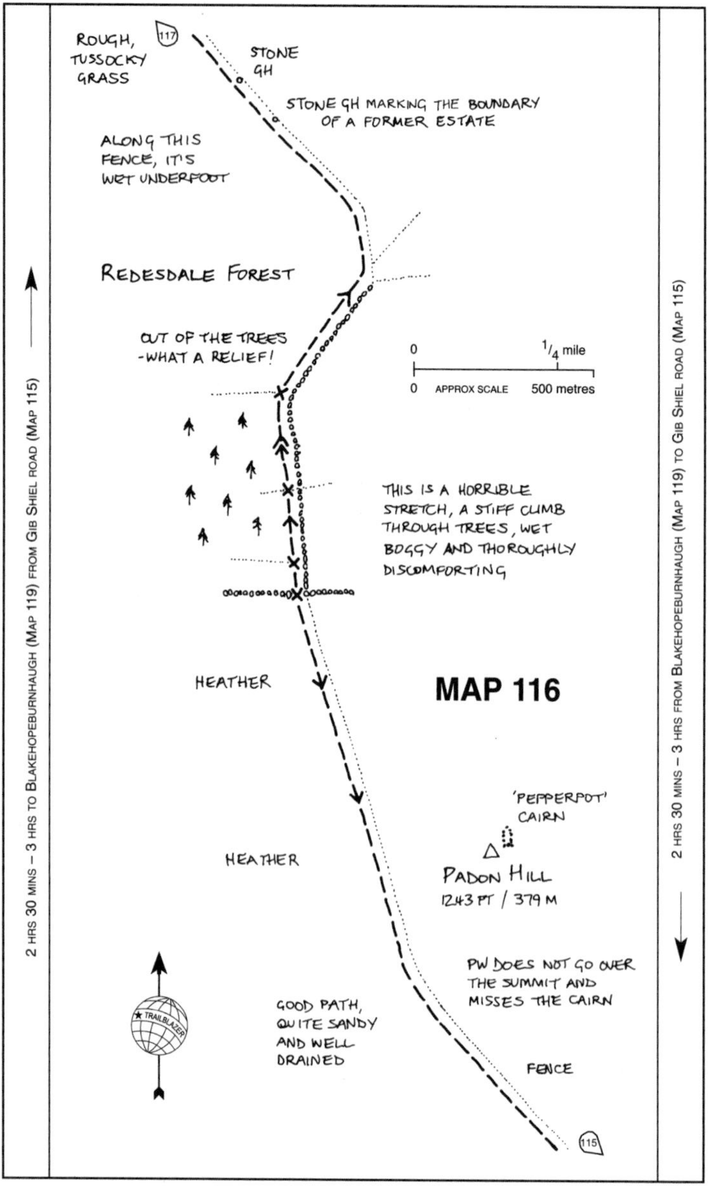

ROUGH, TUSSOCKY GRASS

(117)

STONE GH

STONE GH MARKING THE BOUNDARY OF A FORMER ESTATE

ALONG THIS FENCE, IT'S WET UNDERFOOT

REDESDALE FOREST

OUT OF THE TREES - WHAT A RELIEF!

0   ¼ mile

0   APPROX SCALE   500 metres

THIS IS A HORRIBLE STRETCH, A STIFF CLIMB THROUGH TREES, WET BOGGY AND THOROUGHLY DISCOMFORTING

HEATHER

MAP 116

'PEPPERPOT' CAIRN

△

PADON HILL
1243 FT / 379 M

HEATHER

PW DOES NOT GO OVER THE SUMMIT AND MISSES THE CAIRN

GOOD PATH, QUITE SANDY AND WELL DRAINED

FENCE

(115)

★ TRAILBLAZER

2 HRS 30 MINS – 3 HRS TO BLAKEHOPEBURNHAUGH (MAP 119) FROM GIB SHIEL ROAD (MAP 115)

2 HRS 30 MINS – 3 HRS FROM BLAKEHOPEBURNHAUGH (MAP 119) TO GIB SHIEL ROAD (MAP 115)

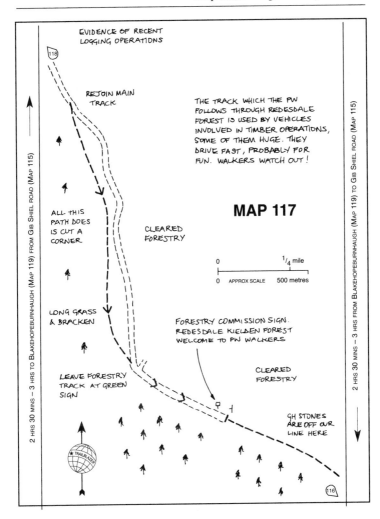

EVIDENCE OF RECENT LOGGING OPERATIONS

118

REJOIN MAIN TRACK

THE TRACK WHICH THE PW FOLLOWS THROUGH REDESDALE FOREST IS USED BY VEHICLES INVOLVED IN TIMBER OPERATIONS, SOME OF THEM HUGE. THEY DRIVE FAST, PROBABLY FOR FUN. WALKERS WATCH OUT!

MAP 117

ALL THIS PATH DOES IS CUT A CORNER

CLEARED FORESTRY

0 _____ ¼ mile
0 APPROX SCALE 500 metres

LONG GRASS & BRACKEN

FORESTRY COMMISSION SIGN. REDESDALE KIELDER FOREST WELCOME TO PW WALKERS

CLEARED FORESTRY

LEAVE FORESTRY TRACK AT GREEN SIGN

★ TRAILBLAZER

GH STONES ARE OFF OUR LINE HERE

116

2 HRS 30 MINS – 3 HRS TO BLAKEHOPEBURNHAUGH (MAP 119) FROM GIB SHIEL ROAD (MAP 115)

2 HRS 30 MINS – 3 HRS FROM BLAKEHOPEBURNHAUGH (MAP 119) TO GIB SHIEL ROAD (MAP 115)

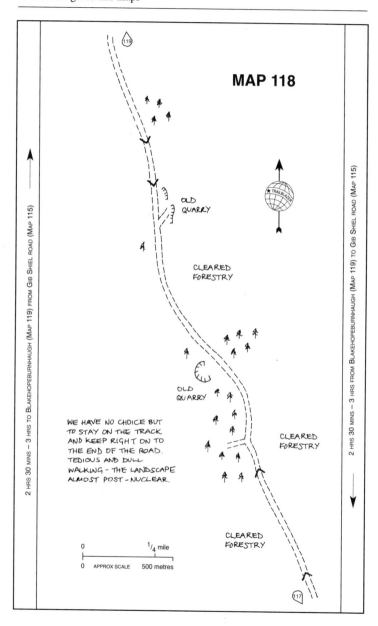

MAP 118

OLD QUARRY

CLEARED FORESTRY

OLD QUARRY

CLEARED FORESTRY

CLEARED FORESTRY

WE HAVE NO CHOICE BUT TO STAY ON THE TRACK AND KEEP RIGHT ON TO THE END OF THE ROAD. TEDIOUS AND DULL WALKING – THE LANDSCAPE ALMOST POST-NUCLEAR.

0   1/4 mile

0   APPROX SCALE   500 metres

2 HRS 30 MINS – 3 HRS TO BLAKEHOPEBURNHAUGH (MAP 119) FROM GIB SHIEL ROAD (MAP 115)

2 HRS 30 MINS – 3 HRS FROM BLAKEHOPEBURNHAUGH (MAP 119) TO GIB SHIEL ROAD (MAP 115)

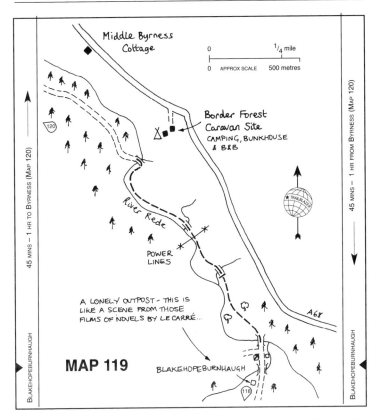

Middle Byrness Cottage

0   1/4 mile

0   APPROX SCALE   500 metres

Border Forest Caravan Site
CAMPING, BUNKHOUSE & B&B

River Rede

POWER LINES

A LONELY OUTPOST - THIS IS LIKE A SCENE FROM THOSE FILMS OF NOVELS BY LE CARRÉ...

★ TRAILBLAZER

A68

MAP 119

BLAKEHOPEBURNHAUGH

45 MINS – 1 HR TO BYRNESS (MAP 120)

45 MINS – 1 HR FROM BYRNESS (MAP 120)

BLAKEHOPEBURNHAUGH

BLAKEHOPEBURNHAUGH

BYRNESS TO KIRK YETHOLM   MAPS 120-135

Of all the challenges met so far these **27 miles (43km, 10½-13hrs)** across the deserted Cheviot massif will be the most demanding, stretching your endurance to near its limits. It is as though every day to date has been a preparation for this one and your mental preparation must be right. You can do it. Keep telling yourself that. The proud fraternity of Pennine Way Walkers has done it before you and there is no reason why you should not take your place among them.

If you decide to make two days of it, the options available to you are few. Campers can manage with a wild camp part way across but it might be necessary to get out of the wind by dropping down off the more exposed parts of the plateau. You could spend the night in one of the two **Mountain Refuge Huts** where there is room for three or four sleeping bags stretched out on the benches or floor where you will be dry and protected from the elements. There is no water at either although a note pinned up tells you where water can be found. There's also a point at which a B&B can be reached (see Uswayford below), but it's 1½ miles (2km) off route and booking would be essential.

The going underfoot is usually wet although some slabbing has been carried out and more is being done, in gradual stages, when weather and labour allow. In places boardwalks have been constructed for short distances but for most of the time you will be dodging boggy areas. There is no serious climbing once you have gained height early in the day, the route following fence lines most of the time. The severest test is the distance. Few walkers normally tackle 27 miles (43km) in a single day. You seem to plod on endlessly, each fence corner exactly like the last, the view ahead, if you can see ahead, opening up few suggestions that salvation is at hand. Without the two refuge huts in which to lick your wounds and take a rest it would be practically impossible to reach journey's end.

At last the divide in the path arrives where a decision has to be made whether to go off left on the so-called low-level route or continue over several more hills before joining up again a couple of miles out of Kirk Yetholm. Believe me, with darkness falling and the end in sight, more hills are the last thing you want and the low-level route will do for all but iron men and women.

At last, you pull back your shoulders and pick up your dragging feet. No point in looking beaten. The villagers in **Kirk Yetholm** don't care one way or the other, but you have your pride. It's over, your walk. At the Border Hotel they'll give you their book to sign. You read there the comments of fellow lengthsmen and women, mostly nonchalant or triumphant, some philosophical. Add yours as you celebrate with a beer, the traditional end to what you'll probably now agree is still Britain's most challenging long-distance trail.

USWAYFORD [Map 128]
Uswayford Farm (☎ 01669-650237, 1T/1D/1F) is 1½ miles off the trail and is the only B&B between Byrness and Kirk Yetholm. Turning up on spec would be a major mistake since you could well find them fully booked during the summer months. B&B costs £20 or £30 with an evening meal; there is nowhere else to eat. To reach it take the footpath signed 'Uswayford' one mile north-east of Russell's Cairn.

KIRK YETHOLM [Map 135]
It's probably fair to say that only a fraction of the people who have heard of this pleasant, quiet village would have done so if the Pennine Way did not end here.

Transport
There are regular **buses** throughout the day to Kelso (20-35 minutes) from where you can catch the service to Berwick-upon-Tweed (60 mins) (see public transport map, pp36-9). Berwick is on the mainline rail network to Newcastle and Edinburgh and also on the National Express coach route between those two cities.

For a **taxi** to Berwick contact Robert Dickson on ☎ 01890-882410.

Services
On your way in you pass *Valleydene* (☎ 01573-420286, 1T/3D/1F), a friendly establishment which charges £25 for B&B. They offer a very useful service of picking you up at Cocklawfoot halfway along the leg from Byrness and dropping you back there the next morning. Through the village and tucked away at the end of the road is *Blunty's Mill* (☎ 01573-420288, 🖳 www.st-cuthberts-way.co.uk/bluntysmill,

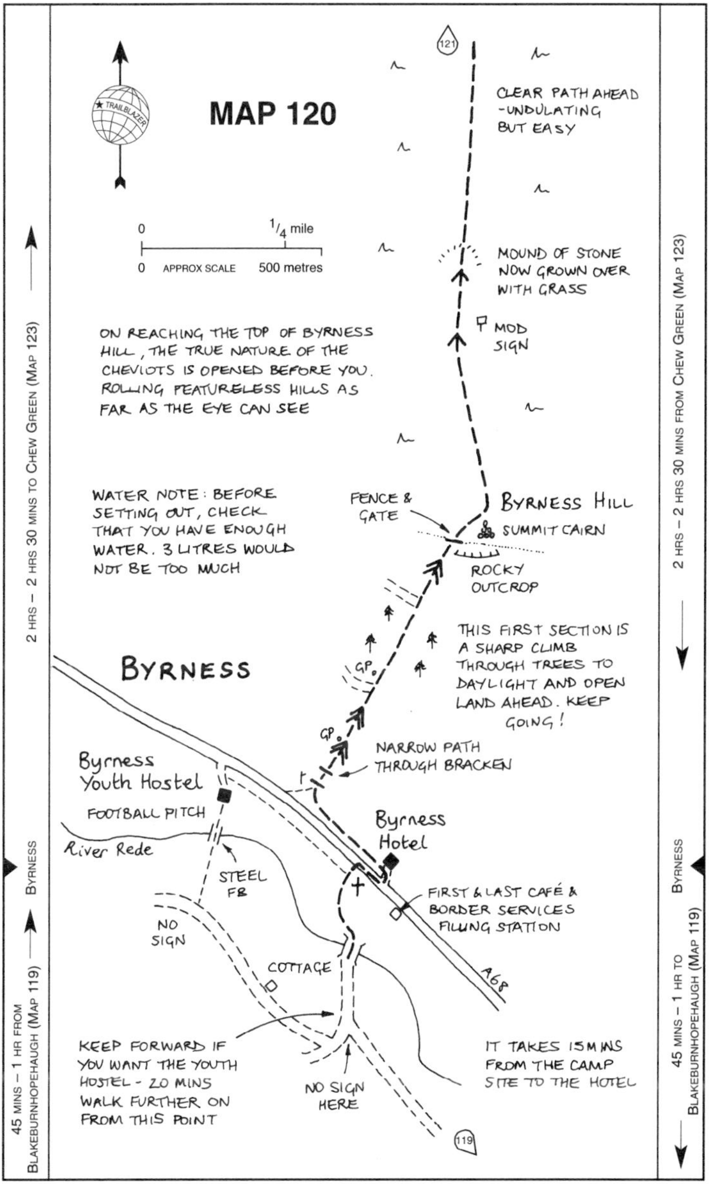

MAP 120

TRAILBLAZER

0   1/4 mile

0   APPROX SCALE   500 metres

CLEAR PATH AHEAD – UNDULATING BUT EASY

MOUND OF STONE NOW GROWN OVER WITH GRASS

MOD SIGN

ON REACHING THE TOP OF BYRNESS HILL, THE TRUE NATURE OF THE CHEVIOTS IS OPENED BEFORE YOU. ROLLING FEATURELESS HILLS AS FAR AS THE EYE CAN SEE

WATER NOTE: BEFORE SETTING OUT, CHECK THAT YOU HAVE ENOUGH WATER. 3 LITRES WOULD NOT BE TOO MUCH

FENCE & GATE

BYRNESS HILL
SUMMIT CAIRN

ROCKY OUTCROP

THIS FIRST SECTION IS A SHARP CLIMB THROUGH TREES TO DAYLIGHT AND OPEN LAND AHEAD. KEEP GOING!

BYRNESS

GP

GP

NARROW PATH THROUGH BRACKEN

Byrness Youth Hostel

FOOTBALL PITCH

River Rede

STEEL FB

NO SIGN

COTTAGE

Byrness Hotel

FIRST & LAST CAFÉ & BORDER SERVICES FILLING STATION

A68

KEEP FORWARD IF YOU WANT THE YOUTH HOSTEL – 20 MINS WALK FURTHER ON FROM THIS POINT

NO SIGN HERE

IT TAKES 15 MINS FROM THE CAMP SITE TO THE HOTEL

119

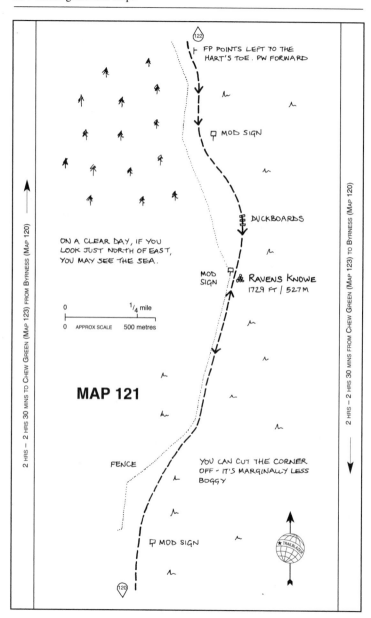

122

⊢ FP POINTS LEFT TO THE HART'S TOE. PW FORWARD

⌶ MOD SIGN

DUCKBOARDS

ON A CLEAR DAY, IF YOU LOOK JUST NORTH OF EAST, YOU MAY SEE THE SEA.

MOD SIGN

RAVENS KNOWE
1729 FT / 527M

0   1/4 mile
0   APPROX SCALE   500 metres

MAP 121

FENCE

YOU CAN CUT THE CORNER OFF - IT'S MARGINALLY LESS BOGGY

⌶ MOD SIGN

★ TRAILBLAZER

120

2T) with drying and laundry facilities in a lovely house. B&B costs £22. *The Border Hotel* (☎ 01573-420237, ▤ 01573-420549, ▤ borderhotel@aol.com, 2T/3D or F, all en suite) has a characterful bar where you'll receive a warm welcome. B&B costs from £40 per person (£45 for single occupancy). Pub food is served every day in summer, but only Wed-Sun in winter, 12-2pm and 6.30-9pm. *Kirk Yetholm Youth Hostel* (☎ 01573-420631, bookings ☎ 0870-155

3255, ▤ reservations@syha.org.uk, open Apr-Sep) costs £10 (£8 under 18s) and has washing and drying facilities.

If you continue to **Town Yetholm** you will find a **shop** (Mon-Sat 7am-12.30pm, 1.30-5pm, closed Wed afternoon, Sun 9am-12 noon) for tinned food, eggs, cheese etc and a **post office** (closed afternoons Wed and Sat). There is also the *Plough Hotel* (☎ 01573-420215) where B&B costs £18.50. Evening meals are served 6.45-8.45pm.

❏ **St Cuthbert's Way**

If you want to extend your walk, St Cuthbert's Way is a long-distance trail that runs between Kirk Yetholm and Holy Island on the Northumberland coast. It goes via Wooler in Northumberland and arrives, somewhat dishevelled, at Lindisfarne on the east coast where the castle, reached via a causeway, would round off your adventure in great style.

If you just can't stop walking there is a link to the Southern Upland Way and with a certain amount of ingenuity to the West Highland Way and then on to the Great Glen Way. It is therefore possible to walk from Derbyshire to Inverness, a great challenge for anyone with the feet and the time.

The pastime of walking the long-distance trails grows on you. Getting back to normal life is hard. You are likely to find that everyday cares are less important now that you have heard the curlews and felt the wind on Windy Gyle. One of the attractions of walking is the tangible sense of being out of the everyday world yet bonded to a community with different values from the common herd:

We are Pilgrims, Master; we shall go
Always a little further: it may be
Beyond that last blue mountain barred with snow,
Across that angry or that glimmering sea.

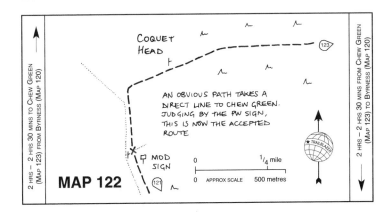

COQUET HEAD

AN OBVIOUS PATH TAKES A DIRECT LINE TO CHEW GREEN. JUDGING BY THE PW SIGN, THIS IS NOW THE ACCEPTED ROUTE

MOD SIGN

0   ¼ mile
0   APPROX SCALE   500 metres

★ TRAILBLAZER

MAP 122

123

123

2 HRS – 2 HRS 30 MINS TO CHEW GREEN (MAP 120) FROM BYRNESS (MAP 120)

2 HRS – 2 HRS 30 MINS FROM CHEW GREEN (MAP 120) (MAP 123) TO BYRNESS (MAP 120)

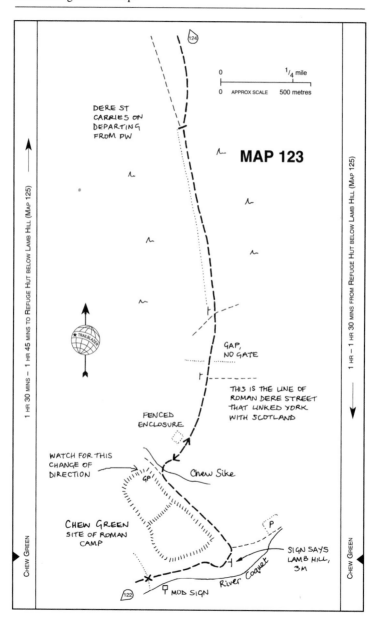

0   1/4 mile

0   APPROX SCALE   500 metres

DERE ST
CARRIES ON
DEPARTING
FROM PW

MAP 123

GAP,
NO GATE

THIS IS THE LINE OF
ROMAN DERE STREET
THAT LINKED YORK
WITH SCOTLAND

FENCED
ENCLOSURE

WATCH FOR THIS
CHANGE OF
DIRECTION

GP

Chew Sike

CHEW GREEN
SITE OF ROMAN
CAMP

SIGN SAYS
LAMB HILL,
3M

River Coquet

MOD SIGN

1 HR 30 MINS – 1 HR 45 MINS TO REFUGE HUT BELOW LAMB HILL (MAP 125)

1 HR – 1 HR 30 MINS FROM REFUGE HUT BELOW LAMB HILL (MAP 125)

CHEW GREEN

CHEW GREEN

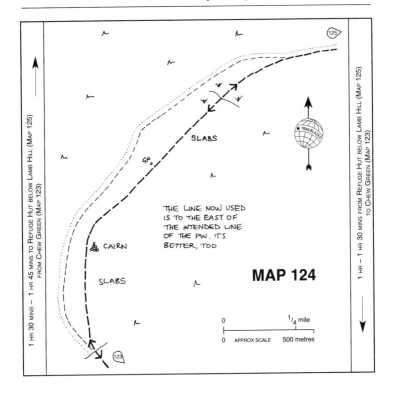

SLABS

GP

THE LINE NOW USED
IS TO THE EAST OF
THE INTENDED LINE
OF THE PW. IT'S
BETTER, TOO

CAIRN

SLABS

MAP 124

0   1/4 mile

0   APPROX SCALE   500 metres

1 HR 30 MINS – 1 HR 45 MINS TO REFUGE HUT BELOW LAMB HILL (MAP 125) FROM CHEW GREEN (MAP 123)

1 HR – 1 HR 30 MINS FROM REFUGE HUT BELOW LAMB HILL (MAP 125) TO CHEW GREEN (MAP 123)

★ TRAILBLAZER

125

123

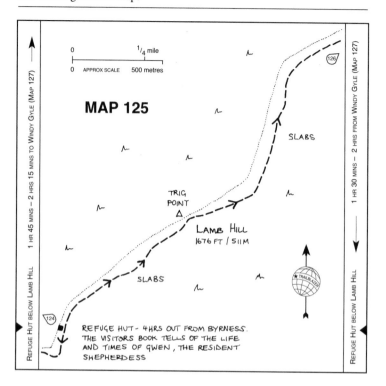

REFUGE HUT BELOW LAMB HILL | 1 HR 45 MINS – 2 HRS 15 MINS TO WINDY GYLE (MAP 127)

1 HR 30 MINS – 2 HRS FROM WINDY GYLE (MAP 127) | REFUGE HUT BELOW LAMB HILL

0   ¼ mile

0   APPROX SCALE   500 metres

MAP 125

SLABS

TRIG
POINT
△

LAMB HILL
1676 FT / 511 M

SLABS

TRAILBLAZER

REFUGE HUT- 4HRS OUT FROM BYRNESS.
THE VISITORS BOOK TELLS OF THE LIFE
AND TIMES OF GWEN, THE RESIDENT
SHEPHERDESS

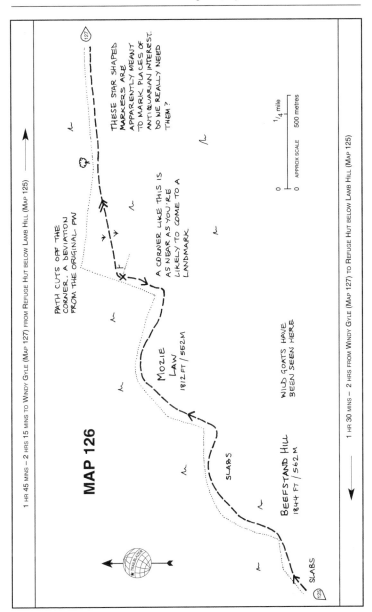

1 HR 45 MINS – 2 HRS 15 MINS TO WINDY GYLE (MAP 127) FROM REFUGE HUT BELOW LAMB HILL (MAP 125)

MAP 126

THESE STAR SHAPED MARKERS ARE APPARENTLY MEANT TO MARK PLACES OF ANTIQUARIAN INTEREST. DO WE REALLY NEED THEM?

PATH CUTS OFF THE CORNER. A DEVIATION FROM THE ORIGINAL PW

A CORNER LIKE THIS IS AS NEAR AS YOU'RE LIKELY TO COME TO A LANDMARK

MOZIE LAW
1812 FT / 562 M

BEEFSTAND HILL
1844 FT / 562 M

WILD GOATS HAVE BEEN SEEN HERE

SLABS

SLABS

0   APPROX SCALE
0   500 metres
1/4 mile

1 HR 30 MINS – 2 HRS FROM WINDY GYLE (MAP 127) TO REFUGE HUT BELOW LAMB HILL (MAP 125)

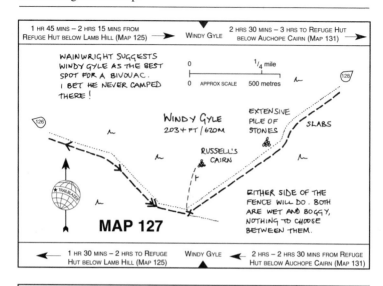

1 HR 45 MINS – 2 HRS 15 MINS FROM REFUGE HUT BELOW LAMB HILL (MAP 125) → **WINDY GYLE** 2 HRS 30 MINS – 3 HRS TO REFUGE HUT BELOW AUCHOPE CAIRN (MAP 131) →

WAINWRIGHT SUGGESTS WINDY GYLE AS THE BEST SPOT FOR A BIVOUAC. I BET HE NEVER CAMPED THERE!

0 ¼ mile
0 APPROX SCALE 500 METRES

126

WINDY GYLE
2034 FT / 620M

RUSSELL'S CAIRN

EXTENSIVE PILE OF STONES

SLABS

128

EITHER SIDE OF THE FENCE WILL DO. BOTH ARE WET AND BOGGY, NOTHING TO CHOOSE BETWEEN THEM.

MAP 127

← 1 HR 30 MINS – 2 HRS TO REFUGE HUT BELOW LAMB HILL (MAP 125) **WINDY GYLE** ← 2 HRS – 2 HRS 30 MINS FROM REFUGE HUT BELOW AUCHOPE CAIRN (MAP 131)

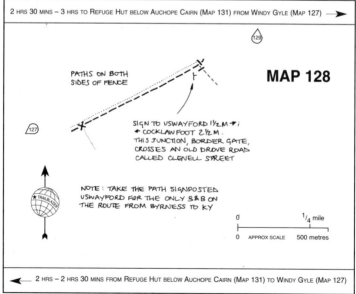

2 HRS 30 MINS – 3 HRS TO REFUGE HUT BELOW AUCHOPE CAIRN (MAP 131) FROM WINDY GYLE (MAP 127) →

129

PATHS ON BOTH SIDES OF FENCE

MAP 128

127

SIGN TO USWAYFORD 1½ M →;
← COCKLAW FOOT 2½ M.
THIS JUNCTION, BORDER GATE, CROSSES AN OLD DROVE ROAD CALLED CLENELL STREET

NOTE: TAKE THE PATH SIGNPOSTED USWAYFORD FOR THE ONLY B&B ON THE ROUTE FROM BYRNESS TO KY

0 ¼ mile
0 APPROX SCALE 500 METRES

← 2 HRS – 2 HRS 30 MINS FROM REFUGE HUT BELOW AUCHOPE CAIRN (MAP 131) TO WINDY GYLE (MAP 127)

Opposite Top and bottom right: Hadrian's Wall, near Caw Gap (see p213). **Bottom**: The well-preserved Roman latrines at Housesteads Fort (see p211). (Photos © Bryn Thomas.)

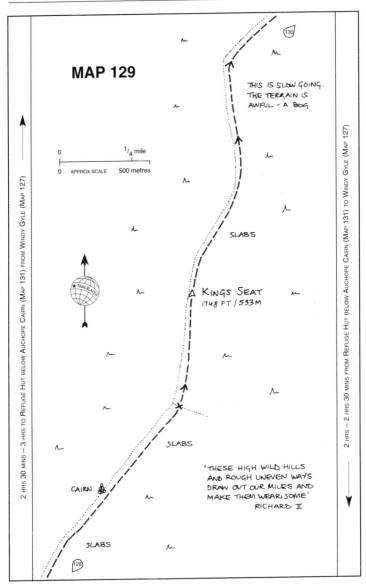

MAP 129

0 — ¼ mile
0 — 500 metres
APPROX SCALE

★ TRAILBLAZER

THIS IS SLOW GOING.
THE TERRAIN IS
AWFUL - A BOG

130

SLABS

△ KINGS SEAT
1748 FT / 533M

SLABS

'THESE HIGH WILD HILLS
AND ROUGH UNEVEN WAYS
DRAW OUT OUR MILES AND
MAKE THEM WEARISOME'
RICHARD II

CAIRN

SLABS

128

2 HRS 30 MINS – 3 HRS TO REFUGE HUT BELOW AUCHOPE CAIRN (MAP 131) FROM WINDY GYLE (MAP 127)

2 HRS – 2 HRS 30 MINS FROM REFUGE HUT BELOW AUCHOPE CAIRN (MAP 131) TO WINDY GYLE (MAP 127)

Opposite Top: Bothy near Auchope Cairn. **Bottom**: Border Hotel, the finish at Kirk Yetholm.

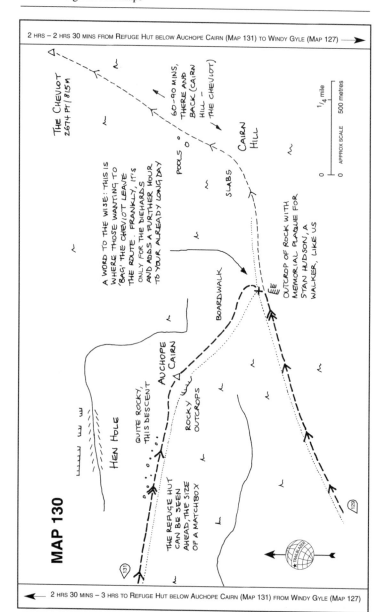

2 HRS – 2 HRS 30 MINS FROM REFUGE HUT BELOW AUCHOPE CAIRN (MAP 131) TO WINDY GYLE (MAP 127) →

MAP 130

THE CHEVIOT 2674 PT 815 M

60-90 MINS, THERE AND BACK (CAIRN HILL – THE CHEVIOT)

CAIRN HILL

¼ mile

500 metres

0   APPROX SCALE   0

A WORD TO THE WISE: THIS IS WHERE THOSE WANTING TO 'BAG' THE CHEVIOT LEAVE THE ROUTE. FRANKLY, IT'S ONLY FOR THE DIEHARDS AND ADDS A FURTHER HOUR TO YOUR ALREADY LONG DAY

POOLS

SLABS

BOARDWALK

OUTCROP OF ROCK WITH MEMORIAL PLAQUE FOR STAN HUDSON, A WALKER, LIKE US

HEN HOLE

QUITE ROCKY, THIS DESCENT

AUCHOPE CAIRN

ROCKY OUTCROPS

THE REFUGE HUT CAN BE SEEN AHEAD, THE SIZE OF A MATCHBOX

131

129

← 2 HRS 30 MINS – 3 HRS TO REFUGE HUT BELOW AUCHOPE CAIRN (MAP 131) FROM WINDY GYLE (MAP 127)

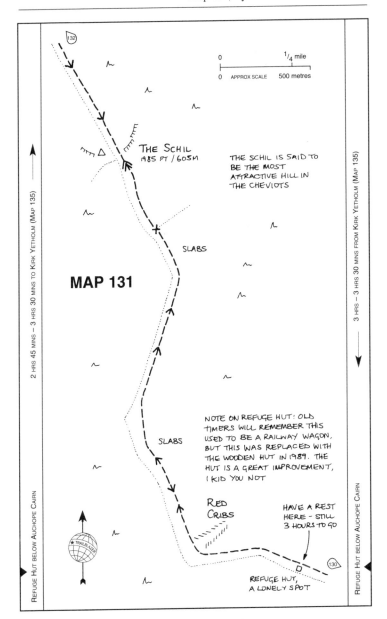

132

0   1/4 mile
0   APPROX SCALE   500 metres

THE SCHIL
1985 FT / 605M

THE SCHIL IS SAID TO
BE THE MOST
ATTRACTIVE HILL IN
THE CHEVIOTS

SLABS

MAP 131

SLABS

NOTE ON REFUGE HUT: OLD
TIMERS WILL REMEMBER THIS
USED TO BE A RAILWAY WAGON,
BUT THIS WAS REPLACED WITH
THE WOODEN HUT IN 1989. THE
HUT IS A GREAT IMPROVEMENT,
I KID YOU NOT

RED
CRIBS

HAVE A REST
HERE - STILL
3 HOURS TO GO

130

★ TRAILBLAZER

REFUGE HUT,
A LONELY SPOT

2 HRS 45 MINS – 3 HRS 30 MINS TO KIRK YETHOLM (MAP 135)

REFUGE HUT BELOW AUCHOPE CAIRN

3 HRS – 3 HRS 30 MINS FROM KIRK YETHOLM (MAP 135)

REFUGE HUT BELOW AUCHOPE CAIRN

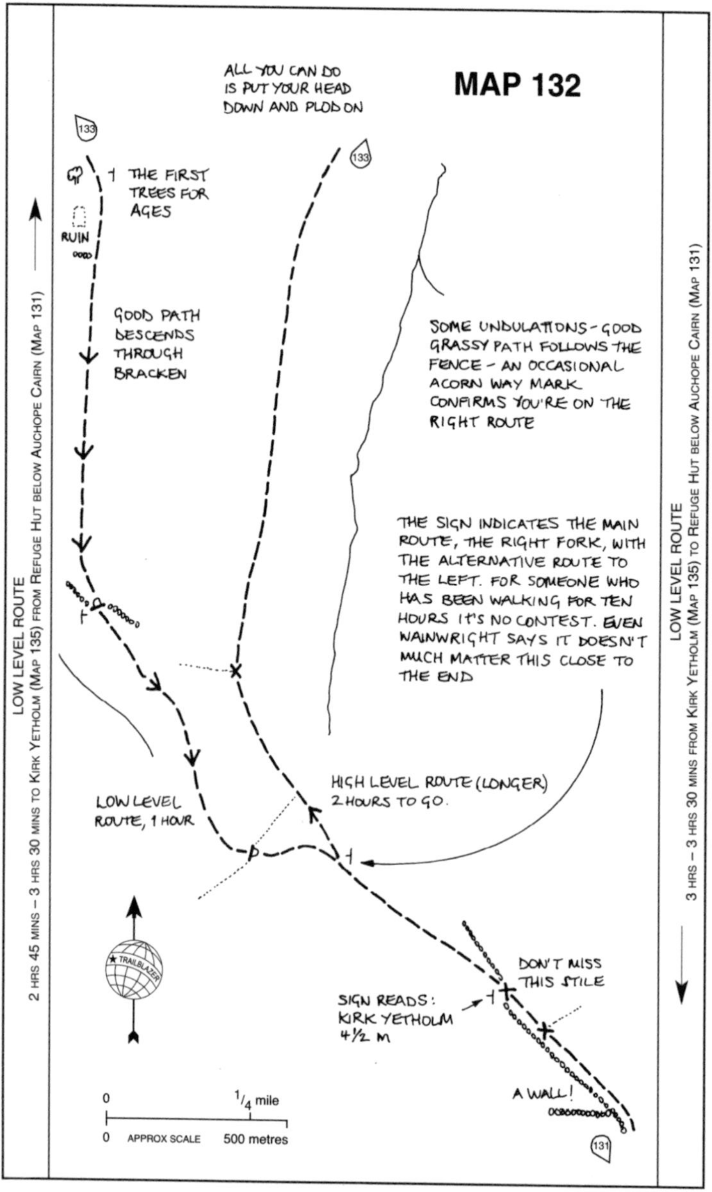
MAP 132
ALL YOU CAN DO IS PUT YOUR HEAD DOWN AND PLOD ON
133
133
THE FIRST TREES FOR AGES
RUIN
GOOD PATH DESCENDS THROUGH BRACKEN
SOME UNDULATIONS - GOOD GRASSY PATH FOLLOWS THE FENCE - AN OCCASIONAL ACORN WAY MARK CONFIRMS YOU'RE ON THE RIGHT ROUTE
THE SIGN INDICATES THE MAIN ROUTE, THE RIGHT FORK, WITH THE ALTERNATIVE ROUTE TO THE LEFT. FOR SOMEONE WHO HAS BEEN WALKING FOR TEN HOURS IT'S NO CONTEST. EVEN WAINWRIGHT SAYS IT DOESN'T MUCH MATTER THIS CLOSE TO THE END
HIGH LEVEL ROUTE (LONGER) 2 HOURS TO GO.
LOW LEVEL ROUTE, 1 HOUR
DON'T MISS THIS STILE
SIGN READS: KIRK YETHOLM 4½ M
A WALL!
TRAILBLAZER
0
1/4 mile
0
APPROX SCALE
500 metres
131
LOW LEVEL ROUTE
2 HRS 45 MINS – 3 HRS 30 MINS TO KIRK YETHOLM (MAP 135) FROM REFUGE HUT BELOW AUCHOPE CAIRN (MAP 131)
LOW LEVEL ROUTE
3 HRS – 3 HRS 30 MINS FROM KIRK YETHOLM (MAP 135) TO REFUGE HUT BELOW AUCHOPE CAIRN (MAP 131)

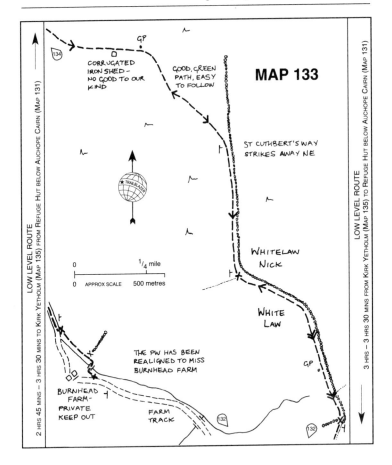

MAP 133

134

CORRUGATED
IRON SHED –
NO GOOD TO OUR
KIND

GP

GOOD, GREEN
PATH, EASY
TO FOLLOW

ST CUTHBERT'S WAY
STRIKES AWAY NE

WHITELAW
NICK

WHITE
LAW

GP

TRAILBLAZER

0   ¼ mile
0   APPROX SCALE   500 metres

THE PW HAS BEEN
REALIGNED TO MISS
BURNHEAD FARM

BURNHEAD
FARM –
PRIVATE
KEEP OUT

FARM
TRACK

132

132

LOW LEVEL ROUTE
2 HRS 45 MINS – 3 HRS 30 MINS TO KIRK YETHOLM (MAP 135) FROM REFUGE HUT BELOW AUCHOPE CAIRN (MAP 131)

LOW LEVEL ROUTE
3 HRS – 3 HRS 30 MINS FROM KIRK YETHOLM (MAP 135) TO REFUGE HUT BELOW AUCHOPE CAIRN (MAP 131)

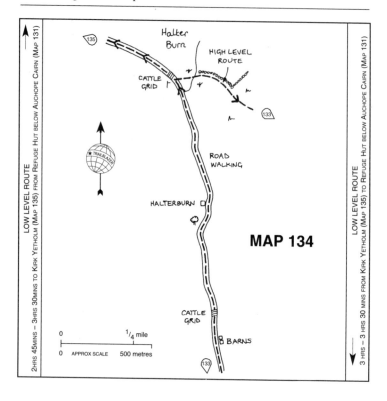

Halter Burn

HIGH LEVEL ROUTE

135

CATTLE GRID

133

ROAD WALKING

★ TRAILBLAZER

HALTERBURN

MAP 134

CATTLE GRID

0   ¼ mile

0   APPROX SCALE   500 metres

BARNS

133

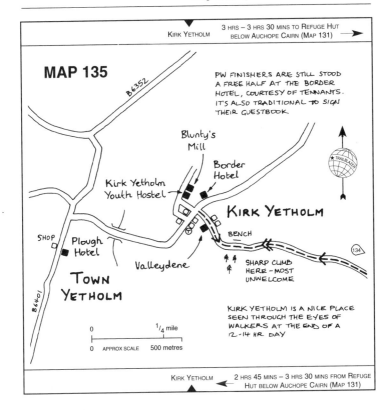

MAP 135

B6352

KIRK YETHOLM

3 HRS – 3 HRS 30 MINS TO REFUGE HUT BELOW AUCHOPE CAIRN (MAP 131) →

PW FINISHERS ARE STILL STOOD A FREE HALF AT THE BORDER HOTEL, COURTESY OF TENNANTS. IT'S ALSO TRADITIONAL TO SIGN THEIR GUESTBOOK

Blunty's Mill

Border Hotel

Kirk Yetholm Youth Hostel

KIRK YETHOLM

★ TRAILBLAZER

SHOP

Plough Hotel

BENCH

134

Valleydene

SHARP CLIMB HERE – MOST UNWELCOME

TOWN YETHOLM

B6401

KIRK YETHOLM IS A NICE PLACE SEEN THROUGH THE EYES OF WALKERS AT THE END OF A 12-14 HR DAY

0   ¼ mile

0   APPROX SCALE   500 metres

KIRK YETHOLM ← 2 HRS 45 MINS – 3 HRS 30 MINS FROM REFUGE HUT BELOW AUCHOPE CAIRN (MAP 131)

APPENDIX: HEALTH AND OUTDOOR SAFETY

AVOIDANCE OF HAZARDS

The Pennine Way is a long and at times arduous walk. It takes you through some very bleak and exposed terrain where good navigation skills are essential. You must take a **map** and **compass** with you and, of course, know how to use them. If the weather closes in, which it can do in moments, particularly in winter when blizzards have caught unsuspecting walkers off guard and nearly killed them, you need to know either a good escape route or how to look after yourself. Always make sure you have sufficient **clothing** to keep you warm and dry, whatever the conditions, and a spare change of inner clothes. A **whistle**, **torch** and **first-aid kit** should also be carried, as well as **hat** and **gloves** and possibly a **survival bag** too.

Take enough **food** to sustain you during the day and a little bit more in case you get caught out, and always set out with at least one litre of **water**. You will find that you will eat more than normal because you are using up more energy. High-energy snacks are worth considering, either proprietary brands or chocolate, nuts and dried fruit. Remain alert and try to keep track of exactly where you are throughout the day. The easiest way is to use the map to **check your position**. If bad weather comes in you will then be able to make a sensible decision on what action to take based on your location. A GPS can be useful, particularly as the better ones will give you a grid reference (if you've plugged in the map before the start of the walk) but should not be a substitute for a map and compass. You won't see many places selling batteries up high, nor many places to get it fixed if you drop it in a stream.

If you like **walking alone** the risk is greater and you must be capable of getting yourself out of trouble. It's a good idea to leave word with somebody about where you're going. One way of doing this is to telephone your booked accommodation and let them know you are walking alone and what time you expect to arrive. Don't forget to contact whoever you left word with to let them know you have arrived safely.

WEATHER INFORMATION

Anyone familiar with the British weather will know that it can change quickly. What started out as a warm sunny day can be chilly and wet by lunchtime, so don't be fooled. The daily newspapers, television and radio will always give the forecast for the day ahead and local people will have plenty of advice on the subject.

Telephone and web forecasts

If you are particularly interested you can call Weathercall ☎ 09068-5004 plus 12 for Derbyshire; 16 for North West England; 17 for Yorkshire; 18 for Northumberland. Calls are charged at the expensive premium rate. You can also contact them (☎ 0870-600 4242, ⌨ weathercall@itouch.co.uk) to arrange text messaging of weather reports. Alternatively internet weather forecasts can be found at ⌨ www.onlineweather.com.

WATER

You will need to drink lots of water whilst walking, both to avoid dehydration and to keep your energy levels up. If you're feeling drained, lethargic or just out of sorts it may well be that you haven't drunk enough. You need to drink between two and four litres a day when walking. Always start the day well hydrated and keep topping yourself up until you get to your next destination. You shouldn't wait until you're thirsty before you drink; by then you've already got drier than you should. A good way of checking your hydration level is to check the colour of your urine and the maxim, 'the mountaineer always pees clear', can be worth following. Tap water is safe to drink unless a sign specifies otherwise. In upland areas above habitation and away from intensively-farmed land walkers have traditionally drunk straight from the stream and many continue to do so with no problems. However, there is a small risk of a dead sheep lying upstream so it may be worth sterilizing the water first. There is also a very small but steadily increasing risk of catching giardia from drinking straight from streams. Just a few years ago this disease was only a threat to third world travellers. As more people travel some are returning to the UK with the disease. If one of these individuals defecates too close to a stream that water source can become infected and the disease transmitted to others who drink from it. To minimize the risk purify the water using purifying tablets, iodine, or a portable water filter.

Far more dangerous to health is drinking from natural water sources in the lowlands. The water may have run off roads, housing or agricultural fields picking up heavy metals, pesticides and other chemical contaminants that we humans liberally use. Such water should not be drunk; find a tap instead.

BLISTERS

You will prevent blisters developing by wearing boots that are well worn-in before you start. How many people set out on a long walk in new boots and live to regret it! Look after your feet; air them at lunchtime, keep them clean and change your socks as often as you can. If you notice any hot spots on your feet while you are walking, stop as soon as possible to treat them. Apply a strip of zinc oxide tape and leave on until the area is pain-free or the tape comes off of its own accord.

If you've left it too late and a blister has developed you should apply some 'moleskin', or other blister kit available from pharmacies to stop any more rubbing. Blisters shouldn't be lanced or popped as it can lead to infection. If the skin is split, keep the area clean with antiseptic and cover it with gauze held down with adhesive tape. Blisters are seldom a problem once covered up and will quickly recover, but if you can't treat them you'll be going nowhere, regardless of your fitness. The native Alaskans have a saying about their huskies when they get sore feet, 'no paw, no dog'; and so it is with you.

❏ Lyme Disease

Ticks are small blood-sucking insects that live on cattle, sheep and deer and cannot fly. When walking with bare arms or legs through long grass or bracken small ticks can brush off and attach themselves to you, painlessly burying their heads under your skin to feed on your blood. After a couple of days of feasting they will have grown to about 10mm and drop off.

There is a very small risk that they can infect you with Lyme Disease. Because of this you should check your body thoroughly after a walk through long grass, heather or bracken; the tick's favoured habitat. If you find a tick remove it promptly. Use fine point tweezers and grasp the tick where its head pierces your skin, do not squeeze its body. Tug gently and repeatedly until the tick lets go and falls off. Be patient, this will take time. Keep the area clean with disinfectant and over the next month watch for any flu-like symptoms, a spreading rash or lasting irritation at the site of the bite which could indicate Lyme Disease. If any of these symptoms appear see a doctor and let them know you suspect Lyme Disease. It is treatable with antibiotics but the sooner you deal with it the easier this will be.

Prevention is always better than cure so wear boots, socks and trousers when walking through or sitting on long grass, heather and bracken. For further information look up ▢ www.lymediseaseinformation.com.

HYPOTHERMIA

Also known as exposure, this occurs when the body can't generate enough heat to maintain its normal temperature, usually as a result of being wet, cold, unprotected from the wind, tired and hungry. Moving air has a much greater cooling effect than still air, hence the phrase 'wind-chill'. It is easily avoided by wearing suitable clothing, carrying and eating enough food and drink, being aware of the weather conditions and checking the morale of your companions. Moderate hypothermia can normally be reversed. Deep hypothermia is often fatal. That said, it is always worth persisting with the resuscitation of someone who does get deep hypothermia until a doctor arrives.

Early signs to watch for are feeling cold and tired with involuntary shivering, and cold, pale, dry skin. Apathy is a good indicator too. Find some shelter as soon as possible and warm the victim up with a hot drink and some chocolate or other high-energy food. If possible give them another warm layer of clothing and allow them to rest until feeling better.

If allowed to worsen, strange behaviour, slurring of speech and poor co-ordination will become apparent and the victim can quickly progress into unconsciousness, followed by coma and death. Quickly get the victim out of wind and rain improvising a shelter if necessary. Rapid restoration of bodily warmth is essential and best achieved by bare-skin contact: someone should get into the same sleeping bag as the patient, both having stripped to their underwear, any spare clothing under or over them to build up heat. Send urgently for help.

DEALING WITH AN ACCIDENT

- Use basic first aid to treat the injury to the best of your ability.
- Work out exactly where you are in case you have to send for the emergency services.
- Try to attract the attention of anybody in the area. To summon help, use the standard emergency signal of six blasts on the whistle, repeated if necessary, or in the dark, six flashes with the torch.
- If possible leave someone with the casualty while others go to get help. If there are only two people, you have a dilemma that will call for judgement to be exercised, depending on the severity of the injuries. If you decide to go for help yourself, leave all your spare clothing and food with the casualty.
- Telephone ☏ 999 and ask for the police and mountain rescue. Report the exact position of the casualty and his or her condition.
- Remember to **keep the casualty warm**. Put them in a sleeping bag and get in with them if necessary. If they are physically able to take hot drinks make some for them if you can.

Town plan key				
	ⓘ Tourist Information		£ Bank / ATM	
	Ⅹ Camping Site		◻ Public Toilet	
⟳ Place to stay	✝ Church / Cathedral		ⓣ Public Telephone	
○ Place to eat	⊞ Museum		⑧ Bus Stop	
⊠ Post Office	⊞ Bookshop / Library		● Other	

Trail map key

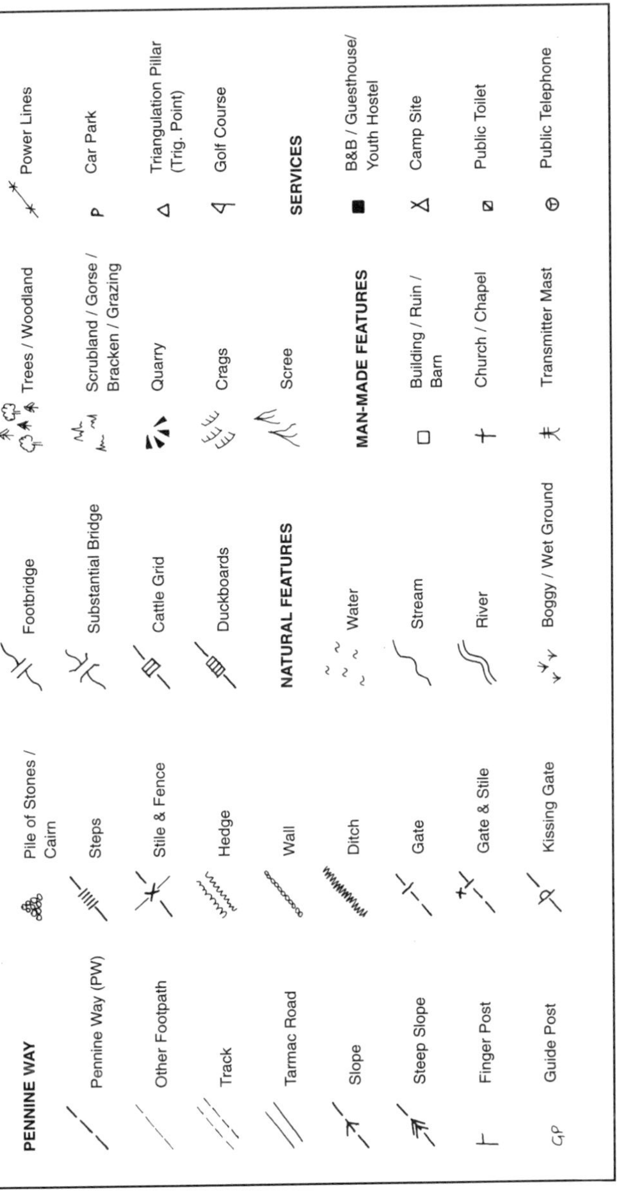
PENNINE WAY
Pennine Way (PW)
Other Footpath
Track
Tarmac Road
Slope
Steep Slope
Finger Post
GP
Guide Post
Pile of Stones / Cairn
Steps
Stile & Fence
Hedge
Wall
Ditch
Gate
Gate & Stile
Kissing Gate
Footbridge
Substantial Bridge
Cattle Grid
Duckboards
NATURAL FEATURES
Water
Stream
River
Boggy / Wet Ground
Trees / Woodland
Scrubland / Gorse / Bracken / Grazing
Quarry
Crags
Scree
MAN-MADE FEATURES
Building / Ruin / Barn
Church / Chapel
Transmitter Mast
Power Lines
P
Car Park
Triangulation Pillar (Trig. Point)
Golf Course
SERVICES
B&B / Guesthouse / Youth Hostel
Camp Site
Public Toilet
Public Telephone

INDEX

Europe
Trekking in Corsica
Trekking in the Dolomites
Trekking in the Pyrenees
(and the British Walking Series)

South America
Inca Trail, Cusco & Machu Picchu

Australasia
New Zealand – Great Walks

Africa
Kilimanjaro
Trekking in the Moroccan Atlas

Asia
Trekking in the Annapurna Region
Trekking in the Everest Region
Trekking in Ladakh
Trekking in Langtang
Nepal Mountaineering Guide

Trekking in Ladakh *Charlie Loram*   Due mid 2004
3rd edition, 288 pages, 75 maps, 24 colour photos
ISBN 1 873756 75 5, £12.99, Can$27.95, US$18.95
Fully revised and extended 3rd edition of Charlie Loram's practical
guide to trekking in this spectacular Himalayan region of India.
Includes 75 detailed walking maps, guides to Leh, Manali and Delhi
plus information on getting to Ladakh.
                'Extensive...and well researched'. **Climber Magazine**

Trekking in Corsica *David Abram*
1st edition, 320pp, 74 maps, 48 colour photos
ISBN 1 873756 63 1, £11.99, Can$26.95, US$18.95
A mountain range rising straight from the sea, Corsica holds the
most arrestingly beautiful and diverse landscapes in the
Mediterranean. Among the many trails that penetrate its remotest
corners, the GR20, which wriggles across the island's watershed,
has gained an international reputation. This guide also covers the
best of the other routes.   *'Excellent guide'.* **The Sunday Times**

New Zealand – The Great Walks *Alexander Stewart*
1st edn, 272pp, 60 maps, 40 colour photos
ISBN 1 873756 78 X, £11.99, Can$28.95, US$19.95
New Zealand is a wilderness paradise of incredibly beautiful landscapes. There is no better way to experience it than on one of the nine
designated Great Walks, the country's premier walking tracks which
provide outstanding hiking opportunities for people at all levels of fitness and proficiency. Also includes detailed guides to Auckland,
Wellington, National Park Village, Taumaranui, Nelson, Queenstown,
Te Anau and Oban.

The Inca Trail, Cusco & Machu Picchu *Richard Danbury*
2nd edition, 288pp, 54 maps, 35 colour photos
ISBN 1 873756 64 X, £10.99, Can$24.95, US$17.95
The Inca Trail from Cusco to Machu Picchu is South America's most
popular hike. Includes the **Vilcabamba Trail** to the ruins of the last
Inca capital, plus guides to Cusco and Machu Picchu. *'Danbury's
research is thorough...you need this one'.* **The Sunday Times**

Kilimanjaro: a trekking guide to Africa's highest mountain
Henry Stedman, 1st edition, 240pp, 40 maps, 30 photos
ISBN 1 873756 65 8, £9.99, Can$22.95, US$17.95
At 19,340ft the world's tallest freestanding mountain, Kilimanjaro is
one of the most popular destinations for hikers visiting Africa. It's possible to walk up to the summit: no technical skills are necessary. This
new guide includes town guides to Nairobi and Dar-Es-Salaam, excur-
sions in the region and a detailed colour guide to flora and fauna.

❏ TRAILBLAZER GUIDES

Adventure Cycling Handbook	1st edn mid 2005
Adventure Motorcycling Handbook	4th edn out now
Australia by Rail	4th edn out now
Azerbaijan	3rd edn out now
The Blues Highway – New Orleans to Chicago	2nd edn out now
China by Rail	2nd edn Nov 2004
Coast to Coast (British Walking Guide)	1st edn out now
Cornwall Coast Path (British Walking Guide)	1st edn out now
Good Honeymoon Guide	2nd edn out now
Inca Trail, Cusco & Machu Picchu	2nd edn out now
Japan by Rail	1st edn out now
Kilimanjaro – a trekking guide to Africa's highest mountain	1st edn out now
Land's End to John O'Groats	1st edn mid 2005
The Med Guide	1st edn mid 2004
Nepal Mountaineering Guide	1st edn Oct 2004
New Zealand – Great Walks	1st edn out now
Norway's Arctic Highway	1st edn out now
Offa's Dyke Path (British Walking Guide)	1st edn out now
Pembrokeshire Coast Path (British Walking Guide)	1st edn out now
Pennine Way (British Walking Guide)	1st edn out now
Siberian BAM Guide – rail, rivers & road	2nd edn out now
The Silk Roads – a route and planning guide	1st end out now
Sahara Overland – a route and planning guide	1st edn out now
Sahara Abenteuerhandbuch (German edition)	1st edn out now
South Downs Way (British Walking Guide)	1st edn out now
South-East Asia – The Graphic Guide	1st edn out now
Tibet Overland – mountain biking & jeep touring	1st edn out now
Trans-Canada Rail Guide	3rd edn out now
Trans-Siberian Handbook	6th edn out now
Trekking in the Annapurna Region	4th edn Oct 2004
Trekking in the Everest Region	4th edn out now
Trekking in Corsica	1st edn out now
Trekking in the Dolomites	1st edn out now
Trekking in Ladakh	3rd edn July 2004
Trekking in Langtang, Gosainkund & Helambu	1st edn out now
Trekking in the Moroccan Atlas	1st edn out now
Trekking in the Pyrenees	2nd edn out now
Tuva and Southern Siberia	1st edn mid 2005
West Highland Way (British Walking Guide)	1st edn out now

For more information about Trailblazer and our expanding range of guides,
for where to find your nearest stockist, for guidebook updates
or for credit card mail order sales (post-free worldwide) visit our web site:

www.trailblazer-guides.com

ROUTE GUIDES FOR THE ADVENTUROUS TRAVELLER

West Highland Way *Charlie Loram*   **Available now**
1st edition, 192pp, 48 maps, 10 town plans, 40 colour photos
ISBN 1 873756 54 2, £9.99, Can$22.95, US$16.95
Scotland's best-known long distance footpath passes through some of the most spectacular scenery in all of Britain. From the outskirts of Glasgow it winds for 95 miles along the wooded banks of Loch Lomond, across the wilderness of Rannoch Moor to a dramatic finish at the foot of Britain's highest peak – Ben Nevis. Includes Glasgow city guide.
'*...the same attention to detail that distinguishes its other guides has been brought to bear here*' *The Sunday Times*

Cornwall Coast Path *Edith Schofield*   **Available now**
1st edition, 192pp, 81 maps & town plans, 40 colour photos
ISBN 1 873756 55 0, £9.99, Can$22.95, US$16.95
A 160-mile (258km) National Trail around the western tip of Britain with some of the best coastal walking in Europe. With constantly changing scenery, the footpath takes in secluded coves, tiny fishing villages, rocky headlands, bustling resorts, wooded estuaries and golden surf-washed beaches. It is an area rich in wildlife with seabirds, wild flowers, dolphins and seals.

Pembrokeshire Coast Path *Jim Manthorpe*   **Available now**
1st edition, 208pp, 96 maps & town plans, 40 colour photos
ISBN 1 873756 56 9, £9.99, Can$22.95, US$16.95
A magnificent 186-mile (299km) footpath around the stunning coastline of the Pembrokeshire Coast National Park in south-west Wales. Renowned for its unspoilt sandy beaches, secluded coves, tiny fishing villages and off-shore islands rich in bird and marine life, this National Trail provides some of the best coastal walking in Britain.

Coast to Coast *Henry Stedman*   **Available now**
1st edition, 224pp, 108 maps & town plans, 40 colour photos
ISBN 1 873756 58 5, £9.99, Can$22.95, US$16.95
A classic 191-mile (307km) walk across northern England from the Irish Sea to the North Sea. Crossing three fabulous National Parks – the Lake District, the Yorkshire Dales and the North York Moors – it samples the very best of the English countryside – rugged mountains and lakes, gentle dales and stone-built villages; country lanes and wild moorland; sea cliffs and fishing villages.

Offa's Dyke Path *Keith Carter*   **Available now**
1st edition, 208pp, 88 maps & town plans, 40 colour photos
ISBN 1 873756 59 3, £9.99, Can$22.95, US$16.95
A superb National Trail from the North Wales coast to the Severn Estuary following the line of Offa's Dyke, an impressive 8th-century earthwork along the English/Welsh border. The ever-changing landscape is steeped in history providing 177 miles of fascinating walking.

South Downs Way *Jim Manthorpe*   **Available now**
1st edition, 192pp, 60 maps & town plans, 40 colour photos
ISBN 1 873756 71 2, £9.99, Can$22.95, US$16.95
This 100-mile (160km) National Trail follows the line of chalk hills stretching from Winchester to Eastbourne. Walking the length of the Downs is the best way to experience this beautiful landscape with its mixture of rolling hills, steep hanging woodland and windswept fields. You'll also pass through picture-postcard villages with welcoming pubs, thatched cottages and quintessentially English country gardens.

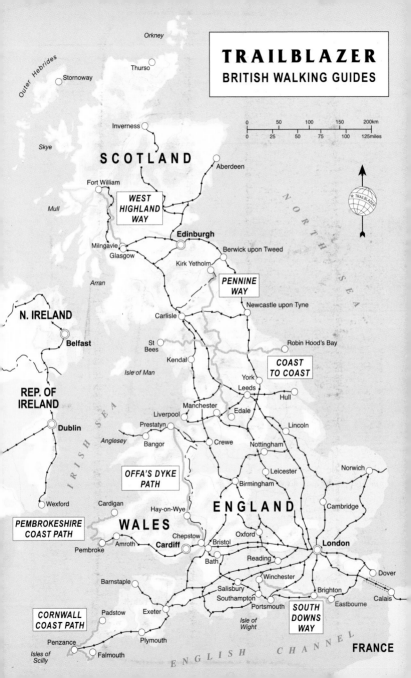

Pennine Way

EDALE – KIRK YETHOLM